The Dialogic and Difference

GENDER AND CULTURE

Carolyn G. Heilbrun and Nancy K. Miller, editors

GENDER AND CULTURE
A SERIES OF COLUMBIA UNIVERSITY PRESS
Edited by Carolyn G. Heilbrun and Nancy K. Miller

IN DORA'S CASE: Freud, Hysteria, Feminism
Edited by Charles Bernheimer and Claire Kahane

BREAKING THE CHAIN: Women, Theory, and French Realist Fiction
Naomi Schor

BETWEEN MEN: English Literature and Male Homosocial Desire
Eve Kosofsky Sedgwick

ROMANTIC IMPRISONMENT: Women and Other Glorified Outcasts
Nina Auerbach

THE POETICS OF GENDER
Edited by Nancy K. Miller

READING WOMAN: Essays in Feminist Criticism
Mary Jacobus

HONEY-MAD WOMEN: Emancipatory Strategies in Women's Writing
Patricia Yaeger

THINKING THROUGH THE BODY
Jane Gallop

GENDER AND THE POLITICS OF HISTORY
Joan Wallach Scott

SUBJECT TO CHANGE: Reading Feminist Writing
Nancy K. Miller

PLOTTING WOMEN: Gender and Representation in Mexico
Jean Franco

ANNE HERRMANN

The Dialogic and Difference

"AN/OTHER WOMAN" IN
VIRGINIA WOOLF AND CHRISTA WOLF

COLUMBIA UNIVERSITY PRESS
New York

COLUMBIA UNIVERSITY PRESS

NEW YORK   GUILDFORD, SURREY

Copyright © 1989 Columbia University Press

ALL RIGHTS RESERVED

LIBRARY OF CONGRESS CATALOGING-IN-PUBLICATION DATA

Herrmann, Anne.

The dialogic and difference.

(Gender and culture)

Bibliography: p.

Includes index.

1. Feminist literary criticism.

2. Woolf, Virginia, 1882–1941—Characters—Women.

3. Wolf, Christa—Characters—Women.

4. Bakhtin, M. M. (Mikhail Mikhailovich), 1895–1975.

5. Women in literature.

6. Women authors.

7. Women—History.

8. Literature and history.

I. Title.   II. Series.

PN98.W64H47   1989   823'.912   88-25772

ISBN 0-231-06642-2

Printed in the United States of America

*Casebound editions of Columbia University Press books
are Smyth-sewn and printed on permanent and
durable acid-free paper*

IN MEMORY OF
Elizabeth Rütschi Herrmann

CONTENTS

ACKNOWLEDGMENTS

*T*his project's history has been long, the outcome of my bilingual upbringing and the emergence of feminist critical theory as a legitimate field of study. I remain indebted to my mother for the first Virginia Woolf novel I ever owned (purchased in a one-room bookstore in Colorado) and for later introducing me to Christa Wolf's works. It was she who taught me how to read and write German as I grew up speaking Swiss-German in an English-speaking country.

I would like to thank Peter Brooks, for introducing me to Mikhail Bakhtin, and Ingeborg Glier, for offering (as a medievalist) the only class on contemporary German women writers at Yale. They supported me as I pursued a research project that largely lay outside their expertise and might have seemed premature, given the then current state of feminist criticism. I am indebted as well to Margaret Homans for the class she taught on feminist literary criticism and to her, Margie Ferguson, and Hélène Wenzel, for commenting on early versions of the manuscript. Most memorable are the many hours I spent with members of the Feminist Literary Group in New Haven, especially Danna Blesser, Mary Leoffelholz, and Nancy Becket, all of whom provided inspiration and contributed greatly to my intellectual growth and feminist commitment. Danna, in particular, was always prepared to exchange information and ideas. Andrea Snell assisted greatly with mechanical details.

I owe much to Peg Lourie for helping me to transform the manuscript into a book and for encouraging me to be formally innovative. I would also like to thank the National Endowment for the Humanities for a Summer Stipend, the University of Michigan Committee for Gender for a Faculty Fellowship, and the University of Michigan English Department for an in-house research leave. I am also grateful to Karen Mitchell, my editor at Columbia University Press, for her informed reading and incisive comments.

My thanks to Martha have been and will be expressed many times outside this book. It is she who makes it all possible and worthwhile.

A shorter version of chapter 2 appeared as " 'Intimate, Irreticent, and Indiscreet in the Extreme': Epistolary Essays by Virginia Woolf and Christa Wolf," *New German Critique* (Spring–Summer 1986), vol. 38.

The Dialogic and Difference

INTRODUCTION

*A*ny comparison between Virginia Woolf (1882–1941) and Christa
Wolf (1929–) requires an explanation, inasmuch as this book offers
neither an influence study nor a critical reappraisal of each author's complete works. Although my text focuses largely on the relation between
the female author and her female characters, it does not do so through a
psychoanalytic description of the development of the female subject; in
spite of its insistence on history as an essential category, it is not a historical
study. By creating a dialogue between Woolf and Wolf I seek to give voice
to at least two critiques of masculinist political and literary practices—
critiques governed by the social and historical conditions which have produced each author. At the same time, I juxtapose Woolf and Wolf in order
to foreground the theoretical contradiction they unwittingly produce.
Taken synchronically, they come to represent the two opposing positions
in the debate within feminist critical theory surrounding the construction
of the female subject: Woolf deconstructs the centered, unified subject as
such, while Wolf rewrites the traditionally male subject as female.

In spite of their dissimilar representations of the female subject, Woolf
and Wolf are two modern women writers who have positioned themselves
in their respective literary traditions in similar ways, although at different
historical moments. They are among the most incisive inheritors of a

dominant masculine culture, the result of self-education and a privileged relation to literary precursors. At the same time they place themselves as their culture's harshest critics, as women for whom gender and class remain inseparable from each other and from forms of male power whose exclusionary practices culminate in war. Woolf is the casualty and Wolf the offspring of World War II, the temporal moment which symbolically separates what we now call modernist and postmodernist aesthetic practices.

Virginia Woolf inherits a male literary tradition steeped in biographical discourses which includes the work of her father, Leslie Stephen, the editor of the *Dictionary of National Biography,* and is continued by her own biographer and nephew, Quentin Bell. She is also born into a female lineage dominated by visual forms of representation: her great-aunt, Julia Margaret Cameron, immortalized the image of her mother, Julia Pattle-Duckworth, in her photographs; while Vanessa Bell, her sister, became a painter. Woolf breaks out of this traditional dichotomy between language (the speech of men) and the visual (the silence of women) by becoming a female author. In choosing words rather than images, she attempts to alter language so that it both "adapts itself to a woman's body" and critiques the body politic of male oppression.

This dual inheritance parallels Christa Wolf's, although Wolf's traditions do not take the form of a familial legacy.[1] Her investigation into the dichotomy between masculine and feminine is not the origin but the logical culmination of an investigation into the cultural splittings which emerge with the division of Germany. Woolf's opposition between linguistic signs and visual images thus acquires for Wolf a larger political meaning. No longer do writing and painting exist as unequal modes of representation in a cultural hierarchy; rather, for Wolf, visual images become metaphors for memories stabilized for ideological purposes. Only language has the capacity to rewrite history and reintegrate a severed past into the consciousness of the present. Wolf's divergence from tradition thus lies not in rewriting a generational difference in terms of sexual difference (Georgians vs. Edwardians) but in the introduction of gender as a critical category within Marxist cultural practices.[2]

The response of each writer to a dominant literary culture lies in breaking with a literary tradition by totally immersing herself within it, at once appropriating and interrogating it. Woolf and Wolf's construction of a female subject which questions the very notion of subjectivity takes place within a highly developed aesthetic. For the sake of simplicity, one might say that Woolf's modernism alludes to an established literary tradition in order to react against it, while positing the supremacy of language in the face of history's demise; Wolf's postmodernism borrows from a multitude of cultural discourses, no longer privileging language as a sign system but exposing the impossibility of an authentic or adequate representation. While the modernist seeks to transform modes of representation to rewrite the world, the postmodernist seeks to reveal the systems of power in the world that legitimize certain representations and not others. Thus Woolf decenters the Victorian realist novel by seeming to displace the center of the narrative from the omniscient, omnipotent, omnipresent narrator to the consciousness of the individual fictional subject; while Wolf rewrites the novel of socialist realism by replacing an absent with a self-conscious narrator, who produces both a socialist and a novelistic subject while reflecting on the status of her own subjectivity.

Whereas the novelistic narrative of nineteenth-century realism almost always ends in the marriage or death of a middle-class heroine, the protagonist of socialist realism has traditionally been the male worker. If one wished to counter these traditions, one could close the book differently or simply change the sex of the protagonist, but Woolf and Wolf far more radically alter the structure of the narrative: the female artists in Woolf manage to bring their work to completion; the female protagonist in Wolf is not a worker but a writer.

The conceptual point of intersection in both authors' discourses between their dominant literary aesthetics and their woman-centered or feminist ideologies is what I have chosen to call "an/other woman": the other woman as "another" woman in the form of an addressee, a member of the audience, a literary precursor; or woman as both self and "other" in the author's construction of her own subjectivity and that of her female fictional subjects. I use "woman" to refer to the "real" woman as both the author and her female protagonists, in contrast to "the feminine"— what is left when the male subject has been deconstructed—which repeatedly forgets that real women exist.[3] The figure of "an/other woman" makes it possible for the woman writer to rewrite "the feminine" in the form of a female subjectivity, by inscribing herself in her own text as gendered and as fictional subject.

The production of the other woman takes the form of intra- and intertextual dialogues which construct "her" in the interstices of dialogized discourses. She exists for Woolf and Wolf most concretely as fictional subject, as female artist who either never marries or never completely succeeds at her art. This figure of the marginalized female subject is in a dialogic relation to both "the feminine," as represented in the looking glass and the portrait, and the historical subject, the author's sister or female friend. A dialogic relation also connects the woman writer and her literary precursor, since the precursor, largely absent from history, comes into existence only as fiction. Both authors reconstruct their precursors as literary heroines—Woolf in her creation of Judith Shakespeare, who has no historical basis, and Wolf in her rewriting of Karoline von Günderrode (1790–1806) as dramatic heroine. Ultimately the relations between women become more and more eroticized as they begin to acquire an affiliation based on their art, although the "other" woman never openly exists as lesbian.

I borrow the term "dialogic" neither to legitimize a feminist critical practice with a reputable, even fashionable male theory, nor to apply a theoretical construct systematically to a group of literary texts. The dialogic, because of its asystemic nature and its insistence on the social significance of discourse, is a term which embraces both a comparative and an ideological interrogation of literary practices.[4] Any comparison between Woolf and Wolf takes place against the background of the differences between a British and a German national history, capitalism and socialism as political and economic systems, and modernism and postmodernism as moments in the history of aesthetics. The comparison itself is predicated on the dialogue between Woolf and Wolf about the implications of women writing, as well as on the dialogic nature of their particular discourses, on their dialogue as women writers with the discourses of a dominant culture, and on my own dialogue as a feminist reader with their discourses and with those of a gender-blind theory, the dialogic. My own dialogized relation to the texts under discussion requires that I provide a structure for the dialogue between these two authors without either erasing myself or subjugating them. In addition, it requires that I address the debate between French post-structuralists and Anglo-Amerian feminist critics on the nature of female subjectivity.

The controversy surrounding the practice of "sexual/textual politics"[5] lies in the contradiction between the deconstruction of the subject and the construction of a female subjectivity. It centers on the problem of referentiality: does "woman" refer to an entity in the real world, a reference based on the assumption of a fixed gender identity and the possibility of its reflection in language, or does "woman" refuse a referent, as does "the feminine," by signifying the disruption of meaning which follows the deconstruction of the sovereign subject? In other words, how does one reconcile one's ideological position as a feminist, conscious of the fact that women as a group are differently and unequally inscribed as legal subjects, and one's knowledge as a theorist that subjectivity itself functions as discursive fiction?[6] Theorists who have entered the debate have left this contradiction largely unresolved. Some feminist critics have sought textual closure through an interrogative mode, which asks questions of each side without attempting to provide answers;[7] others have chosen a deconstructive mode, which through an almost limitless word play unveils the precariousness of any discursive system.[8]

By introducing the dialogic I hope to establish a dialogue which avoids this double bind by moving it from the realm of logical inconsistency to that of historical specificity. Even though the emergence of the female historical subject in the modern period coincides with the disappearance of the philosophical or knowing subject, women have continued to construct female subjects, in both fictive and nonfictive texts. Modernist and postmodernist fictions, by relying on some semblance of plot and character, interrogate subjectivity in ways that are denied to theoretical discourses, which tend to inscribe and reinscribe their own inability to achieve resolution. The female character provides the space for a potentially new kind of subjecthood, because the female author has an investment in the conditions of her representability. The female fictional subject exists as subject and as gendered, and thus is no longer the site of unrepresentability; and yet because she exists as fiction, she represents only a discursive, not a prescriptive possibility. The dialogic avoids the double bind of the feminist critical theorist's position by rewriting the debate as dialogue, a form of discourse whose contradictions are decided not in the text but in history. By postponing the possibility of a resolution within her own text, the critic interrogates the historicity as well as the present status of the theoretical debate.

The construction of the female subject reflects modernist or postmodernist literary practices; but it also reflects the status of the individual subject within each national culture, as the intersection of aesthetic and political practices at a particular historical moment. Woolf deconstructs the subject in order to subvert the male biographical subject, which represents for her a tradition of British middle-class individualism; Wolf reconstructs the subject in the German Democratic Republic (GDR) by exposing the veiled ideology of both idealism (which ignores the social construction of the subject) and socialism (which ignores the identity of the subjects who constitute the social order). To the named, remembered, and self-referential male "I," Woolf opposes the anonymous female subject whose anonymity was first historically imposed and then freely chosen to avoid reinscribing the tyranny of the subject as such. In response to the suppression of subjectivity for the sake of a socialist collectivity, Wolf focuses on the effacement of individual historical subjects, most often female, whose heroism lies in their critique of rather than their conformity to the social order which produced them.

Woolf and Wolf come to represent each side of the dialogue by reinserting both subjectivity and its discursive inscription into history. The construction of the subject takes a different form if it has been reified in history, as in Woolf's patrilineage, or denied, as in the socialism of the GDR. It also acquires a different configuration if the omniscient narrator has been replaced by the self-consciousness of multiple fictional subjects, as in modernist fiction, or the self-consciousness of a self-reflexive narrator, as in postmodernist fiction. Woolf deconstructs the subject because all subjectivity has been defined as masculine; Wolf reconstructs the subject as female in order to reinsert it into history. Yet Woolf's subjects also have a historical specificity which locates them in terms of gender and class, while Wolf problematizes subjectivity as the conflict both between the individual and the state, and between self-realization and the possibility of its representation.

In either case the female subject is posited as structurally different from the male subject. Absent from history, "she" embodies the possibility of a different subjectivity, based on a recognition of the other not as object but as "an/other" subject. The dialogic names the discursive relation between two subjects, understood as a dialogue in which the subject constitutes itself without the annihilation or assimilation of the other. This dialogue posits itself as a struggle between the two subjects' respective discourses. For Woolf and Wolf these discourses are predicated on male and female subject positions which result in the sexual oppression of "real" women and which ultimately lead to military conflict, the most extreme imposition of one subject on another.[9] Still different from men, yet no longer barred from dominant cultural practices, Woolf and Wolf rely on double-voiced discourses to rewrite sexual difference.

The dialogic as a rewriting of difference escapes the hierarchical binary opposition of sexual difference, which can either be deconstructed and displaced, thus leaving the feminine eternally deferred, or left in place but revalorized in order to celebrate Woman. Whereas the concept of difference implies a hierarchy between masculine and feminine, the dialogic disrupts that hierarchy by positing the other as another subject rather than as object. But Bakhtin's dialogic represses gender by assuming two gender-neutral, that is, masculine, subjects. Specularity, a concept I borrow from Luce Irigaray, infuses the dialogic with a notion of gender by imagining the constitution of the subject as female.[10] The specular subject constitutes itself simultaneously as subject and object, as woman and the "other woman"; that is, woman's own otherness in language and the other women of her sex. For Irigaray the "speculum" as the locus of both the psychoanalytic and the philosophical construction of the subject represents the "curved" mirror as the site not of woman as visual object but of female representability.

In order to reinscribe the specular subject in a political discourse I return to a notion of alterity, which refers to the power relation between two subjects of different gender and/or class positions. The construction of the female subject does not involve introducing gender as a supplementary category; it redefines alterity by deconstructing the power relations which reserve the position of the other for women and the position of the object for the woman who is represented. To represent a female subject as the object of discourse is to engage in the same process of objectification by which one has been oppressed. To produce the female subject as necessary fiction is to privilege textual production and the figurative status of truth. The question remains: how does a woman writer deconstruct the female subject as mimetic fiction without relegating her to the position of absence occupied by "the feminine"?

The texts I have chosen to compare encompass both fictive and non-fictive works by Woolf and Wolf. The similarity of their literary production lies in formal and thematic affinities: the use of the epistolary essay; a concern with female literary history; the novel as elegy; and the interpolation of history within novelistic fiction. The forms I have chosen for various chapters—the self-interview, the letter, the dialogue—foreground the dialogized position of the writer as reader, particularly in the production of feminist readings. The readings themselves rely on intertextual connections and focus on visual representations of the feminine which Woolf and Wolf first reconstruct and then deconstruct by means of a feminist ideology. In blurring the boundaries between fiction and nonfiction, reader and writer, I hope to bridge the gap between theoretical discourse and literary practice.

Chapter 1 offers a discussion of the dialogic in the form of a self-interview, emphasizing the double-voiced position of the feminist critical theorist which stems from the dialogue between feminism and critical theory. My inquiry into the dialogic traces its origins to Mikhail Bakhtin, its initial appropriation to Marxist critics, and its current popularity to the possibility it offers as an alternative to an apolitical post-structuralism. I explore the dialogic's possibilities for feminism via Kristeva's notion of intertextuality, which purges the dialogic of its psychological and theological underpinnings by rewriting the subject as split subject. And I conclude by postulating a female dialogic through Irigaray's notion of specularity, which insists on the construction of "an/other woman" as essential to the representability of the female subject.

In chapter 2 I examine three sets of epistolary essays: Woolf's *Three Guineas,* and Wolf's "Come! Into the Open, Friend!"; Woolf's "A Letter to a Young Poet" and Wolf's "A Letter, About Unequivocal and Ambiguous Meaning, Definiteness and Indefiniteness; About Ancient Conditions and New View-Scopes; About Objectivity"; and Woolf's introduction to *Life as We Have Known It,* written by working-class members of the Women's Co-operative Guild, and Wolf's "Nun ja! Das nächste Leben geht aber heute an: Ein Brief über die Bettine" [Granted! But the Next Life Begins Today: A Letter About Bettine].[11] This chapter, written in the form of a letter in order to reflect on the differences between my reading of the epistle and another feminist critic's, explores the dialogic relation of the author to an addressee as a rhetorical strategy for "visualizing" the other as another speaking subject. The epistle, by constituting a private discourse, allows the author to engage in a public critique of a masculinist culture made manifest through war, hegemonic literary production, and the suppression of women's writings. By constructing the addressee either as antagonist or as ally, the author addresses "an/other woman" as dialogic other or as specular image. The dialogue between epistle and essay juxtaposes the literal letter as "feminine" to the history of female letter writing.

In chapter 3 I focus on Woolf's *To the Lighthouse* and Wolf's *The Quest for Christa T.* An allegorical reading of Woolf's "Lady in the Looking-Glass" provides the subtext for a discussion of the female fictional subject in the text of the novel; here she appears as absence rather than as split subjectivity. I read both novels as elegies, where the absence of the female other is predicated not on the rhetorical status of the addressee but on the premature death of the heroine. Once she dies, the female subject becomes "visible" in order to provide a specular image for both the author and another female character. A series of intertextual readings reveals the relation to "an/other woman" as the author's relation to a sister or female friend, to her own previous subjectivity, and to a prior self-authored text.

In chapter 4 I examine the relation to the other woman as literary precursor: Judith Shakespeare in Woolf's *A Room of One's Own* and Karoline von Günderrode in Wolf's "Der Schatten eines Traumes: Karoline von Günderrode—Ein Entwurf" [The Shadow of a Dream: Karoline von Günderrode—A Sketch]. The dialogue I construct between Woolf and Wolf foregrounds the debate over the invention or recovery of the female historical subject. The precursor achieves "visibility" only as an absence which lies both "elsewhere," outside history, and "nowhere," never to be recovered from the past. The literary precursor as literary heroine exists as both fact and fiction, inscribed in a female literary history (i.e., a novel narrative) or story which has never been told. The intertextual dialogue of the literary history juxtaposes literature, in which the author has disappeared except as discursive position, and women's history, in which the subject has appeared as female historical subject.

Chapter 5 continues the dialogue between literature and history in two historical fictions: Woolf's *Between the Acts* and Wolf's *No Place on Earth*. In another allegorical reading, this time of a passage from Jane Austen's *Northanger Abbey,* I focus on the readings of verbal texts and visual scenes produced by male and female readers. History enters the text as dramatic event rather than as "novel narrative." The novelistic heroine, in the guise of the female dramatist, writes the silenced feminine (represented by the portrait) into history by staging gender oppositions as arbitrary, and ultimately as changeable through costume. The female subject enters history not as a female "I" but as the voice of a communal "we," understood as both the promise and the threat of the disappearance of the subject as such.

I conclude with a discussion of the implications of either deconstructing the subject or rewriting the subject as female, for both Woolf and Wolf and their protagonists. In either case the possibility of a utopian subjectivity which transcends the conflict of sexual difference in discourse cannot exist in culture. Woolf and Wolf, in confronting this disjuncture, must necessarily inscribe themselves in that conflict as historical subjects.

CHAPTER ONE

THE FEMALE DIALOGIC
A Self-Interview

Every reader seems to make his [her] own Bakhtin.
— GARY SAUL MORSON

Q: I understand that you have been working on "the dialogic and difference." Have you finally decided what you mean by the "dialogic"?

A: The term "dialogic" was coined by Mikhail Bakhtin (1895–1975), a philosophical anthropologist[1] who published under his own name and assumed names borrowed from two friends, V. N. Volosinov and P. N. Medvedev. The extent to which Volosinov and Medvedev were authors, coauthors, or pseudonyms remains largely undecided.[2]

Q: And, I assume, ultimately undecidable. How do you interpret this controversy surrounding Bakhtin's authorship?

A: On the one hand, it draws attention to the crushing effects of repressive political regimes on literary production. Publishing during the Stalin era required the use of pseudonyms to avoid political censorship, resulting in the belated appearance of Bakhtin's work, both in his own time and later in French and English translations. On the other hand, Bakhtin's ambiguous authorship has come to function as a figure for the theoretical debate surrounding authoring, the relation between the author as historical subject and the status of the author as signature.[3]

Q: Who are the participants in this controversy?

A: Michael Holquist, Bakhtin's biographer, argues that Bakhtin authored virtually all work under discussion, yet did so as "ventriloquist,"[4] using language as ideological disguise to circumvent political repression. As biographer, Holquist is forced to privilege the ventriloquist over his dummies by insisting on the single signature of the biographical subject.[5] At the same time the status of historical truth in biographical discourse requires that behind the linguistic mask there lie an authentic, recoverable subjectivity. Unable to ask whether there is a "real" Bakhtin, the biographer can only unify the fragmented Bakhtin so that readers will finally be able "to see him whole."

Q: What about Todorov?

A: Todorov, in *The Dialogical Principle,* shifts the focus from author to addressee: Volosinov and Medvedev are not posited as coauthors but as actual or imagined recipients of Bakhtin's texts. As addressees they participate in a dialogized discourse which sees every utterance as equally determined by sender and receiver. Todorov is able to acknowledge his own ambiguous authorship, as translator, commentator, and anthropologist, and thus to feel more at ease with a split signature, designated typographically by a slash: "Medvedev/Bakhtin. The slash is chosen specifically for the ambiguity it authorizes: is it a relation of collaboration? of substitution (pseudonym or mask)? or of communication (the first name identifying the receiver, and the second, the sender)?"[6]

Q: How, then, do you see the relationship between the dialogic as split signature and as a rewriting of sender/receiver communication?

A: In its most general terms, the dialogic views language as social practice, as the struggle between language systems within a particular sociohistorical context. When that struggle ends, the word becomes monologic, limited to a monolithic symbolic system characterized by arbitrary political power and literary convention. To enter that struggle as a language user means to engage in speech as citation, for any linguistic utterance involves the adoption of as well as the response to prior speech. Speech as interlocution becomes an ideological form which both reveals and produces the subject's position within a social system.

Q: Are you suggesting, then, that we author ourselves rather than the texts we produce?

A: This remains a topic of debate even among the Bakhtinians. Caryl Emerson writes: "Whatever stable definitions the 'I' possesses are inevitably acquired from the other. Thus one cannot author oneself."[7] Holquist, in contrast, concludes: "The suggestion of Bakhtin's total oeuvre, conceived as a single utterance, is that our ultimate act of authorship results in the text which we call our self."[8] According to Emerson it is the gaze of the other which constitutes the subject, while for Holquist the subject answers the world by authoring it. One could go so far as to say that the repressed origins of the first formulation lie in existentialism, the second in Christian theology. In each case authorship as the relation between historical subject and signature has been replaced by authoring as ethical responsibility, to an other or to the self in its relation to others.

Q: But this seems to detract us from a notion of the subject not as split signature but as speaking subject constituted by a splitting in the act of enunciation.

A: You mean the split between the enunciator and the enunciated in the appropriation of the first person pronoun. To return to the discursive dimension of the dialogic, Volosinov says of the word: "*word is a two-sided act. It is determined equally by whose word it is and for whom it is meant. As word, it is precisely the product of the reciprocal relationship between speaker and listener, addresser and addressee.* Each and every word expresses the 'one' in relation to the 'other.' I give myself verbal shape from another's point of view, ultimately, from the point of view of the community to which I belong. A word is a bridge thrown between myself and another. If one end of the bridge depends on me, then the other depends on my addressee. A word is territory shared by both addresser and addressee, by the speaker and his interlocutor."[9] Every word, saturated in contextual meaning, becomes a word about the word of another addressed to someone else.

Q: The tropic structure of Volosinov's statement, the implications of words such as "bridge" and "territory," posits a model of communication less concerned with an ideal of intersubjectivity than with one of social community, which was being suppressed, from what you said, by an authoritarian state.

A: But a community which constitutes itself through language, discourse providing both the context and the text of social formations. As Todorov reminds us, the dialogic presupposes not two physical bodies but two or more social entities.[10] Even though Todorov insists that intersubjectivity logically precedes subjectivity and that a dialogic relation posits an other as another subject, the dialogic remains the structure of a relation rather than a content. The relation between two subjects is a semiotic one, one based not on empathy inspired by ethics but on a power differential.

Q: This becomes particularly clear in Todorov's *The Conquest of America,* where the lack of dialogue between the Indians and the Spanish leads to genocide not because of military inferiority but because of a clash between symbolic systems: that is, an oral rather than a written tradition, the use of images rather than writing, the presence rather than the absence of the referent. Do you mind if I quote a rather lengthy passage which will make the semiotic content of this relation clearer?

A: Not at all.

Q: Columbus in his encounter with the Indians could adopt one of two attitudes:

> Either he conceives the Indians (though without using these words) as human beings altogether, having the same rights as himself; but then he sees them not only as equals but also as identical, and this behavior leads to assimilationism, the projection of his own values on the others. Or else he starts from the difference, but the latter is immediately translated into terms of superiority and inferiority (in his case obviously, it is the Indians who are inferior). What is denied is the existence of a human substance truly other, something capable of being not merely an imperfect state of oneself. These two elementary figures of the experience of alterity are both grounded in egocentrism, in the identification of our own values with values in general, of our *I* with the universe—in the conviction that the world is one.[11]

The Indian as other fails to retain a status as subject because he/she is never seen as "comparable to what I am myself."[12]

A: It is important to reiterate that equality as a corrupt form of identity is no better than difference which deteriorates into inequality. And it is only by speaking *to* rather than *about* the other that I acknowledge him/her as another subject.

Q: If the dialogic is a semiotic structure and not a model of communication, "a fierce social struggle" rather than "a friendly and polite discussion,"[13] how and where are we to locate it?

A: Bakhtin distinguishes between at least five different types of dialogic relationship. Double-voiced discourse arises between individual words, "if that word is perceived . . . as a sign of someone else's semantic position, as the representative of another person's utterance; that is, if we hear in it someone else's voice."[14] It also arises between whole utterances, between language styles or social dialects, in relation to aspects of one's own previous utterance, and among different semiotic phenomena such as images belonging to different art forms. Dialogism finds its most explicit expression in the novel, in the relation between author and character. There the author and character approach the same theme through two different discourses, entering a semantic bond based on the intersection of two embodied meanings.[15]

Q: Why the novel?

A: Because the novel has always been both a noncanonical genre, which prevents it from congealing into one of the genres of the canon, and a mixed genre, which allows it to incorporate so-called "extraliterary genres," the most common being the letter, the diary, and the confession.

Q: Before I ask you about the relation between "extraliterary genres" and intertextuality, how do you differentiate between dialogic and dialogue?

A: In the direct speech of characters no bond is established with the author because dramatic dialogue represents an objectified discourse against which other objective discourses are directed. Dramatic dialogue splits a single discourse into two or more represented voices without threatening the unity of the author's semantic position;[16] the dialogic represents the struggle between opposing discourses arising out of different contexts, either semantic or sociohistorical. Unlike the dialectic, which seeks to transcend oppositions by means of a synthetic third term, the dialogic resists the reconciliation of opposites by insisting on the reciprocity of two or more antagonistic voices. Both the dialectic and the dialogic are based in theories of conflict, but the former attempts to resolve antitheses in a utopian synthesis while the latter seeks to disrupt the assimilation of differences sought by a monologic discourse.[17]

Q: The most distinguishing characteristic of *this* dialogue seems to be its propensity for digression; and so far we have used the dialogic to describe the word, the novel, and the conquest of America. You distinguish it from dialogue and the dialectic, but I'm still not quite sure what its relationship is to intertextuality and difference, not to mention alterity.

A: I think this confusion or dialogue between levels of semiotic analysis is precisely what has made the dialogic so attractive as a theory and yet so elusive as a term. But the inclusion of Julia Kristeva in our discussion will lead us on to intertextuality.

Q: It was Kristeva who introduced Bakhtin to the French-speaking world . . .

A: By writing the introduction to the French translation of *Dostoevsky's Poetics*.[18] And it was she who coined the term "intertextuality" to mean "intertextual dialogue" and who pointed out an inadequate theory of the subject in Bakhtin's text. This she traces to its psychologism, a missing theory of the language user, and the influence of Christianity in a humanist terminology which still speaks of such things as heroes' "souls." She replaces the psychological with the psychoanalytic, intersubjectivity with intertextuality, and the nineteenth-century realist novel with the avant-garde modernist text.

Q: And emphasizes the other "logic" of the dialogic.

A: The logic of the dream, a logic which exceeds codified discourse because it is no longer predicated on causality. This "other" logic is seen as subversive, as anti-Christian and antirationalist, as a transgression of linguistic and social codes, similar to Bakhtin's notion of the carnival.[19]

Q: By carnival you mean . . . ?

A: Both the carnival and the dream offer recurrent disruptions of a seemingly stable order: that of the ruling class and that of the unified ego. The carnival as pageant abolishes the distinction between spectator and performer (i.e., the distinction between art and life), and as symbolic event temporarily reverses the hierarchical order of birth and death, high and low, male and female, and so on. The "carnivalization of literature," which appears most explicitly in the novels of Rabelais, reveals "that 'normalcy,' order, orthodoxy, hierarchy, and determined, monolithic social relations should themselves be considered momentary, and arbitrary, even if they are serious reductions of social and political possibilities, powerful defenses against alterity and change."[20]

Q: Why has the carnival in particular had such an appeal for Marxist critics?

A: Because of its roots in popular culture and its reversal of social hierarchies. Yet like the dialogic, which fails to offer a model of communication, the carnival unsuccessfully provides a mode of political intervention. Both refer to discursive events, not to intersubjective or revolutionary moments. In essence, Marxist critics have appropriated

Bakhtin because they see him as adding history to post-structuralism, yet they have done so largely by dehistoricizing the carnival itself.[21]

Q: One could even argue that the role of the folk as the idealized other in the carnival has a similar function to "the feminine" in the psychoanalysis of Kristeva.

A: But Kristeva begins by rewriting the dialogue between author and hero in terms of the Lacanian split subject. If we turn back for a moment to the novel, we discover that the author constitutes his character as autonomous discourse rather than as objectified image. Bakhtin writes: "For the author the hero is not 'he' and not 'I' but a fully valid 'thou,' that is, another and other autonomous 'I' ('thou art'). The hero is the subject of a deeply serious, *real* dialogic mode of address, not the subject of a rhetorically *performed* or *conventionally* literary one."[22]

Q: For Kristeva such a statement would certainly border too closely on the theological as well as the psychological.

A: Which is why she replaces the relation between author and hero as writing subject and addressee with a notion of the addressee as discourse itself: "The writer's interlocutor, then, is the writer himself, but as reader of another text. The one who writes is the same as the one who reads. Since his interlocutor is a text, he himself is no more than a text rereading itself as it rewrites itself. The dialogical structure, therefore, appears only in the light of the text elaborating itself as ambivalent in relation to another text."[23] The other speaking subject becomes the other of the split subject and both exist as plural and fragmentary texts within an intertextual discourse.

Q: So intertextual refers to the relation not only between texts but also between subjects, who themselves are written and read.

A: Subjects who are divided by their listening and by their reading in their writing of the other, the other both as interlocutor and as sociohistorical context. For Kristeva, intertextuality occurs in the "in-between" of texts, in the nonlinguistic, the negative, the rupture, what she calls the "unreadable" of modernist writing.

Q: Before we pursue the relation between the modernist text and "the feminine," we might review Lacan's splitting of the subject in the Imaginary and its relation to the dialogic.

A: The distinction you seem to be referring to is the difference one might make between a Lacanian misrecognition of the other as self in the mirror and a Bakhtinian recognition of the self in the gaze of the other.

Although both theorists use visual metaphors, for Lacan looking leads to alienation because the object of sight is an illusion, while for Bakhtin it leads to dialogue because only the response of the other guarantees one's visibility.[24]

Q: How would you characterize each theorist's representation of self and other in terms of a system of differences?

A: In Lacan the entrance into the Symbolic destroys the narcissistic identification of the Imaginary by marking the entrance into language as a system of differences; for Bakhtin, in order to maintain the differences necessary for dialogue, the speaker's discourse must constantly struggle against its tendency to assimilate the speech of the other. For Lacan the Symbolic dissolves the mother-child dyad in order to insert a third term in the figure of the Father as Language, the Law, the Institution, a paradigm still largely indebted to the dialectic. Bakhtin begins with a synthesis, the inclusion of both speaker and addressee in any utterance, but the usurpation of one position by the other transforms the dialogic into a monologic voice, a discourse which is closed, authoritarian, and absolute.

Q: Could one say that for Bakhtin we are all authors, potential participants in the reversed hierarchies, suspended privileges, and relativized norms of the carnival, and for Lacan we are always already authored, assigned a position in a system of differences marked by the two doors which require that we position ourselves in front of one or the other?

A: You mean the two doors marked masculine and feminine,[25] which finally brings us to the issue of gender. I think Caryl Emerson's statement provides the best articulation of the differences between Lacan and Bakhtin: "speech is based on the idea of lack, and dialogue, on the idea of difference."[26] The other defined as lack or as different has enormous implications for notions of "the feminine" and for the practices of feminist criticism.

Q: But difference has also been unveiled as the repetition and displacement of the same.[27]

A: Yet I would argue that the dialogic is the only theory which situates difference discursively, as a social practice rather than a theoretical construct, as the product of ideological formations rather than personal experiences.

Q: What about the French feminists, like Kristeva?

A: One could argue that her semiotic, as the other of the Symbolic, also signifies its lack.[28]

Q: Or its disruption.

A: But certainly the lack of women writers in Kristeva's list of avant-garde authors (which include writers such as Mallarmé, Artaud, and Joyce) makes a difference in terms of feminist criticism.

Q: Why? Where does she locate "the feminine"?

A: Kristeva focuses on "the feminine" primarily in terms of male writers' identification with the mother,[29] which takes the form of fetishism or homosexuality, depending on whether they adopt the masculine or the feminine position. Female writers enter her discourse principally as the victims of suicide. Since for a woman literary production cannot provide the narcissistic gratification it does for a man, the disruption of language leads to madness rather than innovation.[30] And since female homosexuality can be conceived of only as the virilization of "the feminine," women writers' lack of access to a maternal figure leads to premature death.[31]

Q: But do we want to posit a specifically female subject or what Kristeva calls a subject "en procès" [in process/on trial][32]—one which challenges the authority of a monologic God, a transcendental ego, and a representational discourse?

A: You would have no qualms with Alice Jardine's reading of Kristeva: "For Kristeva, it is not a question of whether women write differently from or the same as men, but rather it is a question of examining how the dialectization of the two functions is different in texts written by those on the margins of our culture."[33] But how legitimate is it to collapse historical differences based on race, class, and gender into a generalized notion of "marginality"?[34]

Q: Which brings me to another point, namely that Kristeva imagines "the difference between the sexes not as a fixed opposition ('man-woman') but as a process of *differentiation.*"[35]

A: The undecidability of gender is an important concept for feminist critical theory but a problematic one for feminist criticism. On the one hand, the undecidability of gender displaces difference not by eternally deferring the feminine but by destabilizing the terms masculine and feminine. On the other hand, if we retain an interest in the production and reception of literary texts, then the gender of the author as historical subject can never remain undecidable.

Q: Which brings us to another signature, split between the male patronym of the female historical subject and the male pseudonym of the female author.

A: That should probably bring us back to Bakhtin.

Q: Does Bakhtin make any mention of gender?

A: Quite the contrary. His interest lies in the canonized male authors of Western literary history: Sophocles, Dante, Cervantes; and he unproblematically conceptualizes both author and hero as masculine. If the dialogic relation is viewed primarily as an antagonistic one,[36] rather than as courteous conversation in the drawing room (the only discursive situation in which the sexual difference of the speakers is mentioned),[37] the question remains as to what extent it might inscribe "the feminine."

Q: Or include women, given that the inclusion or exclusion from military conflict and decision-making remains one of the primary figures for the difference in the social inscription of men and women.

A: Several readers of Bakhtin have found it necessary to excuse Bakhtin's use of militarized language, claiming that it reflects "the general militarization of Soviet life and language during the prewar and war years"[38] or that the conflict between languages represents "a *happy* war . . . So while voices 'do battle' they do not die out—that is, no authority is established once and for all."[39] But no one has examined how this type of rhetoric is inscribed in a text which fails to thematize a sex-gender system, or what its implications might be for the status of sexual difference in theoretical discourse.[40]

Q: What about Wayne Booth?

A: His findings are far from revolutionary: "The truth is that nowhere in Rabelais does one find any hint of an effort to imagine any woman's point of view or to incorporate women into a dialogue. And nowhere in Bakhtin does one discover any suggestion that he sees the importance of this kind of monologue, not even when he discusses Rabelais' attitude toward women."[41] Booth takes feminist criticism back to its historical beginnings by focusing on images of women in male texts. His coming-to-consciousness as a feminist reader, whose "pleasure in the canon" has been greatly diminished by the discovery that it is male-dominated, remains a dialogue primarily with himself.

Q: So what is the alternative? Woman as lack? Gender as absent in virtually every major male theory?

A: Now you're beginning to sound like me.

Q: One could ask the question differently: why the dialogic when there have been so many feminist articulations of woman's "double consciousness"?

A: You mean, for instance, Nancy Chodorow, who borrows her paradigm from Freud: "Women define and experience themselves relationally. Their heterosexual orientation is always in internal dialogue with both oedipal and preoedipal mother-child relational issues."[42]

Q: Or Michèle Barrett, who expresses it in Marxist terms: "the relationship she has to the class structure by virtue of her wage labour (or her ownership of the means of production) will be substantially influenced by the mediation of this direct relationship through dependence on men and responsibility for domestic labour and childcare."[43]

A: The most obvious model for literary practices would be Elaine Showalter's, which, borrowing from Edwin Ardener's model, posits women as a muted group whose cultural boundaries coincide with, yet are not completely contained by, the dominant male group. As a result: "women's writing is a 'double-voiced discourse' that always embodies the social, literary, and cultural heritages of both the muted and the dominant."[44]

Q: Why, then, is it important to distinguish the dialogic from this "double-voiced discourse"?

A: Primarily because of its implications for feminist criticism. The dominant and the muted have most often been read as "the dominant and the muted story," as told above all in the novel—a reading that began, of course, with Gilbert and Gubar's *Madwoman in the Attic*. But the emphasis has been on the rewriting of literary conventions, principally those of plot and character. There has been little concern with a more radical breaking of form, with rhetorical strategies which fall outside standard genres, with a rewriting of gender which does not presuppose the heterosexual romance plot.[45]

Q: What seems to be missing is a notion of language itself as "double-voiced," the other as the other of the split subject, the other as text.

A: Exactly. These readings leave out the inscription of the other not just as the hegemonic male text but as the reappropriation of the "other" woman, that is, in the reappropriation of conventionally female literary forms, in the construction of female characters, and in the very act of saying "I."[46] Monique Wittig, for instance, begins at the level of the pronoun. She problematizes the act of speaking by inscribing female subjectivity in a doubly split first-person pronoun: "J/e is the symbol of the lived, rending experience which is m/y writing, of this cutting in two which through literature is the exercise of a language which does not constitute m/e as subject. J/e poses the ideological and historic question of feminine subjects."[47]

Q: In other words, the female subject is doubly split because when it appropriates the first-person pronoun, it vacillates between a subject position which is masculine and the function of the feminine which is that of object.

A: At the same time, the first-person pronoun is the least stable of all linguistic signifiers, since its referent changes with every utterance; every person who says "I" refers to a person with a different name. By masking its gender it obscures the fact that any subject speaks from a position marked by sexual difference; by masquerading as genderless it embodies the possibility of disrupting difference by eliminating gender altogether.

Q: So where does Irigaray fit in?

A: Irigaray attempts to disrupt symbolic discourse not by positing the semiotic as a second signifying system but by reimagining the female Imaginary. Rather than locating the disruption of dominant discourse in the poetic language of male modernist texts, she deconstructs the figures of philosophical discourse, "the discourse on discourse."[48] She reopens, unveils, and exposes these figures as predicated on a single libidinal economy, a male homosexual one, or "l'hom(m)o-sexualité."[49]

Q: What are the implications of this "hom(m)o-sexualité" for the female subject?

A: She writes that we must "interpret, at each 'moment,' the *specular make-up* of discourse, that is, the self-reflecting (stratifiable) organization of the subject in that discourse. An organization that maintains, among other things, the break between what is perceptible and what is intelligible, and thus maintains the submission, subordination, and exploitation of the 'feminine.'"[50] Woman remains imperceptible, therefore unintelligible, because her sexual organ offers "nothing to see."

Q: And "the feminine"?

A: "The feminine" exists as the "repetition-representation-reproduction of sameness,"[51] that is, not different from but the same as the masculine. Woman in a male libidinal economy "mimics" the posture of "femininity" which has been assigned to her. Her mimetic function prohibits engagement in self-representation because it requires participation in the autorepresentation of the masculine. Alienated from her own desire, her position becomes one of "in-difference": nondifferentiation from the masculine and unresponsiveness to her role as impostor. At the same time "in-difference" also contains the possibility of difference as alterity in her eventual indifference to the masculine (subject).

Q: Alterity?

A: Alterity as the radical difference between two subjects, as a difference not predicated on the a priori hierarchy of sexual difference which posits a universal subject and thereby writes the other as the repetition of the same.

Q: How would you distinguish this "in-difference" from Kristeva's "intertextuality"?

A: Whereas Kristeva locates the splitting in the mirror within the modernist text as the rewriting of the text as "intertextual" (i.e., as that which is produced between texts and in the "in-between" of the text), Irigaray rewrites the figure of the mirror (i.e., the flat mirror of masculine self-representation) as the speculum.

Q: The speculum?

A: The gynecological instrument, used by the male medical establishment to appropriate the female body, has been reappropriated as figure for the self-representation of the female subject in discourse. The speculum would "put into place a mode of specularization that allows for the relation of woman to 'herself' and to her like. Which presupposes *a curved mirror*, but also one that is *folded back on itself*, with its impossible reappropriation 'on the inside' of the mind, of thought, of subjectivity. Whence the *intervention of the speculum and of the concave mirror*, which disturb the staging of representation according to too-exclusively masculine parameters."[52] The speculum, by conforming to the shape of the object it reflects, allows the female subject to represent itself as specular image: as self-reflecting image which represents the female subject as *both* self *and* other, not as a self which exists only in the Lacanian Other as language, already appropriated by the masculine subject who represents the other as feminine.

Q: What does woman "see" in this specular image?

A: She sees "nothing," but not the "nothing to see" of her sexual lack. She resists all definition, being neither one nor two, analogous to her lips, both oral and vaginal, the figure for her desire as well as its representation.

Q: Hasn't Irigaray repeatedly been accused of returning to a form of biological essentialism, reifying the "two" and substituting it for the original one?

A: This can be attributed to the fact that the figure she borrows is a biological one. Like Lacan's "phallus" the lips have both an anatomical and a symbolic function, instrumental in the articulation of speech as well as desire. Thus speech becomes an expression of female rather than male desire, and desire is linked to the labia rather than the uterus; that is, to linguistic production rather than biological reproduction, to the spoken rather than to hysterical symptoms. In addition, speech becomes the product of the individual (female) subject, rather than remaining the property of a linguistic system already governed by the Law.

Q: Once again the insistence on the symbolic status of the phallus and the referential value of the lips betrays the equation of the masculine with the figurative and the feminine with the literal.[53]

A: And as Jane Gallop reminds us: "Belief in simple referentiality is not only unpoetic but also ultimately politically conservative, because it cannot recognize that the reality to which it appeals is a traditional ideological construction, whether one terms it phallomorphic, or metaphysical, or bourgeois, or something else."[54] Irigaray offers a mode of perceiving the feminine which is other to the masculine, not as the "other," not as another "one," but as the simultaneity of subject and object in a state of reciprocity.

Q: Reciprocity as discursive exchange, similar to the dialogic?

A: Before we describe it as dialogic, we might introduce a discursive activity specific to women conversing in unmixed company, what Irigaray calls "parler-femme": "Speaking (as) woman is not speaking of woman. It is not a matter of producing a discourse of which woman would be the object, or the subject. That said, by *speaking (as) woman,* one may attempt to provide a place for the 'other' as feminine."[55]

Q: And where does she locate that place?

A: In an Imaginary which has not yet been disrupted by the Symbolic, where woman can still look at herself.

Q: Similar to Eve in *Paradise Lost* gazing at her reflection in the pool before she is made to valorize the superior "beauty" of Adam.

A: Precisely.

Q: Does Irigaray herself write such "female" texts?

A: She has produced various dialogic discourses, some of them deconstructions of male theoretical texts, such as those by Nietzsche and Heidegger;[56] others, short dialogues between voices of either the female or an indeterminate sex.[57] *Speculum of the Other Woman* is a reply to the position of the feminine in Lacanian psychoanalysis; *This Sex Which Is Not One* responds to the difficulties encountered by the readers of *Speculum*. *Speculum* is divided into three parts: the first on Freud and the third on Plato mirror each other, while at the same time disrupting historical chronology. The center section speaks from "the other side of the looking-glass" by offering an alternative to a self-reflecting male philosophical discourse. *This Sex* contains an essay entitled "Questions" which offers responses to questions asked in a series of letters, at a doctoral defense, in an interview.

Q: Can you give us an example of the last type of discourse?

A: In "When Our Lips Speak Together," a voice addresses its specular other as follows: "We live by twos beyond all mirages, images, and mirrors. Between us, one is not the 'real' and the other her imitation; one is not the original and the other her copy. Although we can dissimulate perfectly within their economy, we relate to one another without simulacrum. Our resemblance does without semblances: for in our bodies, we are already the same. Touch yourself, touch me, you'll 'see.' "[58]

Q: What does Irigaray mean here by "seeing"?

A: She rewrites the dominant metaphor of the visual in order to establish a link between philosophical speculation—cognizance as a form of self-reflection—and psychoanalytic specularization as the splitting of the subject in the mirror stage. The specular both constitutes the subject as speaking subject in the mirror and represses or silences the feminine because it offers "nothing to see." For Irigaray "to see" means to see oneself other than in the mirror of someone else's self-representation; that is, for the female subject to "see" (i.e., represent) itself in relation to itself and its own sex.

Q: Which places the emphasis on the discursive reproduction of the subject rather than on the discourse between two subjects.

A: Dialogue implies two subjects, but since "any theory of the subject has always been appropriated by the 'masculine,' "[59] this has only been imaginable between two masculine subjectivities. For a subject to speak, it must be able to represent itself neither as "masquarade" nor as "mimicry" but as specular image. Specularity requires that the female subject be able to represent itself by representing the other as feminine, not itself as the other of the masculine. Irigaray's female specular subject finds its most succinct articulation in the statement: " 'She' is indefinitely other in herself."[60]

Q: Can you explain this?

A: "She" appears in quotation marks, implying that the female subject functions as syntactic subject but has no identity as a sexually different subjectivity. To be "other" in oneself prohibits the possession as object by an "other" which puts itself in the position of the subject. To be so "indefinitely" implies a lack of closure, of completeness, of narcissistic self-containment.

Q: Are you proposing, then, a redefinition of narcissism?

A: If not a redefinition, then at least a reconsideration of the inscription of narcissism in two different (i.e., male and female) libidinal economies. At the very moment when the universal (male) subject experiences the dissolution of a narcissistic identification through his entrance into the Symbolic, the female subject has her identity as narcissistic woman culturally guaranteed. In Freud's terms: "[narcissistic] women love only themselves with an intensity comparable to that of the man's love for them. Nor does their need lie in the direction of loving, but of being loved."[61] By never substituting her desire for herself with the desire for a male other, she inscribes herself as the other for the male self. The narcissistic woman remains the most fascinating to men because she represents a prior state, that of an unfissured subjectivity.

Q: So on the one hand the narcissistic woman is never divided, and yet as speaking subject she is always already divided. What do you do with this contradiction?

A: The as yet undivided narcissistic woman is nevertheless part of a division as the other of man, "the feminine" as the unconscious, as the unrepresentable, as lack. But rather than being more narcissistic, woman actually undergoes what Irigaray calls a process of "denarcissization."[62] She is denied the possibility of re-presenting herself because of the "unrepresentable" nature of her origin: born lacking (a penis), the daughter of a castrated mother, she comes to recognize her sex as scarred and insufficient.

Q: So how does she reverse this unpresentability? Through a process of "renarcissization"?

A: Or what I would call specularization, the possibility of representing the female subject as self-reflexive act. This requires not only a political, but also a discursive understanding of the female subject as ideological construct. It requires an awareness, with every inscription of the feminine within a text, of one's own inscription as female author, both as historical subject and as the product of a female literary history. It exacts an apprehension of the female subject as theoretical construct, appropriating the position of the masculine in a discursivity which has repeatedly objectified "the feminine" as other.

Q: How, then, would you distinguish between a "dialogized" and a "specularized" discourse?

A: The dialogic imagines the discourse between two subjects; specularity posits the subject as dialogized. For Bakhtin the word is double-voiced; any utterance contains the word of both sender and receiver, and language remains the struggle between utterances. For Irigaray the struggle for the female subject begins before the entrance into a language which has already foreclosed the possibility of a female subjectivity; and yet that subject cannot exist outside language. The subject struggles to rewrite itself as a subjectivity by representing both a subject and an object position. For Bakhtin this means responding to and anticipating the word of another; for Irigaray it means being neither one nor two, neither open nor closed, never the copy of someone else's original.

Q: Given that one discourse seems highly practical and the other highly theoretical, what do you see as their point of intersection?

A: Both the dialogic as a theory without a system and specularity as the deconstruction of a psychoanalytic theory are concerned with perceptions of the "other," with epistemological and discursive representations of alterity. For Bakhtin otherness is threatened by the authority of a totalitarian regime: the monologic represents the assimilation and thus the annihilation of difference as conflicting voices; for Irigaray "the feminine" is subsumed under the hierarchy of sexual difference: phallologocentrism relies on the erasure of "the feminine" to guarantee the masculine as sovereign subject. For Bakhtin the danger lies in turning another subject into an other; for Irigaray it lies in being that other as well as in being the subject predicated on the construction of an other.

Q: How do you propose translating between one critical discourse and the other?

A: By dialogizing them, by creating a dialogue between Bakhtin's dialogic and sexual difference as it is currently being debated within feminist critical theory.[63] The outcome would be a female dialogic, not as synthesis but as struggle.

Q: A female dialogic?

A: The female dialogic imagined both as the dialogue between Bakhtin's gender-blind theory and Irigaray's deconstruction of a male-biased theory and as the debate within feminist critical theory between the deconstruction of the subject as such (Kristeva) and the reconstruction of a subject as female (Irigaray). This debate will find its parallel in the dialogue between Virginia Woolf and Christa Wolf, where Woolf envisions the disappearance of the individual subject and Wolf imagines its reemergence as female.

Q: Before we get to Woolf and Wolf, would you briefly explain the relation between specularity and the female dialogic?

A: Specularity allows for the possibility of a female dialogic: it constructs the subject as gendered in dialogue with itself as other.[64] On the one hand, it retains the visual as an epistemological category integral to a mimetic theory of representation necessary for a feminist politics; on the other hand, it inscribes the specular subject in specifically literary categories such as the epistle, the novel, a female literary history.

Q: Can you be more specific?

A: The visual remains an important category not just as a metaphor of cognition but also for a feminist critique of contemporary forms of popular culture such as film, advertisement, and pornography. At the same time, forms of high culture such as literary genres inscribe the specular subject as fictional character rather than as theoretical construct.

Q: We've briefly discussed the role of the visual in distinguishing between the Lacanian and the Bakhtinian gaze. What difference does a gendered subject make?

A: The introduction of a gendered subject into either model reveals an asymmetry of looking: if the gaze of the other, either in the mirror or on the street, constitutes the subject, the female subject has repeatedly been constituted by the male gaze. And as Anthony Wilden reminds us: "no man is for woman simply her other in the mirror. He is also her master and exploiter; he is the Other."[65]

Q: Woman is made visible only through the male gaze, which renders her invisible except where she elicits an erotic response as visual object.

A: Which she does by representing herself as the object of desire of both her own gaze and that of the masculine subject. As John Berger first described it in *Ways of Seeing:* "You painted a naked woman because you enjoyed looking at her, you put a mirror in her hand and you called the painting *Vanity,* thus morally condemning the woman whose nakedness you had depicted for your own pleasure."[66]

Q: In other words, the mirror splits the female subject while retaining her essential narcissism, and the act of looking requires her to adopt both gendered positions, simultaneously masculine as subject and feminine as object of the gaze.

A: Or as Berger concludes: "*men act* and *women appear.* Men look at women. Women watch themselves being looked at. This determines not only most relations between men and women but also the relation of women to themselves. The surveyor of woman in herself is male: the surveyed female. Thus she turns herself into an object—and most particularly an object of vision: a sight."[67]

Q: And to take it one step further, woman both reproduces herself as other and reproduces the otherness of sexual difference.

A: Precisely. This vacillation between masculine and feminine as a function of looking has been examined by feminist film theorists, who have used the asymmetry of the gaze to theorize the vacillation rather than the relation between gender positions. Almost all this work has rewritten Laura Mulvey's theory, which posits man as bearer of the look and woman as icon. According to Mulvey, woman as spectator either masochistically overidentifies with the female image or narcissistically becomes her own object of desire.[68]

Q: So woman has finally lost her invisibility as "nothing to see" to become a spectator in the process of looking.

A: Mary Ann Doane attempts to address the problem of the female spectator by replacing woman's narcissistic overidentification with the female image with her oscillation between a feminine and masculine spectator position characteristic of the transvestite. In "Film and the Masquerade: Theorising the Female Spectator" she replaces the spectacle, where man is the subject and woman the object of the gaze, with the masquerade: "The masquerade, in flaunting femininity, holds it at a distance. Womanliness is a mask which can be worn or removed. The masquerade's resistance to patriarchal positioning would therefore lie in its denial of the production of femininity as closeness, as presence-to-itself, as, precisely, imagistic."[69]

Q: But how is femininity as "imagistic" different from femininity as "specular"?

A: Femininity as "imagistic" equates the image with the feminine, while the masquerade allows for distance from the image by unmasking the feminine as fictive. Behind the image lies another image, but this time a self-reflexive one which reveals itself as mask. Through this distancing the female viewer destabilizes the image and thereby defamiliarizes traditional forms of female iconography.

Q: How would you apply this to literary forms of fiction which involve linguistic rather than visual modes of representation?

A: The specular image reveals itself as mask when it leaves the realm of theory and enters the realm of literary production. There, not only does the relation between author and character take the form of a specular image—the character as both self and other—but the character functions as mask, allowing for a critique of subjectivity, leading to innovations in discursive structures.

Q: What remains of the visual?

A: The visual remains as a metaphor for the process of representing the "other" woman. "Seeing" her means seeing her for the first time as female subjectivity rather than as idealized image; it also means seeing her so that she can appear as subject, in spite of her status as the object of discourse. In addition, visual forms such as the mirror, paintings, and the dramatic scene are thematized as realms which include the feminine as icon, thereby excluding her as speaking subject. These forms are rewritten as specular images which allow the female subject to represent herself as something to be seen within a self-reflexive act.

Q: By self-reflexive you mean?

A: Highly aware of its process of production and therefore of its fictionality. Whether the female author borrows from traditional modes of representing subjectivity and simply changes the gender or whether the representation of subjectivity itself is transformed, the female subject remains a fiction, historically because she has been elided by the representations of men, theoretically because the feminine is the marked term in the binary opposition of sexual difference, and discursively because the female literary character offers the only space for a potentially new kind of subjecthood.

Q: Which takes us back to the theoretical fictions of Kristeva and Irigaray . . .

A: And forward to the debate over the female subject in feminist critical theory. Irigaray returns the feminine to its presymbolic origins, thus positing a moment before speech, whereas Kristeva places the feminine on the margin, thus imagining it outside speech. For Irigaray the absence of a female subject leads to a female subject which is neither one nor two; for Kristeva it leads to a subject which is both masculine and feminine.

Q: In either case the female subject is absent as well as divided.

A: Because it continues to represent the site of the very problem of the subject rather than a subjectivity determined by a different sexual identity. Gayatri Spivak describes this dilemma of the feminist critical theorist most aptly: "If she confines herself to asking the question of woman (what is woman?), she might merely be attempting to provide an answer to the honorable male question: what does woman want? She herself still remains the *object* of the question. To reverse the situation would be to ask the question of woman as a subject: what am I? That would bring back all the absolutely convincing deconstructive critiques of the sovereign subject."[70]

Q: The alternative?

A: To dialogize the theoretical double-bind by returning to the site of the female character as female subject and as fiction.

Q: In the novel?

A: Not just in the novel. The female subject functions as necessary fiction in the epistolary essay and in literary history as well.

Q: The difference?

A: The difference would be that the hierarchy of difference as sexual difference would be replaced by the dialogic. The dialogic would be rewritten on the one hand as specularity, to guarantee the inclusion of the female subject as dialogized, and on the other hand as alterity, to inscribe the subject as such in a different ideology.

Q: The other woman?

A: Is the woman who is both self and other in the interview.

CHAPTER TWO

THE EPISTOLARY ESSAY
A Letter

The letter can be either portrait or mask.
—JANET ALTMAN, _Epistolarity_

Dear D.,

What a relief, finally, to speak to someone else. The inevitable theoretical introductions one produces to somehow legitimize one's position. The sense, too often, that one is speaking to those who would rather not be listening, or listen because they assume they do it temporarily, waiting for us to let go of our resistance, and thus of our differences. But will it ever be the same?

It's been years since you read to me the draft of an essay entitled "The Relationship Between Epistolary History and Edith Wharton's Fiction."[1] (I'm still not quite sure why you insisted on reading it aloud, that afternoon suspended between the exposed brick and the hanging ferns, on a busy street in that early industrial town.) In its final form (the one you eventually turned in), you placed your indebtedness in a footnote. I'm writing to you in an attempt to turn that debt into a dialogue by naming the addressee not in the subtext (where we too often relegate it) but in the text of the essay. (It was you who most often spoke of the monologic tendencies of academic discourse, of its hegemony, its exclusionary practices.)

I hope you will also find the female dialogic useful for examining the epistolary essays of Virginia Woolf and Christa Wolf. As you know, Woolf and Wolf have each come to represent a side of the debate over the construction of the female subject (something I could never have anticipated then, in those days, when it was just a few of us thinking about such things, and each of us caught in the exigencies of our own disciplines). They both address an individual interlocutor in order to position themselves in opposition to the institutions most responsible for their formation, the patriarchal family and the socialist state, yet do so for different purposes. Woolf constitutes her addressee as antagonist in order to diminish her own position as female speaking subject, thus undermining the stability of the subject itself; Wolf constitutes her interlocutor as ally in order to construct the female subject as alternative subjectivity, thus writing herself and her literary precursors into history. I'm writing to you because you have thought about women and letters and specifically about the circulation of letters and the circulation of women as signs.

In your essay you examine the tension between the letter as gift and the letter as commodity when a woman begins to make a living by her gift, by publishing her labor in the world of letters as fiction: "When a woman can support herself, sidestepping the inevitable fate of the movement from father to husband by peddling her own falsified versions of her self, not only is the gift economy in which she is implicated subtly deconstructed and reworked into commodity capitalism, but an entirely new fictional character is created: a woman who perceives the commercial system she is implicated in and begins to manipulate it to her own pleasure and advantage. Thus the woman's ultimate gift of herself, the passionate missive, becomes consciously crafted for commercial gain."[2] As you suggest, to enter the economy as gift-giver, rather than as gift, requires not the construction of a more authentic female subjectivity but a more skillful manipulation of the female persona, which requires displacing desire from the body onto the text.

Rather than circulating the signs of discourse and desire and the signs of capitalism within the same economy, my own interest lies in the rhetorical strategies modern women writers adopt when they simultaneously inscribe themselves in a feminine tradition of letter writing (here I rely largely on Woolf) and a masculine tradition of the written essay (here I rely largely on my own reading). You mention that in 1901 the love letters from a woman were still thought to be the "spontaneous unconscious outpouring of true feeling."[3] How then are we to read the epistle in our own age, an age in which telecommunications have largely replaced written correspondence and women are now the respected authors of scholarly books?

Both Woolf and Wolf, as you know, repeatedly return to the epistolary essay as a self-conscious strategy for engaging in a public critique of masculinist culture while presuming to engage in a private correspondence.[4] Their essays foreground the theoretical problem of woman's relation to the literal letter and to literary language as the discourse of the canonized male author; they also insert themselves into a historical tradition of women as the writers of personal epistles. This simultaneous inscription in a theoretical and a historical discourse produces a double-voiced text which examines both the practices of domination of a hegemonic culture and its exclusionary stance toward the literary production of women. The woman writer, simultaneously included in and excluded from discursive practices, positions herself dialogically; that is, by constituting herself in relation to an other, in this case, the epistolary addressee.

I thought I would begin with a review of the debates on the letter within language and the unconscious, while at the same time acknowledging, as you insist upon doing, the history of women's letter writing as a form of conscious, codified behavior. I have therefore decided to return to the texts which precede Barbara Johnson's essay "The Frame of Reference: Poe, Lacan, Derrida," from which you selected the epigraph to your own paper, by beginning with Jacques Lacan.

According to Lacan, a letter can be a character from the alphabet, an epistle, or what distinguishes a man of letters. It can also refer to surface meanings, the literal, as in "the letter versus the spirit of the law." In his "Seminar on 'The Purloined Letter'" Lacan equates the letter with the signifier: the signifier and the epistle are both symbols of an absence. In Poe's tale "The Purloined Letter," the letter whose message is never revealed intimates that the queen has committed sexual treason against the king. Doubly absent, as stolen material object and as the missing discourse of female desire, the letter serves as a sign of woman as lack, whose circulation threatens the law of the signifier; that is, of the phallus (i.e., the king). Purloining the letter robs woman of her significance, making it possible to elevate her to the sign of signification as such. The feminine becomes equated with truth, with being as absence, as emptiness, as "hole."[5] In Derrida's words: "Truth is 'woman' as veiled/unveiled castration."[6]

Derrida does not read "The Purloined Letter" as an allegory of the signifier; it is rather a literary tale that reflects on its own rhetorical status, problematizing truth as fiction rather than as feminine. Arguing against Lacan's "idealization of the signifier" and his conclusion "that a letter always arrives at its destination"[7] (i.e., has an unequivocal meaning), Derrida suggests that a letter has no status as the literal since it already functions as division: it is the substance not of an absence but of a difference. As Barbara Johnson describes it in "The Frame of Reference": "A letter as a signifier is thus not a thing or the absence of a thing, not a word or the absence of a word, not an organ or the absence of an organ, but a *knot* in a structure where words, things, and organs can neither be definably separated nor compatibly combined."[8]

Johnson's deconstructive reading of Poe, Lacan, and Derrida addresses the problem of gender (as you perceived) by recognizing that anatomical difference creates an "irreducible dissymmetry to be accounted for in every human subject," but that this dissymmetry is irrelevant to the letter, which is not located in a geometrical or anatomical space but in the Symbolic, "a structure that can only be perceived in its effects. . . ."[9] The effect of the letter lies with its reader: "The letter's destination is thus *wherever it is read:* the place it assigns to its reader as his own partiality. Its destination is not a place, decided *a priori* by the sender, because the receiver is the sender, and the receiver is whoever receives the letter, including nobody."[10]

If the effect of the letter lies with the reader, then the epistle becomes the literary form which most consciously inscribes, even describes, its reader as addressee. The epistolary sender and receiver enter a power relation as gendered subjects that reenacts the sexual relations of a particular historical moment. The progression from Lacan's lack to Derrida's "difference" to Johnson's "knot" reveals a movement away from the feminine as negative Other to the marked term in a binary opposition to an element in the nonhierarchical figure of the knot. Nevertheless, the attempt to separate sexual difference from the Symbolic fails to address the particular relation to the letter of historical women. If anatomical difference in fact does "not matter to the letter," women writers would neither be remembered primarily as letter writers nor attempt to peddle their fictions as actual epistles.

While the letter as alphabetic character and letters as literature or learning have excluded women from the Symbolic by positing woman as the sign of signification, the epistle has enabled women to enter literary history as prolific writers of letters. Women's participation in the epistolary begins with a confusion between the letter and the literary, through the female impersonations of male authors. In the *Heroides* Ovid "writes like a woman" by authoring the letters of fifteen heroines, including Sappho, to the lovers who have seduced and betrayed them. *The Letters of a Portuguese Nun* (1669), attributed alternatively to Mariana Alcoforado and the Count of Guilleragues, have been read as letters when attributed to a woman and as literature when attributed to a man.[11] In both cases the letters from abandoned women to the lovers whom they refuse to relinquish participate in a repetitive structure of desire, seduction, and betrayal which inscribes itself textually as monologue.[12] The monophonic epistle portrays the failure of a female voice to establish an actual dialogue given her enforced solitude, coded as unrequited love.[13]

With the rise of the epistolary novel in England in the eighteenth century, writers such as Samuel Richardson continue to represent the politics of female desire by circulating a text of male authorship under a female name, such as *Pamela* (1740) or *Clarissa* (1748). Using the language of seduction rather than confession, the novel depicts the male lover as villain rather than enigma. The heroine's position in the discourse of the novel is again a reactive one, responding here to contested virtue. The letter continues to circulate as a sign for the female body, to be "purloined" if not freely given. The epistolary novel allows for a reciprocated discourse by providing both sides of the correspondence, inscribing female desire in a network of power relations legislated by the patriarchal family and commodity capitalism.[14]

As you point out in your paper, when female novelists, such as Mary Manley (1672?–1724) and Eliza Haywood (1693?–1756), enter the economy as popular writers, they do so by circulating their fictitious letters as authentic correspondences. In so doing the woman writer impersonates a romantic heroine far removed from her assigned position as a model of domestic virtue. No longer does a man impersonate a woman, but a woman impersonates "an/other woman," a woman she pretends to be in order to fulfill monetary rather than sexual demands. The confusion between the letter and the literary leads not to an appropriation of the discourse of female desire by the male author but to economic gain for the woman writer. In turn, economic gain, a sign of literary popularity, effectively bars the entrance of these women writers into literary history.

In the nineteenth century, when the letter becomes the sign of a privatized discourse, we encounter a sharp distinction between the novel written by women who impersonate men through the use of male pseudonyms and letters written by women which were never meant for publication. As Virginia Woolf reminds us: "Letters did not count. A woman might write letters while she was sitting by her father's sick-bed. She could write them by the fire whilst the men talked without disturbing them."[15] Letters were the only form of writing that did not require formal education and in their length and scope conformed to the expectations of a woman's life. In *Women, Letters, and the Novel*, Ruth Perry writes: "This was, in fact, one of the few kinds of writing which had long been encouraged in women since—to make the appropriate distinction—letter-writing had always been thought of as an accomplishment rather than as an art."[16]

As you know, as long as women had few alternatives to marriage, letter writing remained an important line of communication with the outside world and one of the few compensations for women's lack of participation in the public sphere. Letter writing allowed a woman to create a network of relations maintained primarily on paper and to construct a subjectivity tailored to the expectations of the addressee. She gave pleasure by artificially composing a self that posed as artless, as the product of involuntary self-revelation. The discursive activity remained a private one, which "required, not the admiration of the world, not even the expectation of posthumous fame, but the undelayed intimate response of a loved person."[17] Female letter writers often wrote in the presence of others, thereby relinquishing the solitude traditionally required for artistic activity, while the absence of a direct verbal response forced them to live in the imaginings of other's thoughts.

The letter, as we both know, written in solitude yet directed toward an addressee, lies somewhere between speech and silence (marked by the fact that you insisted on reading your paper out loud); it lies between the speech required of women in the absence of a male lover and the silence women assume when men speak. (Why, then, did you choose to read your writing, rather than speak about how and why you had come to write it? Was it the presence of a male lover, whom you could silence by reading your epistolary essay to me, to whom you would never have written?) Historically, Mikhail Bakhtin tells us, the arts of letter writing and conversation arose together, allowing him to create a direct link between the rhetoric of the familiar letter and that of the drawing room:

> In this intimate and familiar atmosphere (one that was, of course, semiconventionalized) a new private sense of self, suited to the drawing room, began to emerge. A whole series of categories involving self-consciousness and the shaping of a life into a biography—success, happiness, merit—began to lose their public and state significance and passed over to the private and personal plane.[18]

On the one hand, the letter and the drawing room mark a privatization of public life; on the other hand, as the private sphere gains prominence, women acquire influence. (In our case it was just the reverse. As more women entered the public arena of the university, more of us retired to private spaces to create our own "salons" in the form of feminist reading groups governed by political as well as literary interests. There we read what had just been written, long before it achieved wider circulation.) In countries such as France and Germany, the salon of the eighteenth and nineteenth centuries provides a public, although still privatized, arena in which men and women participate in cultural production by means of a physical presence. (We as a group also sought each other's physical presence, but at the expense of the other sex.)

Helen Fehervary goes so far as to read the salon as a rewriting of an epistolary mode, suggesting that conversation provides a "literal" representation of the letter:

> In the salon women took the art of letter writing one step further and came face to face in order to speak and simultaneously listen to each other. . . . Yet unlike the epistolary genre, written in domestic isolation, the salon was a public institution which established domesticity and conversation as the center of literary life. The salon imagined that there could not be literary authenticity or authorship without reciprocity.[19]

Although the salon breaks down the isolation of the solitary room, reciprocity cannot be equated with authenticity. If one regards speech as another form of "writing" or codified discourse, then the presence of the listener restricts rather than expands the possible utterances of the speaker.

(Did we know this in those days?) Unable to hide behind the gender neutrality of the letter in the Symbolic, the speaker in the salon is exposed as physical presence, and therefore as sexually different. (We sought to eliminate that difference, ignorant of the fact that indifference would create other differences between us.) The salonières are primarily remembered for their affiliations with prominent men; nevertheless, they did provide a place, along with the convent, where women could encounter each other.[20]

Fehervary reads the salon not just as the "literalization" of the epistolary but also as a recoding of dramatic performance:

> It was a new kind of "theater" in which there was no need for an audience, for this theater was not the representation of life but its verbal enactment. . . . Like the epistolary form, the salon can be seen as a genre: women's conception of the drama perhaps—which, incidentally, would answer the tedious question as to why women don't often write plays.[21]

Women fail to write plays because of a lack of access to the theater as public institution, not because of a privileged relation to speech. (We understood at least that much about our institution, although it was difficult to assess whether we could change it or whether it would eventually change us.) The blurring of distinctions between actors and audience (reminiscent of Bakhtin's carnival) reinforces gender hierarchies rather than reversing them. It includes women in a social structure which it fails to expose as arbitrary by "naturalizing" it as authentic. The achievements of the salon have been forgotten where they have failed to enter written discourse and marginalized where they have been recorded in letters. (Is that the fate I tempt, in choosing you as my addressee?)

In contrast to the salon, which offers no distinction between audience and spectacle, and the stage, which requires an audience but prefers a mute one, the single epistle interpolates an anticipated response. For Bakhtin, the letter, which falls under the rubric of the word oriented toward another person's word, is predicated on a hidden internal polemic, not on polite conversation. The hidden polemic of the author's word is oriented both toward the object and toward the other person's word about the object. The other's word is not reproduced but implied, altering the original word through intonation and syntax:

> In a hidden polemic . . . the other's words are treated antagonisti-

cally, and this antagonism, no less than the very topic being discussed is what determines the author's discourse. This radically changes the semantics of the discourse involved: alongside its referential meaning there appears a second meaning—an intentional orientation toward someone else's words.[22]

This antagonistic relationship stands in sharp contrast to the ideal of peaceful intersubjectivity associated with the female subject in the salon or the sitting room. Although Bakhtin's notion of the letter fails to foreground the hidden polemic intrinsic to the relation between the sexes, it nevertheless dialogizes the single epistle and posits the epistolary as a discourse of (political) demand, rather than (amorous) desire.

Thus we are left with a series of questions: what happens when women resort to the epistolary not for an amorous but for a dissident discourse; when they no longer seek to retrieve a male lover unchanged but seek to change the exclusionary practices of a male-dominated culture; when the letter no longer finds its inscription in a repetitive structure of desire but in a unique opportunity to advocate social change? An obsession with sexual passion has been replaced with a passion for political intervention; the dialogue made possible by an absent lover has been made necessary by the growing participation of women in the nation state. To better understand the rhetoric of the epistolary essay, we need to examine how the private discourse of the epistle intersects with the public aspect of the essay. But first it might be useful to reexamine the little theorizing that has been done about the essay.

The essay, like the epistle, suggests an attempt (*essaie*) at writing, as opposed to an art. Both forms remain limited in their subject matter, both need to state explicitly their reasons for opening and reaching closure, and both interpolate endless digressions. The aims of the essay at the same time contradict those of the epistle: the essay aspires to publication rather than to the intimacy of a secret correspondence and celebrates the public virtue of male friendship rather than the private passions of heterosexual love.[23] The essay converges with the epistle in the dedicatory letter addressed to a patron or reader at the beginning of a literary work. François Rigolot, in his essay on Montaigne, has provided the most extensive deliberations on the connection between the essay and the letter by focusing on "the effect of the non-use of the letter as signifier" in Montaigne's *Essaies*. There he writes: "Montaigne wished his essays were letters and he was tempted to use the letter form for some of his chapters."[24]

The epistolary essay creates a tension between the two genres, which results in "the fundamental structure of *exchange* between letter and essay: the letter makes the essay the best possible substitute for the symbolically 'purloined letter'"[25] (i.e., the letter of the primal scene as an original loss, since it marks the entrance into language as division). This moment of intimacy can never be re-presented except in the idealized "epistolary style," since, according to Lacan, "the unconscious is [always already] the discourse of the Other." In Montaigne's case the primal scene of writing takes place on the occasion of the death of his friend La Boetie. Because of his friend's absence, the letter is addressed instead to his father and marks the beginning of Montaigne's vocation as essay writer.

What Rigolot's essay fails to articulate are the implications of a single-sex (male) triangle, of a primal scene that, in Montaigne's case, involves not the loss of the mother but the death of a male friend. Rigolot translates Lacan's understanding of the letter as lack into Montaigne's inability to conceive of the essay in epistolary terms. Woolf and Wolf, I would argue, follow a different strategy, a repeated return to the epistolary as a way of structuring the essay. Rather than appropriating the letter as a sign of their lack, they use it as a way of legitimizing their entrance into language. As Woolf once again reminds us:

> The art of letter writing is often the art of essay-writing in disguise. But such as it was, it was an art that a woman could practice without unsexing herself. It was an art that could be carried on at odd moments, by a father's sick-bed, among a thousand interruptions, without exciting comment, anonymously as it were, and often with the pretense that it served some useful purpose.[26]

For Montaigne the essay inadequately substitutes for the symbolically "purloined letter," the letter of the unconscious which already belongs to the Other; for Woolf time consciously must be "stolen" from domestic duties and the essay must pose as letter for the others in the room. "Disguised" and "pretense" no longer involve an impersonation of the opposite sex but an impersonation of the epistle by the essay.

What does it mean for the essay to impersonate the epistle? (Or does the epistle impersonate the essay?) On the one hand, the epistolary essay offers a semblance of intersubjectivity associated with traditional forms of the feminine; on the other hand, it posits subjectivity as the product of the power relations between subjects. The letter, in each case solicited by the addressee, in the form of a request for information, an opinion, or an answer, demands that the subject respond, and that the respondent problematize the position from which she speaks. That position reveals itself as precarious, owing to the historical construction of the female subject as inferior and the insertion of the female subject into history as unstable, vacillating between a subject and object position. Whether the addressee is male (ensuring a male audience for a female critique of male domination), or female (creating a discourse between women subversive in its exclusion of men), the epistolary essay undermines monologic discourse as the failure to question its source of authority and recognize its own authoritarian impulses. One might conclude, then, that the dialogic of the epistolary essay lies not only in the inclusion of an addressee but in the dialogue between the letter and the literary, the public and the private, historical and theoretical discourses.

Having come to the end of this lengthy digression, we finally arrive at a discussion of the essays themselves. (Is this where we should have begun?) As you know, Virginia Woolf and Christa Wolf have written numerous essays in letter form and have appropriated the form on similar occasions: in response to real or fictive letters asking for ways to prevent war; as a means of reflecting on the role of the subject in modern literature; and in response to editors' requests for introductions to collections of women's writings. Both Woolf's *Three Guineas* (1938)[27] and Wolf's "Come! Into the Open, Friend!" (1982)[28] respond to male concerns regarding the prevention of war, given the rise of fascism on the eve of World War II and the current role of nuclear missiles in Germany in the arms race between the United States and the Soviet Union. Woolf's "A Letter to a Young Poet"[29] and Wolf's fourth Cassandra lecture, entitled "A Letter, About Unequivocal and Ambiguous Meaning, Definiteness and Indefiniteness; About Ancient Conditions and New View-Scopes; About Objectivity,"[30] both use examples from modern poetry to discuss the inscription of the author's subjectivity in the lyric poem. Finally, Woolf's introductory letter to *Life as We Have Known It* by Co-operative Working Women (1931)[31] prefaces a collection of private papers written by working women, while Wolf's "Nun ja! Das nächste Leben geht aber heute an: Ein Brief über die Bettine"[32] [Granted! But the Next Life Begins

Today: A Letter About Bettine] inaugurates the recent republication of Bettina von Arnim's epistolary novel *Die Günderode* (1839).

I've arranged the three sets of essays so that they progress in subject matter from the masculine activity of war to the male-dominated sphere of literary production to the alternative literary forms and social formations produced by women writers. The rhetorical difference lies in the role of addressee: Woolf constructs her addressee as antagonist, whose otherness is attributed to differences in gender or class; Wolf constructs her interlocutor as ally, as someone who mirrors her own point of view. Although both authors address male as well as female interlocutors, for Woolf epistolarity implies a dialogue between two subjects marked by social differences which ultimately even sympathy fails to bridge; for Wolf any construction of the subject implies the inclusion of another subjectivity as a way of guarding against objectification.

Today letter writing no longer provides the only form of communication with an outside world but rather facilitates a critique of that world from the position of the outsider. The female lover who mourns her sexual abandonment and prolongs desire through writing has been replaced by the female writer who feels she has been abandoned by history in her ignorance of previous women of letters. For Woolf gender fails to break down the otherness of the addressee: "an/other woman" enters her text as radical other and thus appears not radically different from the male interlocutor. For Wolf the otherness presupposed by a split subjectivity becomes mitigated through gender so that the lack of sexual difference allows for the disappearance of at least one structural opposition.

I've recently discovered that these epistolary essays have much in common with Derrida's "carte postale," which he describes as "une lettre ouverte mais illisible,"[33] that is, a text that is legible but unintelligible to its reader. The critique of an existing social order remains comprehensible only to those ready to embrace its implications and implement its recommendations. Like the postcard (which is both image and text) the epistolary essay combines the image of the interlocutor with the text of the locutor. By visualizing the addressee, the text contributes to the legibility of the other, even if the locutor's own position of otherness continues to remain unintelligible to history. One might say that the epistle has finally been "purloined" by those it once dispossessed, the female writer who uses it to unmask the patriarchal letter as a dead one, founded on class and sexual exploitation and maintained through discourses of domination. Like the postcard, the letter belongs not to its place of origin, reproduced as image, nor to its recipient, but to its reader—that is, to no one.

In fact, the apparent formlessness of the epistolary essay demands that an author thoroughly identify the originator of the letter, while leaving the reader to marvel at the outcome of the essay. Woolf's *Three Guineas* and Wolf's "Come! Into the Open, Friend" both offer replies to the appeals of men concerning war (World War II for Woolf and nuclear war for Wolf), an enterprise which has excluded women historically. The single epistle emphasizes the exclusionary practices of a male hegemony by resting on two assumptions: that women can speak legitimately only when asked to do so by personal request; and that they are asked to speak about war precisely because they have never been conscripted. (Does it always require a state of emergency for the outsider to step temporarily inside?) The letter gives the illusion of a "spontaneous" response, while providing a complex reading of the past through the inclusion of historical fact and literary allusion in a logically argued essay.

Woolf answers a letter that begins with the question "How in your opinion are we to prevent war?" by offering three practical solutions: "The first is to sign a letter to the newspapers; the second is to join a certain society; the third is to subscribe to its funds."[34] Woolf constructs *Three Guineas,* her longest and most controversial piece of nonfiction, as fiction, as "a letter perhaps unique in the history of human correspondence, since when before has an educated man asked a woman how in her opinion war can be prevented?" (p. 3).[35] Within the framing letter from a middle-aged male barrister, she embeds two additional letters which require more immediate responses—money for a woman's college and for a female professional organization. Thus she creates a dialogic relation between the requests from one male and two female interlocutors, suggesting that while she finds it necessary to submit to the male interlocutor discursively, politically the material needs of women must be met before the abstract question of war can be addressed. By arguing that wars can be prevented only by first establishing equality between the sexes, Woolf establishes a direct connection between patriarchal power and fascism.[36]

Wolf responds to a letter from a young man who asks three questions: "The first—'May I still hope?' The second—'Are there ways out of the danger?' And the third—'Where can we find the strategies and the

strength to withstand such a future?' "[37] Her essay, published in 1982 in
Süddeutsche Zeitung, a West German newspaper, embeds excerpts from a
letter she actually sent to the young man, thus commenting on her own
prior text by offering both a more optimistic and a more pessimistic
prognosis for human survival. Wolf's essay reinscribes her epistle in order
to limit its authority, the authority of any single voice whose plea for peace
might be too urgent or not urgent enough for the present moment. The
historical significance of the letter lies in its attempt to overcome national
(that is, German) rather than sexual differences, "the tendency of many
people in this century and in this culture—myself included for some
time—to submit unquestionably to authority" (p. 12). The danger of
authority lies not in its arbitrary imposition from the outside but in its
totalitarian impulse which no longer excludes women. Unlike the dialogic
structure of Woolf's text, which subordinates the feminine to the masculine text, the difference between a past and a present subjectivity in
Wolf's essay implies that even the female subject is subject to historical
transformation.

The dialogic takes the form of an epistolary dialogue between a representative male interlocutor and a reluctant female respondent; it also
inscribes itself as intertextual dialogue. In each letter another text (this
time a historical one) mediates between locutor and interlocutor and provides the necessary evidence for a gender-based argument about the causes
of war. The textual allusion places the epistolary as a discourse of the
present moment into a past, which in Woolf's case provides her with a
female ally against a male antagonist and in Wolf's case with a historical
ally against an uncertain future. The additional text does not reconcile or
resolve but further dialogizes the response of the locutor.

As you may recall, Woolf introduces her interlocutor as follows: "You,
then, who ask the question, are a little grey on the temples; the hair is no
longer thick on the top of your head. You have reached the middle years
of life not without effort, at the Bar; but on the whole your journey has
been prosperous" (p. 3). She imagines someone like herself, middle-aged,
of the educated class, supported by an earned income. But likeness quickly
yields to difference and sexual difference to feelings of inferiority. To break
the three-year silence created by the letter left unanswered, Woolf introduces a second voice in the figure of Mary Kingsley. She quotes an excerpt
from her biography about how "German was *all* the paid-for education I
ever had. Two thousand pounds was spent on my brother's" (p. 4). Woolf
is able to enter a correspondence predicated on an unequal power relation

by constructing a specular subject in the form of a female biography. Mary Kingsley represents the sameness of "an/other woman," in opposition to the difference of her interlocutor; yet her word also carries the authority of a written biography. Kingsley subverts the subjectivity of the epistolary by appearing not as an exception but as a member of Woolf's own caste, what she calls "the daughters of educated men." Discursively she appears as lengthy footnote, as objective fact, enabling Woolf to participate in male discourse as an equal.

In Wolf's essay, the sender is personified as intruder rather than antagonist: "'a young person,' as he described himself, a father of three children who works with mentally handicapped children and studies medicine" (p. 12). His otherness stems from his West German nationality and his youth, but his work and his profession have feminized him. He is not the fictive interlocutor of Woolf's text who will guarantee an audience; he is an everyman who demands and deserves an answer. Wolf's response, like Woolf's, is "Why me? Why should *I* know 'ways out of the danger'? Why should *I* in particular be obliged—never mind entitled—to express an opinion that will be taken more seriously than many other opinions of this time?" (p. 12). The rhetorical strategy has been reversed: the female recipient no longer adopts the role of the outsider who has been denied a formal education. On the contrary, Wolf hesitates to respond out of actual complicity, as a participant in National Socialism which produced the war that Woolf had been asked to prevent. She questions her authority because she might have not too little but too much.

Wolf's historical allusion takes the form of the Hölderlin quotation which serves as her title, "Come! Into the open, friend!" (what she calls his "utopian request")—a request for hope at a moment in German history which is as "leaden" as the early nineteenth century. She creates this intertextual dialogue to modify her own views, to have them radically altered so that she too can believe in Europe's survival. Unlike Woolf, who enters the debate on male terms by including the objective, biographical fact, Wolf unveils the fact as the very source of exclusion:

Masses of people have been forced into an "object" existence devoid of reality. The natural sciences, especially, have been co-opted, and the facts they deliver elevated to sole, valid truths. This means that whatever can't be measured, weighed, counted, or verified is, to all intents and purposes, nonexistent. It does not count. And where the

"real" and "really important" things are designed, planned and produced, women do not, and have not counted for the last three thousand years. (p. 13)

Not unequal access to formal education, which has been ameliorated by
the socialist policies of the East German state, but the content of that
education, which privileges the authority of the quantifiable, has led contemporary culture to the missile and the bomb.

Both authors manipulate the solicited critique of war into an unsolicited
critique of male hegemony by presenting the future as the inevitable outcome of the past. Whereas Wolf recognized the extent of women's exclusion from history recently during her trip to Greece in 1982, Woolf begins
her polemic with the year 1919, the year the professions were opened to
women in England by Act of Parliament. In spite of the gap between
these two historical moments and the differences in the political systems,
both writers question the desirability of women's full participation in a
society that has functioned by excluding women and then considers including them on the eve of potential self-destruction. The urgency of the
need to prevent war—the sense that time is running out—enables each
author to cast off forms of self-censorship in order to speak out about an
activity which traditionally has constituted the male, not the female subject. War, like the addressee, exists as absent presence: the anticipation of
war must inform a reading of the present moment, just as the anticipated
response of the addressee informs the writing of the epistolary text.

The answers provided by Woolf and Wolf (as I'm sure you have come
to suspect) are utopian, discursive fictions coined by Woolf and borrowed
by Wolf from the Romantics. They seek to reach closure within the epistolary text as much as they attempt to alter a global future. Instead of
reversing gender roles by having a female locutor tell her male interlocutor
how to avoid annihilation, the locutor feels reluctant to place herself in the
position of "the one who knows." Woolf offers an abstract answer to what
she has constructed as a fictive question: "we can best help you to prevent
war not by repeating your words and following your methods but by
finding new words and creating new methods" (p. 143). This will be the
function of the Outsider's Society, an organization which seeks to unite
men and women in their collective opposition to political oppression.

Woolf ends her letter as apologetically as she began:

Now, since you are pressed for time, let me make an end; apologising three times over to the three of you, first for the length of this letter, second for the smallness of the contribution, and thirdly for writing at all. The blame for that however rests upon you, for this letter would never have been written had you not asked for an answer to your own. (p. 144)

Just as she cannot be held responsible for the series of events that place Europe on the precipice of another world war, Woolf disclaims responsibility for this epistle which so boldly describes how Europe got there. The original interlocutor becomes three, just as the locutor was never one but always one of a group of women or "daughters of educated men." The three apologies respond to the three requests, once again implying that any one question will always lead to another and any single response will always prove irresponsible.

Wolf, knowing that her letter requires a "real" answer because her interlocutor is not a discursive fiction, anticipates the objections readers might launch against her solution, a call for being "especially peaceful": "My letter comes to an end. How shall I conclude? 'Dear Mr. D., I can clearly see the objections that might be raised against my reflections, which—I do not deny—center on our powerlessness and our reaching for a miracle'" (p. 14). But what she as a single individual cannot do, the peace movement will, uniting at least a portion of the two Germanies for the first time since their division. She ends by thanking her sender for his letter, grateful for being coerced into something she might otherwise not have done; that is, creating a dialogue between her hopes and her fears for a nuclear-armed world.

Undoubtedly you will have noticed that both Woolf and Wolf repeatedly rely on the triad, three answers or three questions, to structure an argument that gives the illusion of a possible mediation, as in the *Aufhebung* of the Hegelian dialectic or the resolution of the oedipal triangle.[38] For Woolf the original division lies in the sexually separate spheres of the Victorian household, for Wolf in a divided Germany. From there each author pursues a mode of argumentation that inscribes the sexual in the political: Woolf locates the origin of the fascist dictator in the familial patriarch; Wolf finds the origin of the false dichotomies that lead to military conflicts in women's exclusion from culture.

In each case war functions as a metaphor for the battle between the sexes, the texts' subtext. The initial enemy of man is not other men but woman in her construction as Other. Once a woman has achieved at least partial integration into the dominant culture, her otherness no longer excludes her but demands her inclusion as outsider. (Is this another form of tokenism?) Peace lies in the reconstruction of social institutions rather than a reconciliation between the sexes. Because victory against either fascism or a nuclear attack remains unthinkable, no viable third term exists, either logically or politically. This lack of resolution suggests that the dialogic knows no reconciliation and that any solution to either military or gender conflict remains largely utopian under current conditions.

I'm going to conclude the discussion of these two texts by suggesting that there is a connection between another subject in the form of an addressee and the construction of the other as military enemy. Woman speaks from the position of the enemy as man's other in order to reveal the other as a figure for the denial of difference. Difference as dialogic would require the subject not only to speak *to* another subject but also to define the position from which it speaks. By constructing the addressee as antagonist, Woolf is led to question her position as gendered subject; by constructing the addressee as ally, Wolf puts into question her position as speaking subject. Both positions involve an identification with the other: for Woolf otherness lies in the appropriation of the male subject position as female speaker, for Wolf in the male subject's appropriation of woman as accomplice. Rather than inscribing the enemy in a pseudo-difference, these two authors show how the enemy functions as a reinscription of the self. For Wolf, recognition of the enemy requires "the lengthy and laborious work of self-education and self-knowledge, which, in turn, might lead to no longer needing to transpose one's own fears and weaknesses onto the image of the enemy. . ." (p. 13). Woolf, gazing at a photograph of the Führer, concludes "that we cannot dissociate ourselves from that figure but are ourselves that figure" (p. 142).

The epistolary, historically the sign of the female subject's position in the private sphere, facilitates her entrance into a public sphere by providing a discourse which has both an explicit origin and a specific destination. The female subject positions itself as the site of exclusionary practices, but not as the site of a solution: women are not inherently peace-loving; rather, because they have been excluded from war, they occupy the position which makes it possible to speak for peace. Rhetorically, the epistle allows Woolf and Wolf to pretend that, in their radical critique of male domination, they were not its instigators, they speak it only privately, they think it only now. At the same time it allows them to dialogize their discourse, to pursue intertextual digressions, to reject all claims to the authority of a discourse that might reiterate the certainty of a patriarch or a political dictator.

Woolf in "A Letter to a Young Poet" and Wolf in "A Letter, About Unequivocal and Ambiguous Meaning, Definiteness and Indefiniteness; About Ancient Conditions and New View-Scopes; About Objectivity" shift their attention from the exclusively masculine domain of military conflict to the male-dominated sphere of literary production. You will note that in these essays Woolf and Wolf no longer speak from the position of the outsider but instead confront the reasons for their historical exclusion from the very activity they are engaged in—writing. The title of each essay privileges one of the two terms of epistolarity: "A Letter to a Young Poet" identifies the receiver and "A Letter, About Unequivocal and Ambiguous Meaning . . ." points to the sender. Once again the letter problematizes subjectivity by suggesting that the other as receiver has as much complicity in the production of meaning as the sender. For Woolf otherness lies in the figure of the poet as opposed to her own position as prose writer; for Wolf the inscription of the self as discursive other lies at the very heart of poetic form.

Woolf resumes her by now familiar apologetic stance toward her interlocutor, who this time is not the successful barrister but a young poet fearing for his profession. "Do write and tell me where poetry's going, or if it's dead?"[39] he asks, the only question in his letter Woolf feels comfortable answering publicly. Before broaching the infirmity of poetry, she briefly discusses the health of letter writing, suggesting that the present age is the great age of letter writing because it will not leave a single letter behind. Letters have finally become what they should be, "intimate, irreticent, indiscreet in the extreme" (p. 209), and therefore will have to be burnt. Woolf strengthens her position as letter writer by belittling her position as a woman of letters: "But before I begin, I must own up to those defects, both natural and acquired, which, as you will find, distort and invalidate all that I have to say about poetry. The lack of a sound university training has always made it impossible for me to distinguish between an iambic and a dactyl" (pp. 209–10).

Woolf again problematizes her position under patriarchy by adopting the persona of the uneducated woman (of course, she is not). She then reclaims her authority, not from "the daughters of educated men" but from the community of prose writers, who "are masters of language, not its slaves . . ." (p. 210), as opposed to poets who must follow formal rules. She refers to prose writers as both "we" and "they," thus claiming to be one of them and to despise them for their petty prejudices against poetry. By setting up an adversarial relationship between poets and prose writers, she again perceives her interlocutor as antagonist, this time mediated by the malleability of his youth and a common participation in literary production. At the same time her interlocutor allows Woolf to place herself, this time voluntarily, in the position of the other: "Let me try to put myself in your place; let me try to imagine, with your letter to help me, what it feels like to be a young poet in the autumn of 1931" (p. 212). Thus she adopts the pose of the letter writer who must first construct the other in order to inscribe the self, and locates the epistle as the potential site for difference as alterity.

Wolf, in contrast, refers to her addressee simply as "A.," a female interlocutor who mirrors herself, who neither poses the questions nor provides the answers but allows the locutor to follow the course of her own thoughts in the company of an ally. The dialogic loses its adversarial component not through empathy, as in Woolf's case, but through the elimination of sexual difference. Rather than placing herself in the position of the addressee, Wolf urges her interlocutor to assume her own position: "recite all the great names of Western literature, forget neither Homer nor Brecht, and ask yourself with which of these mental giants you, as a woman who writes, could identify."[40] Unlike Woolf, who as epistolary subject attempts to identify with the young male poet, Wolf, as writing subject, is unwilling to identify with the great male poets of the past. Wolf also apologizes, not for her ignorance concerning poetic form but for the formlessness of her essay: "I must ask you not to lose patience. Don't think I have lost sight of the question I am really trying to get at: Who was Cassandra before people wrote about her?" (p. 287). Unlike Woolf, who still offers advice to a male addressee by pretending that it was solicited, Wolf is able to authorize her passage out of silence by assuming a common language between women.

(In these essays you will find that both Woolf and Wolf thematize the literary process by constructing it as other, by focusing on poetry when both have written only prose. Like the epistle, lyric poetry foregrounds subjectivity by problematizing the relation between the voice of the poet and the poetic persona in the poem. Woolf examines excerpts from an unidentified volume of modern poetry, while Wolf reads a poem by a literary precursor, Ingeborg Bachmann.)

Woolf criticizes modern poetry's preoccupation with the self, offering "a world that has perhaps no existence except for one particular person at one particular moment" (p. 218), the very quality which characterizes the epistle. She asks her young poet: "How can you learn to write if you write only about one single person?" (p. 223), suggesting that even to write a letter means writing from the position of the other. Woolf herself adopts that position, as prose writer speaking to a poet and as letter writer responding to an addressee. But for her poet she has different expectations: "Think of yourself rather as . . . a poet in whom live all the poets of the past, from whom all poets in time to come will spring" (p. 212).

Although Woolf does not directly refer to gender, the allusion to anonymity recalls the historical position of the woman writer who, when writing in the common sitting room, disguises her essay as letter. By eliminating the specificity of the poet, Woolf subverts the reification of the subject as literary dictator and the eradication of countless female subjects from literary history. She follows her own advice by imagining her interlocutor "not as one poet in particular, but as several poets in one" (p. 212), and eventually addresses him as "you and you and you" (p. 225), as all the young poets writing in 1931. Woolf identifies herself and her addressee through specific subject positions, while undermining the position of the individual subject: she disperses the addressee into a multitude and she apologizes for having assumed her own position. As in *Three Guineas,* the multiplicity of interlocutors and the self-effacement of the locutor undermine the subjective nature of the epistle by rewriting intersubjectivity as anonymity.

Wolf, in contrast, seeks to reinstate the female subject not as historical subject nor as authentic subjectivity but as fiction in the form of a first-person narrative, as in her 1984 novel, *Cassandra:* "To be not allowed to be I, not allowed to be you, but 'it': the object of others' purposes" (p. 275). For Wolf the "it" is far from Woolf's ideal of an anonymous, genderless author. Rather it signifies the victim of a process of objectification which takes place in history and in discourse, and continues to do so in its construction of the individual by the socialist state. Wolf chooses a poem by Ingeborg Bachmann, "Explain To Me, Love," to illustrate alterity as a subject-object dichotomy free of domination. She begins by asking: "Whom is she addressing? Love—a personified abstraction—or a woman whom she calls 'Love'? Is she speaking as a woman, is she speaking as a man? . . . Is 'Love' the male lover. . . . Is 'Love' she herself?" (pp. 274–75).

(She asks the same questions you or I might ask of her own epistle: is she speaking as the woman who begins her letter with a description of the domestic chores she so enjoys doing upon arriving at her summer house in the country, or is she speaking as the woman whose access to higher education allows her to engage in a critical reevaluation of Goethe's and Schiller's Cassandra? Wouldn't you agree that Wolf is addressing herself, as much as her addressee or us, that "A." offers a representation of another subjectivity in the form of an abstraction, another woman, an interlocutor?)

Wolf also speculates about the identity of the "you" in the poem, whom she finds equally ambiguous: "Whom is she addressing? Herself, addressed as 'you'? The woman whom she later calls 'Love'? (Assuming that this 'Love' is a woman)" (pp. 275). Again the "you" is both self and other, but more important, perhaps another woman, a specular representation of the speaker. Wolf as reader rewrites the love lyric by no longer assuming that the personification of love is feminine, thereby destabilizing both the unity and the gender identity of the speaking subject: "You are I, I am he, it cannot be explained. The grammar of manifold simultaneous relations" (p. 276). This grammar also produces the syntax of the dialogic as the simultaneity of subject positions. Wolf reads this dialogized discourse as the possibility of an even more radical alterity: gendered subject positions deconstructed as discursive, assumed only for the purpose of historical placement and political intervention.

By focusing on poetry, Woolf and Wolf seek to unmask the literary dictatorship of the male poet who assures his own canonization by assuming an unproblematic subjectivity. Woolf advocates imagining oneself as someone else, while Wolf insists on the instability of the self one imagines being. In both cases the subject has been dialogized to include the many who lose their identity in anonymity and the two who engage in an interchange between subject and object position. (You might wonder at the contradictory solutions to the problem of "the appropriation of the subject by the masculine.") The explanation lies in a consideration of contextual differences: Woolf seeks to escape the supremacy of the male biographical subject as immortalized, for instance, in Leslie Stephen's

Dictionary of National Biography, while Wolf seeks to reinstate the individual subject as intellectual and moral agent following its eradication by the socialist state. In their deconstruction of the subject, both authors introduce a notion of alterity which involves adopting another subject position, either that of an epistolary addressee or that of a differently gendered pronominal signifier.

At the risk of usurping too much of your time, but knowing that this final topic will probably be of greatest interest to you, I will discuss one more set of essays. (In those days time was much less of a commodity, remembering the afternoons that drifted into dusk.) These epistles focus on an exclusively female sphere: the writings of obscure women. Both Woolf and Wolf are asked to introduce and thereby promote the circulation of texts whose authors are remembered primarily as workers, or as wives and mothers, and whose writings fail to fit into the genres specified by literary history. In each case, an editor asks for an introductory essay, but the nature of the request is so unprecedented that both recipients feel the need to respond in the private and inimitable form of the epistle. The position of the speaker is still precarious, but so is the very nature of the enterprise. At issue is not the end of history nor the exclusionary practices of literary history but the problematic entrance into history of female writers.

Woolf's "Memories of a Working Women's Guild" began as the introductory letter to *Life as We Have Known It* by Co-operative Working Women, edited by Margaret Llewelyn Davies, one of the guild's officers. The organization was founded in 1883 as part of the Consumer's Co-operation Movement, "this peaceful revolution from autocratic Capitalism to democratic Co-operation"[41] designed to address the needs of married working women as consumers. Woolf begins, as you might have anticipated, with her characteristic resistance, this time to insist on the secondariness of the preface in relation to the book: "When you asked me to write a preface to a book which you had collected of papers by working women I replied that I would be drowned rather than write a preface to any book whatsoever. Books should stand on their own feet, my argument was (and I think it is a sound one)."[42] The only way to cooperate was to decide that this was not a book, which she does, but what was it then? Unable to decide, she digresses to her own memories of a guild meeting she attended 17 years before: "And as all this had nothing to do with an introduction or a preface, but brought you to mind and certain pictures from the past, I stretched my hand for a sheet of notepaper and wrote the following letter addressed not to the public but to you" (p. xv). Once again the epistolary relationship between Woolf and her addressee is an adversarial one, this time due to class differences. Woolf mitigates the disparity between social classes by relying on her memories of the meeting. This allows her to reconstruct a sympathetic version of the past based on her physical presence as a woman rather than offer an unsympathetic reading of the book based on her training as a (masculine) reader.

Wolf's "Nun ja! Das nächste Leben geht heute an: Ein Brief über die Bettine" provides the introduction to Bettina von Arnim's *Die Günderode,* an epistolary novel based on the actual correspondence between two female Romantics, Bettina von Arnim (1785–1859) and Karoline von Günderrode (1780–1806). In the novel the two women adopt the names Plato and Dion, taken from Plato's Seventh Epistle, in order to establish a teacher/student relation based on an exchange rather than a hierarchy of roles. Again, as you might have predicted, Wolf establishes a bond based on cooperation rather than conflict by diverting the request for an introduction from an anonymous male publisher to an epistolary debt she owes a female addressee, whom she simply calls, "D." By imitating the letter form chosen by Bettina and Karoline, Wolf creates a link between herself and her reader, and between herself, her interlocutor, and two women writers of the previous century:

> Dear D., instead of the letter you are expecting, I will write to you about Bettine. Maybe we will both profit: I will escape the rules demanded by an afterword, you will learn something about a precursor still unfamiliar to you; together we will be able to continue our epistolary dialogue by recognizing it in Bettine von Arnim's epistolary novel *Die Günderode* and by taking advantage of the historical distance.[43]

Whereas Woolf hesitates to promote the belatedness of the preface, Wolf fears her afterword will usurp the position of the primary text. For Wolf the past represents not a series of personal recollections but a series of literary experiments which cannot help but inspire future women writers. Just as Bettina's epistolary novel cannot be considered conventional because it relies on "authentic" letters, Wolf's essay does not conform to the traditional afterword since it derives its authenticity from the epistolary form. The epistolary essay promotes the continuation of an old acquaintance by introducing a new one, and promotes the publication of an old text by putting it back into circulation.

Both writers come to realize that the challenge of writing a preface or an afterword lies in determining the status of the text from which it gains its identity. Wolf celebrates the formlessness of Bettina's book, while Woolf remains suspicious of the status of the book she has been asked to read: "It cannot be denied that the chapters here put together do not make a book—that as literature they have many limitations. The writing, a literary critic might say, lacks detachment and imaginative breadth, even as the women themselves lack variety and play of feature" (p. xxxvii). (Here Woolf betrays herself in "reading as a man"[44] by equating the discursive body with the body of the author.) But Woolf does not read simply as a literary critic. After quoting several passages that she feels no "Doctor of Letters" could have expressed more eloquently, she writes: "Whether that is literature or not literature I do not presume to say, but that it explains much and reveals much is certain" (p. xxxix).

Caught between the aesthetic values inherited from a masculinist culture and her sympathy for all women as an exploited group, Woolf makes a radical distinction between speech and writing, attempting to privilege neither: the written word which reveals the private life of the working woman helps clarify the discourse of the guild meeting, while the memory of the face and voice of the public speaker compensates for her ungrammatical writing. Out of this contradiction grows the possibility of future speech: "These pages are only fragments. These voices are beginning only now to emerge from silence into half articulate speech. These lives are still half hidden in profound obscurity" (p. xxxix). Woolf praises the fact that they were written at all, given the conditions under which they arose. Like the epistolary essay, they serve to translate the personal grievances of the private house into a recognition of institutionalized forms of oppression.

Wolf, in contrast, suggests that the unprecedented content of female experience would betray its novelty and therefore its authenticity were it to conform to conventional literary forms: "The letters Bettine and Karoline exchange do not pretend to be art, and as book, represent in their formlessness that very form in which they are able to communicate their experiences without having to deform them" (p. 310). Neither the epistolary nor the bourgeois novel would have provided an adequate vehicle for the representation of a female friendship based on shared intellectual interests.

Unlike the writers Woolf discusses, these two women reach the full articulation of an unprecedented discourse, inventing new sign systems which they try out on each other. A "Mischform" [mixed form] is the name Wolf gives what she reads and interprets as a conscious redefinition of the literary: "Here you will be able to read about the rebellion against the hegemony of a canon of forms, not only a standard of which the two are conscious but one to which, Günderrode especially submits herself, since to become 'famous' as a male writer involves using it. And as a female writer?" (p. 310). Wolf is not interested in inserting women's writings into an existing canon but in transforming that canon so that the experiments of women writers will be read. She suggests that although the words "literature" and "aesthetic" are feminine in German, female participation in these spheres has been kept to a minimum; and where women have attempted entrance, they have found themselves as constricted as they were in their domestic roles.

The difference in any ultimate evaluation of these two nonbooks, as you might surmise, stems from the class relations they both reflect and engender. In her usual epistolary role, Woolf pretends to be one of the many working-class women who attend the guild meeting, only to discover that the working-class woman is more of an other than either the middle-aged barrister or the young male poet: "One could not be Mrs. Giles of Durham because one's body had never stood at the washtub; one's hands had never wrung and scrubbed and chopped up whatever the meat may be that makes a miner's supper" (p. xxi). The aspirations of the member of one social class can lead only to imitation; and thus the attempt of one class to understand another must lead to fiction: "Therefore, however much we had sympathised our sympathy was largely fictitious. It was aesthetic sympathy, the sympathy of the eye and of the imagination, not of the heart and of the nerves; and such sympathy is always physically uncomfortable" (p. xxvi). The difference between Woolf and working-class women becomes greater than the difference between Woolf and men of her own class. On the one hand, she expects political solidarity based on gender, disregarding the variable of class. On the other hand, the physical difference between Woolf and the working-class woman is not an arbitrary one: Woolf is different because her labor is inscribed in her text, not on her body. She remains what she calls a "benevolent spectator," forced to watch the spectacle in silence because she cannot become a participant.

Wolf describes the sympathy that involves a connection between herself and her precursors as based in a common desire to break out of rather than into the middle class. Wolf calls the relationship between the two female Romantics a "Liebesbund" [bond of love], an experiment, like the Women's Co-operative Guild, which springs not from the material necessity produced by working conditions but from the luxury of the imagination.[45] This bond requires the interchangeability of two friends (reminiscent of the two subject positions of Wolf's last essay), rather than the anonymity of a social organization. Bettina persuades Karoline to participate in her "Schwebereligion" [soaring religion] as an alternative to ossified forms of rhetoric, religion, and female friendship. The model Bettina proposes is innovative, characterized by the neologism "symphilosophieren," a form of sympathy rooted in common intellectual pursuits. They produce a discourse not in the infrequent moments snatched from physical labor but in the empty hours of a leisured existence, writing a language accessible to each other, to the writer of their afterword, and to each subsequent female reader (hopefully to you too): "you and many others will, I think, understand this language as though you had dreamt of it" (p. 313). Once again the addressee is an ally rooted in a common language which does not need to be invented because it has been silenced by history.

In spite of the fact that these two epistles address "an/other woman," each essayist still finds herself in the position of the other: Woolf feels silenced by her presence as a middle-class woman attending a meeting of working-class women and Wolf fears the dominant political voice in the GDR will silence her as it once did Bettina. The Women's Co-operative Guild and Bettina and Karoline's friendship present alternative paradigms to intersubjectivity—one political and one personal—just as the epistle presents a different kind of textuality, one predicated on subjectivity. The intersubjective is rewritten intertextually, as the relation between text and subtext. Like the other essay addressed to a woman—Wolf's "A Letter, About Unequivocal and Ambiguous Meaning . . ."—these letters have been written to return a historical debt, the debt owed by modern women writers to the women who have been obscured by history and to those women who continue to write in spite of the ignorance of this literary past. The historical debt can be repaid only by constructing a dialogue with "an/other woman," woman as other because of her class difference and her historical distance; woman as addressee who will guarantee at least one other subject as reader, thus dialogizing the text rather than condemning it, once again, to obscurity.

Both Woolf's memoirs by working women and Wolf's epistolary novel represent a form of writing too close to a literal representation of experience to spur sufficient interest in the literary. Woolf's working women have not yet mastered grammatical structures; Wolf's Romantics allow their "real" correspondence to pass as epistolary fiction. The dubious status of the text rests with its questionable fictionality; the tentative status of the subtext lies in a resistance to defending these texts as fictions. A defense lies on historical, not literary grounds; the letter returns to its status not as signifier in the Symbolic which knows no sexual difference but as the sign of that difference. The epistle, repeatedly equated with the literal as the sign of women's experience, has been rewritten as epistolary fiction in the form of the essay. The essay pretends to be an epistle in order to reintroduce the writings of women as a discourse produced by a different relation to history.

(This reminds me of your own discussion, regarding Wharton's "The Touchstone," of the confusion between female literary production in the form of actual letters and the female body as author for which these letters circulate.)

The epistolary essays written by Woolf and Wolf reflect an "anxiety of audience" (I'm sure you will catch the pun) characteristic of modern women writers who no longer recognize an inherent incompatibility between gender and authorship. (Does that include us too?) The question of authority has shifted from its illegitimate usurpation to its proper dissemination, resting with its destination, the effect of the text on the reader. Issues of authority continue to be inscribed in notions of power, the power to declare war, the power to decide what is literary; and in complicity, a failure to combat the practices of domination of nation states and cultural institutions. The producers of the epistolary essay repeatedly address issues of authority by foregrounding the power relation between sender and receiver as gendered subjects.

Woolf, in all three essays, constructs her addressee as antagonist, regardless of gender. Her antagonism stems from her difference, which has its roots in sexual difference and results in the adopted position of the outsider: she cannot know about war because she is a woman; she cannot know about poetry because she is a prose writer; she cannot know about working-class women because she herself is middle-class. Woolf's antagonism is the product of her subordinate position as a woman in a patriarchal society, which enters the epistolary essay as the apologetic relation of sender to receiver: Woolf writes only in response to someone else's request, and does so only insufficiently.

Wolf, in contrast, constructs all three addressees as allies. The antagonism has as its target the masking of differences in history, the most grievous differences being gendered ones. Thus Wolf resorts to the epistle not to emphasize her position as outsider but to unveil her complicity as insider. She speaks in order to engage in a dialogue with herself. She constructs several specular subjects so as to reconstruct, in a different way, the various parts of her subjectivity: the pacifist, the woman writer, the female friend.

The antagonism of Woolf's dialogic discourse leads to an inability to escape the opposition subordination/domination, even in her response to a female addressee. The positions are simply reversed: Woolf adopts a position to the woman of a lower class which in certain ways mirrors the position the man of her class adopts toward her. Wolf's dialogic as a form of specularity idealistically suggests that all women, simply because of their gendered position, will produce a "peaceful" discourse. Alterity as the adoption of the other's subject position is not the outcome of epistolarity; rather, the epistle makes possible the conditions for the articulation of the position of the other. The difference between the other as radical other and as specular subject lies in the historical conditions which produce the subject: for Woolf any construction of the subject requires the appropriation of male subjectivity or the disappearance of the subject in anonymity; for Wolf the disappearance of the subject under socialism requires the construction of a dialogized subject as female to differentiate it from the monologic, socialist subject as male.

The debate between the masculine and the feminine, the theoretical and the historical, the letter and the literary (oppositions you and I have so often sought to reconcile), can be resolved only by history. Adorno suggests that the essay overcomes "the depraved profundity which claims that truth and history are incompatible."[46] And yet in spite of what he calls the essay's "discontinuity," its "non-totality," its "unlogicality," it remains a "universal" (male) vehicle for the critique of ideology, by failing to problematize that ideology as predicated on sexual difference. In choosing the epistolary essay, Woolf and Wolf both appropriate the letter as signifier in the essay and append the history of women as letter writers. They do so in order to question a masculinist culture by emphasizing their precarious position within it.

(Whereas you have chosen to confront that male hegemony elsewhere, by leaving the university, I continue to reinscribe myself within it. Now that I have completed this letter, I feel I can finally tell you, after all these years, that it is still you I write to.)

CHAPTER THREE

THE ELEGIAC NOVEL
The Looking Glass

———————◆◆◆———————

But when the self speaks to the self, who is speaking?
—VIRGINIA WOOLF, "AN UNWRITTEN NOVEL"

"THE LADY IN THE LOOKING-GLASS"

*W*hereas the epistolary essay constructs a speaking subject in relation to an addressee, the elegiac novel constructs two fictional characters who function as specular subjects. The female character serves as fictional subject within a novelistic discourse; at the same time she represents the inscription of a female subjectivity within a female-authored text. This inscription takes the form of specularization: the character mirrors the author as subject because she is also female; she necessarily becomes the object of discourse because she dies. Thus the otherness of the novelistic subject lies in the character's presence, for the author, as discursive fiction, as well as in her absence, within the narrative, as elegiac heroine. The death of the heroine, interrupting or closing the narrative, allows the author to inscribe the loss of "an/other woman" as the loss of the mother or female friend.

Woolf in *To the Lighthouse* (1927) and Wolf in *The Quest for Christa T.* (1968) construct their literary heroines as dialogized subjects by representing them in terms of the female artist's relation to her subject: Lily Briscoe paints Mrs. Ramsay, who is the creator of atmospheres rather than of art; and Christia Wolf's narrator, an author, reads the literary fragments left unfinished by Christa T. The position of the artist is defined by her participation in the process of "looking": literal looking in the case of the painter, figurative looking in the case of the narrator. As spectators, they see the female subject not as something to be represented but as "nothing to see": Mrs. Ramsay is not "visible" in the painting because Lily as postimpressionist represents her as purple triangle; Christa T. remains "invisible" because her image will never change, immobilized forever at the age of thirty-five. Thus the construction of the female subject represents the process rather than the product of representation, a process of specularization which problematizes the position of the spectator as possessor of the gaze.[1]

Like the letter, the looking glass constitutes an other; but unlike the epistolary addressee, the reflection has no other name, since it offers a specular image of the self. For Bakhtin the image in the mirror falsifies the true double characteristic of the dialogic: "Even his own external aspect is not really accessible to man, and he cannot interpret it as a whole; mirrors and photographs prove of no help; a man's real external aspect can be seen and understood only by other persons, thanks to their spatial exotopy, and thanks to the fact that they are *other*."[2] Bakhtin suggests that one's own position can be read only from the position of the other, and yet woman has been read repeatedly as man's Other. This pseudo-other has been unmasked as the same, erasing the difference that would allow for the legibility of woman. In order to ensure her representability, woman must construct herself as specular subject, as the split between woman and "an/other woman," who is both herself and not herself, that is, another female subjectivity.

The specular subject takes the form of a female character which inscribes itself dialogically as both autobiographical subject and double-voiced heroine. Lily Briscoe and Christa Wolf's narrator can be read as the autobiographical subjects of their authors; at the same time they exist in dialogic relation to another character in the text, Mrs. Ramsay and Christa T. In each case the specular subject allows for the inscription of female subjectivity as both self and other; in each case it is the otherness of the self which acquires representability. Lily as painter is also Woolf's sister, Vanessa; Wolf's narrator is primarily a discursive position—the one who tells the tale—not a fictional subject. Woolf and Wolf also present the position of the female subject as precarious, by placing her in the role of the unsuccessful artist: in contrast to their authors, Lily's paintings will never be seen and Christa T.'s writings will never be read. At the same time, the authors ground the character's presence in an absence in their choice of the elegy: through death the other woman attains an otherness which remains irreversible. Finally, the writer encourages the reader to reconstruct the female character as not unified, as a series of intertextual splittings.

THE OTHER WOMAN

Lily Briscoe in *To the Lighthouse* and Christa T. in *The Quest for Christa T.* both represent the antiheroic heroine who fails to hold a viable position within a social order, owing to the fact that the position either has become anachronistic—the Angel in the House in post-Victorian England—or has not yet been realized—the subject governed by an individual subjectivity rather than the state in the postwar GDR.[3] The problem of her positionality is mirrored in her marital status: Lily will never marry, "keeping house for her father off the Brompton Road";[4] Christa T. will marry only to find herself a "veterinary surgeon's wife in a small Mecklenburg town."[5] In each case it is the presence of a male figure, as father or as spouse, which will enforce a life of obscurity—an obscurity which will be the fate of the artifact as well as the artist. In both cases this sexual and artistic insufficiency acquires articulation as geographical remoteness.

Just as the heroine is unable to move in from the outskirts of an urban center, the heroine's art fails to enter the realm of public exchange because it remains deficient as commodity. Lily's paintings, hung in attics and stored under sofas, will never be seen; Christa T.'s writings do not circulate: her thesis gathers dust on a library shelf and her letters fail to reach their intended addressees. Nevertheless, Lily completes her painting, attaining her vision in the final moments of the novel, thus providing novelistic closure. So too Christa T.'s writings enter the narrative of Christa Wolf's novel as interpolated texts in spite of their incompletion. The female character's art enters the discourse of the female novelist to acquire a different valence, an intertextual rather than an exchange value.

The impoverishment of these antiheroic trajectories is set against a background of centrality and competence, represented by the second female figure. In the role of the successful female artist, this second, dialogized subject functions as the ground of the heroine's figurative origin. Lily is the friend yet positioned as the nonbiological daughter of Mrs. Ramsay, famous for her physical beauty and impeccable dinner parties; Christa T. was the friend but has become the literary invention of Christa Wolf, the author who also inscribes herself as narrator. The figures of the mother and the author do not engender the heroine, either physically or meta-phorically. Nor do they exert authority from a position of mastery: Mrs. Ramsay dies, leaving Lily her heir and revisionist; Christa Wolf's narrator continuously questions the power she has over the deceased Christa T.

All four characters participate in a chiasma which once again displaces the authority of authorship. Christa T. and Mrs. Ramsey both die, leaving Lily, the artist, and Wolf's narrator, the writer, as successors. In each case a dominant ideology is put into question which privileges, on the one hand, the self-sacrificing mother, and on the other hand, the self-effacing socialist subject. But the female subject also works in opposite ways: Mrs. Ramsay represents the old-fashioned Victorian construction of the femi-nine, while Christa T. represents the possibilities of a not yet constructed subjectivity, imaginable only as feminine. Yet Lily and the narrator are the ones who insist that power resides neither with the deceased nor with the living but in the dialogic relation between the presence and absence of "an/other woman."

Mrs. Ramsay represents the female hostess, the creator of atmosphere and overseer of social gatherings, the author of "this all" which Lily can neither name nor duplicate, to which she can respond only with rapture. Mrs. Ramsay in turn displays little interest in Lily's painting except in-asmuch as it offers an inscription of her own beauty. Her participation in the production of images is circumscribed by her maternal function, which involves encouraging her youngest son James as he cuts pictures out of a sales catalogue. For Mrs. Ramsay there is no conflict between gender and what she considers appropriate forms of production based on the biological reproduction of the mother. She assumes unproblematically her role as consumer of mass-produced goods and as artisan who knits stockings for the poor. By positioning Lily as surrogate daughter, Woolf attempts to diminish the mother's function as biological origin while insisting on her symbolic function as the necessary ground for specularization.

The symbolic function of Christa Wolf's narrator as the originator of Christa T. is embedded within a postmodernist narrative structure which reflects on its own originating processes. The maternal function of the character has given way to the paternal function of the author, and yet Christa T. is not the reproduction but the specular image of the author in name, and of her narrator in trajectory.[6] The narrator recounts Christa T.'s life (terminated at thirty-five by leukemia) in order to preserve and prolong it, in order to duplicate the years she was given to live by constructing an autobiographical double. Unlike Lily and Mrs. Ramsay, whose difference as painter and hostess leads to a conflict in social roles based on marital status, the difference between the narrator and Christa T. is a function of their status as writers. Christa T. fails to write because of an inability to postpone narration until the story is narratable: "when, if not now?" The narrator, by supplementing Christa T.'s fragments with memory and invention, produces a narrative founded on citation: from "diaries, letters, and loose manuscript pages."

The names of both heroines inscribe their lack: the sexual purity and thus fear of painterly sterility of Lily as spinster; Christa T.'s deprivation of an authorial signature marked by the abbreviation of her patronym. Lack is offset by sufficiency: Mrs. Ramsay provides the beauty that inspires Lily's art, just as the narrator supplies the retrospection required to tell Christa T.'s story. Eventually Lily's lack becomes replenished by loss, the loss of the mother which allows for the completion of her painting. For Wolf it is the loss of Christa T. which initiates the narrative process that makes the story narratable. The novel ends with Christa T.'s death, and yet neither her life nor her story is over: her life has been duplicated in the story which relives her life for the reader; her story has been told in order to encourage others in the GDR to realize the possibilities Christa T. represents.

Thus the two heroines do not represent a double trajectory constituted as a choice between wife/spinster or mother/artist;[7] nor do they represent two halves of a single subject which have been externalized in the form of two characters.[8] Rather, the notion of the dialogic as the relation between author and character is inscribed in the text itself: the relation between two characters as the woman and "an/other woman" takes the form of the relation between the artist and her subject. The other woman does not become the object of representation but a dialogized subject: another subjectivity as female, as friend, as fictional subject. Her otherness lies in her incompletion, which the artist inscribes for the sake of an audience: Lily makes permanent the beauty embodied by Mrs. Ramsay by fixing it onto a canvas, albeit an abstract one; Wolf's narrator inscribes the lists and letters left by Christa T. into a story which can be read, although with difficulty. Resistance against completion emphasizes the process rather than the product of either aesthetic or social transformation: Lily works on a painting in both halves of the novel, which she completes by the end of the book; Christa T. prolongs the process of "becoming"— of choosing and fixing an identity—by never inscribing herself as literary subject. The issue of closure acquires such prominence because of both its aesthetic and its political implications: whereas for Woolf the possibility of closure guarantees the female artist's entrance into an established aesthetic tradition, for Wolf it anticipates the possible reemergence of a fascist state.

The impermanence of the domestic arts and a female beauty which is physically—rather than textually—inscribed represent aspects of the "angel in the house" which Woolf must kill.[9] Only then can the female artist enter the male-dominated sphere of artistic production as a nongendered and therefore equal participant. Christa T.'s unwillingness to conform to a socialist system which prescribes forms of social adaptation for the individual subject is a story which Wolf feels urgently needs telling. It represents a personal and political choice which must be kept alive if any form of socialism is to remain a viable social system. The "other woman" as a position to be resisted or embraced lies in its cultural inscription as the maternal or the female friend: for Woolf the maternal must be resisted if the female subject is to make the transition from the private to the public sphere, so that the female artist loses her gender specificity in the artistic process. For Wolf the female friend must be embraced in the process of transforming the socialist state, since she provides a gender-specific ally against the masculinist socialist subject. In either case the "other woman" as specular subject is not the object of a narcissistic mirroring but the necessary ground for a radical revisioning.

THE ELEGY

The specularization of the "other woman" is made possible by her incompletion as fictional subject and by the narratological gap created by her death. The effacement which threatens Mrs. Ramsay and Christa T. requires that they be recreated as visible—in order to "see" them as they once were, but also to anticipate their renewed disappearance. To "see" them involves contemplating them now that they can no longer "be looked at," discovering them from a distance, both geographically and temporally. "Seeing" both serves as a metaphor for an act of cognition and positions the woman epistemologically as spectator, as the beholder of "an/other woman." Yet the other woman escapes constitution as spectacle through the continuous subversion of the processes of looking: Lily "sees" Mrs. Ramsay through the stroke down the center of her painting; the narrator "sees" Christa T. in remembered scenes from her life. The other woman is seen "as she really was," not always in focus, sometimes obscurely, often with tears providing a veil between the viewer and her vision.

In both narratives the absence of the other woman is the outcome of premature death: Mrs. Ramsay's death appears in parentheses in the novel's center section entitled "Time Passes." Her demise emphasizes the passing of chronological time, in contrast to the premature deaths of her children who disrupt it, one dying in childbirth, the other in battle. Christa T. dies of leukemia at the age of thirty-five, a process of deterioration that begins on her wedding night and is momentarily interrupted when she gives birth to a second daughter shortly before her death. Her premature disappearance inverts temporal order by allowing Christa T., who was older than the narrator, to become suddenly younger, and finally to avoid the process of aging altogether. Both Mrs. Ramsay and Christa T. are perceived as dying too soon, to which the mourner responds with an elegy, in order to lament the emotional loss and to inscribe the deceased's symbolic function as specular subject within a narrative process.

Bakhtin categorizes the elegy as a modified form of biography, what he calls the stoic type of autobiography, characterized by a new way of relating to one's self: "This is a new relationship to one's own self, to one's own particular 'I'—with no witnesses, without any concessions to the voice of a 'third person,' whoever it might be."[10] The soliloquy, or solitary conversation with oneself, places particular emphasis on aspects of one's private life, and therefore on the theme of personal death. The soliloquy nevertheless constitutes a dialogized form, replacing the split between author and character with the splitting of the individual subject. For Bakhtin privatization implies the loss of the individual's relation to public life, the possibility of "the voice of a 'third person'"; for Woolf and Wolf it means the entrance of the woman writer into the public sphere;

that is, the possibility of female representability by means of the specular subject.

The elegy, like the epistle, creates a relationship to an absent presence by constituting a second subject as dialogic double. In the case of the elegy, the absence takes the form of permanent loss. Unlike the epistolary addressee which ensures an audience, the subject of the elegy ensures authorship through the self-inscription of the female subject as author and as character. Whereas the epistolary essay enables the entrance into discourse by means of a disguise (the essay which passes for an epistle), the elegy guarantees the inscription of the female subject as specular, as the spectacle which cannot be seen. Rather than foregrounding the dynamics of political power, the power of the living over the dead serves as a figure for authorial power, which for the female author leads to not empowerment but dread.

In 1925 Woolf writes in her diary: "I am making up *To the Lighthouse*— . . . I have an idea that I will invent a new name for my books to supplant 'novel.' A new ——— by Virginia Woolf. But what? Elegy?"[11] Renaming the novel an elegy infuses the fictional form with autobiographical content, since it is predicated on actual loss. The elegy provides a response to death which enables the female writer to author herself as specular subject, articulating her own subjectivity in dialogue with a novelistic heroine. The woman writer does not mourn her dead reflection in the mirror of the male-inscribed literary text, as described by Sandra Gilbert and Susan Gubar, "killed into a 'perfect' image of herself";[12] rather she mourns the passing of the "other woman" who through her death has made possible her own representation. The other woman lacks an identity because she has physically disappeared, and resists definition because she exists only in a process of discursive recovery. What, then, does it mean to mourn, and how is this process interpolated into the narrative process of women's fiction?[13]

Readers generally agree that the models for Mr. and Mrs. Ramsay were Woolf's parents, Sir Leslie and Julia Stephen. Much less attention has been paid to the connection between Virginia's sister, Vanessa Bell, and both Mrs. Ramsay and Lily Briscoe. Following the death of first her mother and then her half-sister, Stella Duckworth, Vanessa took on the role of surrogate mother to her young siblings, substitute wife to her father, and feigned fiancée to her half-brother George Duckworth, while continuing to pursue her training as a painter.[14] Yet the relationship between the two sisters, so often interpreted as a maternal one, can also be read in the complementary relationship of their roles as daughters and as artists. Their familial as well as aesthetic positions are revealed in their respective relationship to the elegy, in their roles as writer and as reader of the text produced by the process of mourning the mother.

For Virginia the writing process involved a final burial of her parents years after their deaths. On what would have been her father's ninety-sixth birthday (he died at seventy-two), she wrote: "I used to think of him and mother daily; but writing the *Lighthouse* laid them in my mind. And now he comes back sometimes, but differently. (I believe this to be true—that I was obsessed by them both, unhealthily; and writing of them was a necessary act.) He comes back now more as a contemporary. I must read him some day."[15] In a letter to Virginia entitled "On first reading 'To the Lighthouse,'" Vanessa writes:

> it seemed to me that in the first part of the book you have given a portrait of mother which is more like her to me than anything I could ever have conceived of as possible. It is almost painful to have her so raised from the dead. You have made one feel the extraordinary beauty of her character, which must be the most difficult thing in the world to do. It was like meeting her again with oneself grown up and on equal terms and it seems to me the most astonishing feat of creation to have been able to see her in such a way.[16]

For both daughters the parental precursor has become a contemporary. The novelistic process has restored an absence by preserving the parent, while transforming the child's perception into an adult's. The two sisters become readers of a text that finally makes the traces of the portrait legible by placing each daughter neither too close nor too far from the parental figure. The literal act of reading reinforces the difference in their positions: Vanessa reads her sister's writing in order to decrease the distance of memory, while Virginia contemplates reading something her father wrote in order to overcome its closeness.

What differentiates the two readings are the antithetical constructions of the text as burial (Virginia): "writing . . . laid them in my mind" and as resurrection (Vanessa): "to have her so raised from the dead." For Virginia the writing of the novel becomes analogous to the psychoanalytic process: "I suppose that I did for myself what psycho-analysts do for their patients. I expressed some very long felt and deeply felt emotion. And in expressing it I explained it and then laid it to rest."[17] Virginia is no surer of what it means to have "explained" an emotion than Vanessa is of how it might be described. For Vanessa the emotion stems from an aesthetic experience aroused by the reading process: "I have somewhere a feeling about it as a work of art which will perhaps gradually take shape and which must be enormously strong to make any impression on me at all beside the other feelings which you roused in me—I suppose I'm the only person in the world who can have these feelings, at any rate to such an extent."[18] Both sisters resort to legitimizing systems, the psychoanalytic and the aesthetic, to explain the very relation those systems seek to suppress—the relation to the mother. Each sister agrees that the father would be easier to represent: "There is more to catch hold of,"[19] having already been inscribed in the various texts he himself authored. Yet it is the elusiveness of the mother they both seek to capture, the mother who already had an eldest daughter from her first marriage when Vanessa was born and who died too quickly after giving birth to Virginia.

Having written about the mother, Virginia can no longer see her, and Vanessa is able to see her once again. Vanessa finds herself confronted with a portrait she as painter would not have been able to make, given the absence of the models: "So you see as far as portrait painting goes you seem to me to be a supreme artist and it is so shattering to find oneself face to face with those two again that I can hardly consider anything else."[20] Virginia, in turn, wonders how she was able to achieve such verisimilitude, given the fact that she had no prolonged access to the original. She writes to Vanessa:

> I'm in a terrible state of pleasure that you should think Mrs. Ramsay so like mother. At the same time, it is a psychological mystery why she should be: how a child could know about her; except that she has always haunted me, partly, I suppose, her beauty; and then dying at that moment, I suppose she cut a great figure on one's mind when it was just awake, and had not any experience of life—Only then one would have suspected that one had made up a sham—an ideal. Probably there is a great deal of you in Mrs. Ramsay; though, in fact, I think you and mother are very different in my mind.[21]

Vanessa uses the terms of her own art, portrait painting, to comment on Virginia's gifts as a writer, while Virginia suggests that if the mother is present once again, it is partially due to the continuing presence of the sister, who in this case serves as portrait rather than as painter for the representation of the maternal.

Although Virginia recognizes that Mrs. Ramsay might in part have been modeled on her sister, not just her mother, the difference between the two women finds its expression in the two female characters who, in the reception of *To the Lighthouse,* have vied for the place of heroine, Mrs. Ramsay and Lily. What undergoes elision is the connection between Vanessa and Lily, the sister rather than the autobiographical subject as model for the female artist. Although repeatedly apologetic for her attempts at literary analysis, what she calls "the imbecile ravings of a painter on paper," Vanessa nevertheless recognizes that unlike the mother (who has become a contemporary), the daughter is ahead of her time: "By the way surely Lily Briscoe must have been rather a good painter—before her time perhaps, but with great gifts really?"[22] Thus Lily comes to represent the unrepresentable as the avant-garde female artist.

If Lily is based on Virginia and Vanessa, and Mrs. Ramsay on Vanessa and Julia, then it is the sister and not the mother who repeatedly returns in the position of the other woman.[23] As sisters, Virginia and Vanessa formed what Virginia has called "a very close conspiracy": "We had an alliance that was so knit together that everything . . . was seen from the same angle; and took its shape from our own vantage point. . . . We were always battling for that which was always being interfered with, muffled up, snatched away. The most imminent obstacle and burden was of course father."[24] The bond was forged against the world of the patriarch as "a gifted couple," since each sister was referred to as the best female painter or writer of her time. Their formation as a couple was founded on a strict division of artistic roles: Virginia working in the study and Vanessa in the studio. The boundaries nevertheless became more fluid as each read the other's art through the terms of her own medium. Just as Vanessa speaks of Virginia as a skilled portrait painter, Virginia calls Vanessa "mistress of the phrase"; and just as Vanessa is reluctant to pronounce any literary judgments, Virginia feels unsure of herself as art critic: "Of course your colour intrigues me, seduces, and satisfies me exquisitely. I do not suppose that I get to the end of the maze by any means: my susceptibilities are freakish and wayward."[25] Each arouses in the other intense feelings which are better left expressed in terms of an aesthetic experience and circumvented by means of the maternal.

The roles of the two sisters as readers are inscribed in the first and final moments of the novel, when Lily's painting of the mother focuses first on her presence, then on her absence. Lily initially sees Mrs. Ramsay from the point of view of the painter but eventually adopts the position of the writer by recreating her in language as the medium of memory. If, as Virginia suggests in 1927, the problem she and her sister share as artists is a formal one—"I think we are now at the same point: both mistresses of our medium as never before: both therefore confronted with entirely new problems of structure"[26]—then that problem is represented by the painting itself, which is as much about the aesthetic questions of post-impressionism as it is about the position of the mother.[27]

The relation to the other woman in Woolf is highly eroticized, whether it takes the form of the relation between the two sisters—"your colour intrigues me, seduces, and satisfies me exquisitely"—or the relation between Lily and Mrs. Ramsay: "Could loving, as people called it, make her and Mrs. Ramsay one?" (p. 79). In both cases "intimacy . . . is knowledge," predicated on the knowledge of the mother and the intimacy between female friends (Lily and Mrs. Ramsay) or siblings (Virginia and Vanessa) mediated by the maternal figure. For Woolf the specular has a sexual component: the other woman not just as spinster but as lesbian, whose otherness lies in her deviance, her suppression, the impossibility of her being written, except as a rewriting of the mother.

Whereas Woolf in *To the Lighthouse* finally lays to rest the haunting presence of the mother, Wolf in *The Quest for Christa T.* attempts to preserve the all too fleeting memory of the female friend. For Woolf the figure of the real mother must be buried so that she can be resurrected as fiction, thus enabling the sister to confront her once again as portrait. For Wolf, the figure of the friend, who exists only as fiction, must not be forgotten so that she can provide an example for future citizens of the GDR. Although both figures are inscribed in a psychological process of mourning, Christa T. is repeatedly read and misread as political figure. Wolf, in turn, defends her by insisting on her fictionality, on her position as a discursive rather than a political subject.

Like *To the Lighthouse*, *The Quest for Christa T.* has been read as an elegy, what Thomas Beckermann calls "an elegiac utopia, a piece of 'remembered future.' The author justifies this new type of literature with 'a new way of being in the world.' In the present moment of writing—and of reading, memory awakens to possibilities that could actually be real-ised."[28] Once again the elegy invokes literary innovation, the search for a language to express the loss of the "other woman" as the emotion that exceeds the formal structures and epistemological assumptions of even the least canonized literary genre, the novel. For Wolf "a new way of being in the world" implies the emergence of the socialist subject as a critical rather than as a compliant subjectivity. Here it is not the writer who invents a new name for her book; rather it is the reader who seeks to provide the book with a legitimizing name. By calling it "an elegiac utopia," the critic places it in the acceptable tradition of socialist fiction, where the death of the individual would be an unacceptable means of resolving social contradictions. Whereas Woolf remembers in order to forget, in order to make the tradition of her mother's beauty and her father's literary achievements seem outdated, Wolf remembers in order to imagine how it will have been when the subject has been authored by the artist, not the state.

Death signifies personal loss, but also allows for the emergence of new signifying practices as a way of differently inscribing the individual sub-ject. Wolf rewrites the novel of socialist realism as postmodernist by in-troducing the self-reflexive narrator who reflects simultaneously on the originating processes of the subject in the narrative and in the socialist state. Unlike the death of Mrs. Ramsay—one of several deaths which remain bracketed by the narrative—the death of Christa T. brings closure to the plot while at the same time initiating the story. The premature death of Christa T. prevents her from realizing her recent formation as a socialist subject within the newly formed German state. The illness that leads to her death is leukemia, but both the narrator and Christa T. won-der whether the essence of all illness lies in an inability or reluctance to conform—a question answered affirmatively by a former student of Christa T.'s, who has since become a physician.

The question was likewise answered by early critics who initially banned Wolf's novel in the GDR because of its subversion of realistic plots (and thus by implication of socialist politics). Woolf subverts traditional narrative strategies by choosing neither (Lily's) marriage nor (Mrs. Ram-say's) death as a form of closure, while Wolf thwarts the conventions of socialist realism by allowing Christa T. to marry, thereby making her nonexemplary, and by allowing her to die, thus making her nonheroic within a socialist-realist text. Like Lily, Christa T. is ahead of her time, as novelistic heroine and as socialist subject, as someone who does not know what she wants to be, who enacts the process of becoming as part of the coming into being of a new social order.

Again like Lily and Mrs. Ramsay, Christa T. is based on a real figure, a friend who studied German with Wolf at the University of Leipzig. Hans Mayer, who was then professor in Leipzig, recalls the thesis Wolf's friend wrote on Theodor Storm.[29] In contrast to Mayer, who remembers a "real" Christa T. as the author of a thesis, Wolf assures us before the novel begins: "Christa T. is a literary figure. Some of the quotations from diaries, sketches, and letters are authentic. I did not consider myself bound by fidelity to external details. The minor characters and the situations are invented. Any resemblance between them and living persons or actual events is purely accidental."[30] The difference between a "historical" and a "literary" figure has less to do with whether she existed in the past than with whether she can be kept alive for the future. Not her resemblance to the real figure but her ability to figure future possibilities determines her authenticity as literary character. In Wolf's list of sources she fails to mention the one document the professor remembers—the thesis—because she seeks the traces of a subjectivity which can inform the present, rather than the verification of an objective existence which can do no more than reify the past.

Wolf has reversed the terms of realism: instead of the people and the events, the writings are real; they are reminiscent of the fictions that passed as "real letters" in the eighteenth century, and of the films of our own century that use "real" people as actors but only coincidentally tell "true" stories (unless advertised as such). The authenticity of the quotations reminds the reader that even historical figures exist only discursively, whether their discursive functions provide evidence of fact or material for fiction. The "literariness" of Christa T. does not imply a retreat into textuality but instead posits textual inscription as a public, not a private act. By fictionalizing a story that already circulated as fact—Christa T.'s death—the author returns a story to the social context from which it sprang. Her death becomes "the quest for" her, performed as socialist act rather than as psychoanalytic process.[31]

In contrast to the autobiographical splittings between Lily and Virginia and Lily and Vanessa based on artistic roles, and to the mirroring between Mrs. Ramsay and Julia and Julia and Vanessa as aspects of the maternal function, Christa Wolf, Christa T., and the nameless narrator mirror one another in their authorial functions. All three life-story trajectories run parallel, while the personal pronouns used to map out their intersections mark their differences. As pronomial signifier, "I" is characterized by slippage, its story never told because it cannot recount its own death. The author inscribes "the difficulty of saying 'I' " by splitting herself between two third-person positions, the narrator and Christa T.,[32] thus inscribing herself dialogically and specularly as other—in the narrator who speaks with her voice and the protagonist who carries her name. Christa T. is both Christa Wolf with an abbreviated patronym, suggesting an aborted identity as author, and a female friend who, by sharing a name, offers the closest approximation to a specular other. By transforming the "I" into a double-voiced "she," Wolf recounts the other's death and at the same time inscribes her own life, so that her story becomes not an autobiographical narrative but the history of an entire generation in Germany.

Unlike the dialogue between the two Stephen sisters within a (then) private correspondence, the dialogue between Wolf and the other woman as self rather than as sister takes place publicly, in front of and for the sake of a reader. In a published text entitled "Selbstinterview" [Interview With Myself], Wolf splits herself between questioner and respondent in order to defend *The Quest for Christa T.* against the anticipated accusation that the book represents "a retreat into inwardness, a flight into private life."[33] The interview begins with the questioner asking the respondent what she is reading, which turns out to be an as yet unfinished version of her own text. The interview proceeds to expose the irrelevant nature of the questions rather than the missing content of the story. Once again the reader, this time as questioner, seeks to give the work a generic name, implying a need for closure which is as inappropriate for Wolf's work as it is for Christa T.'s life. The suggestion of a "posthumes Lebenslauf" [posthumous life story] instead of an "elegy" reinforces the unproblematic nature of (GDR) life which will not allow itself to be put into question through death.

The autobiographical discourse involves the construction of a subjectivity predicated on the split between the subject and the object of discourse:

> I noticed that the object of my story was not at all, or did not remain
> so clearly herself, Christa T. I suddenly faced myself. I had not
> foreseen this. The relations between "us"—Christa T. and the nar-

rator "I"—shifted of themselves into the center; the differences in character and the points at which they touched, the tensions between "us" and the way they dissolved or failed to dissolve. If I were a mathematician I should probably speak of a "function"—nothing tangible, visible, material, but extraordinarily effective.[34]

The "us" refers to the narrator and narrated in the novel, to the questioner and respondent of the interview, and to the participants in a socialist society. It represents the political ideal of a socialist collectivity as well as the discursive reality of a divided subjectivity. In *The Quest for Christa T.* Wolf begins with a "she" and fails to prevent the intrusion of the "I," which leads her to foreground the process by introducing herself through the first-person narrator; Christa T. fails to write because she finds it impossible to transform the "I" of her autobiographical writings into a "she" who would no longer be herself but a fiction. The narrator, whose function it is to mediate between the "I" of the author and Christa T. as a "she," says: "I understand the secret of the third person, who is there without being tangible and who, when circumstances favor her, can bring down more reality upon herself than the first person: I" (p. 170). The "I" and the "she" mark syntactic positions which determine the process of narration and also the social positions which determine the relation of the woman to "an/other woman." The "she" cannot exclude the "I" as producer of discourse, just as the "I" cannot exclude the "she" as both specular and socialist subject. The "other woman" emerges not from the tension between sexual and aesthetic responses but from the processes of production brought to light by a different social system.

Unlike Woolf's diary, which becomes public only after her death and initially only in the form censored by her husband, Wolf attempts to anticipate the political censorship of her work and its subjective impulse by supplying such a public self-interview. The need for the interview is produced by a different narrative, the history of the GDR, which runs parallel to the lives of both the narrator and Christa T. The "other woman" thus figures not as lesbian, a figure which still cannot be written, but as female friend, a comrade in a different history, where literary interests and political commitments are no longer shared mostly by men. The female friend nevertheless dies too soon, leaving her to be inscribed not as suppressed secret but as public knowledge.

THE OTHER TEXT

Both *To the Lighthouse* and *The Quest for Christa T.* can be read as the response to a precursor text which contextualizes the construction of the female subject by inscribing it as intertextual process. Once again the Woolfian context is a personal one, a short story entitled "An Introduction" which emerged during the writing of *Mrs. Dalloway*, recently collected in a short story sequence entitled *Mrs. Dalloway's Party*. The protagonist's name is Lily Everit, read as a precursor of Lily Briscoe, and a figure of the female artist as a young girl who writes essays rather than paints. Wolf's novel refers to and rewrites a literary precursor, Sophie La Roche's *Geschichte des Fräuleins von Sternheim* [The Story of Miss von Sternheim], subtitled "Von einer Freundin derselben aus Original-Papieren und anderen zuverlässigen Quellen gezogen" [Collected by a Female Friend of Hers from Original Papers and Other Reliable Sources].[35] Published in 1771, La Roche's epistolary novel traces the development of a bourgeois female subject who must preserve her virtue against the machinations of the male aristocracy. Both precursor texts stage as their central event a party, Mrs. Dalloway's party and a masked ball organized by the prince in La Roche's novel. The social gathering marks the "introduction" of the adolescent female subject to a masculine order predicated on sexual difference as the inscription of woman as social inferior.

The party or ball places the woman in a dialogized position where she functions both as spectacle and as spectator: literal spectacle for the male gaze and figurative spectator of her own social inferiority. The masked ball most clearly illustrates the effacement of the female subject behind the literal mask. In La Roche's novel the mask of Fräulein von Sternheim matches the prince's in color, thereby unmasking his plot to make her his mistress. Lord Seymour, her virtuous suitor, replaces his original mask with a white one in order to reveal to her the blackness of the prince's plot. He does so by suggesting the heroine's complicity, thereby misreading the fraudulent mask as the true expression of von Sternheim's character. She lays bare her knowledge of the plot by removing first her mask and then the prince's clothes and jewels (which she had been led to believe were provided by her guardians). The heroine, in turn, misreads the generosity of her villainous suitor, Lord Derby, as genuine compassion, rather than as rakish masquerade.

Lord Derby provides the most interesting reading of the mask in a letter he writes to a male friend:

> Without a mask my Sternheim was at all times the image of virtuous beauty, in that her expression and the look of her eyes seemed to pour a loftiness and purity of soul over her entire being; thus all desires which flowed into her were held within the bounds of deference. But then her eyebrows, temples, and half her cheeks were covered and her soul made almost invisible; thus she lost the characteristically virtuous traits of her charm and sank to the general idea of a *girl*.[36]

The rake reads the face of the bourgeoise as a mirror of her soul, equating virtue with sexual purity. Her face becomes the text that distinguishes her from the other members of her sex, thus serving as metonymic displacement of her body. The concealment of the face behind a mask makes the spectacle generically feminine, as it inscribes the woman as faceless body or pure sex. This makes her infinitely reproducible and thus vulnerable to the repetition of sexual promiscuity. The mask also identifies the woman as the possession of another man, in this case a more powerful one, the prince. In her attempt to escape "the traffic in women" that has made her the object of barter between her uncle and the prince, Fräulein von Sternheim encounters a worse fate in her imprisonment and abandonment by Lord Derby. Only by adopting the disguise of Madam Leidens, a young officer's widow who sells all her worldly possessions to found a school for disadvantaged girls, can Fräulein von Sternheim finally become Lady Seymour.

Lily Everit arrives at Mrs. Dalloway's party already aware of the artificiality of her appearance, which masks what she calls "her ordinary being." But like Fräulein von Sternheim, she has been led to believe in the authenticity of her subjectivity, in the significance of what lies beneath the surface: "beneath lay untouched like a lump of glowing metal—her essay on the character of Dean Swift."[37] Not virtue but intellectual accomplishment, an essay which has received three red stars, distinguishes her as female subject. Mrs. Dalloway selects Bob Brinsley, a university student, as the appropriate partner for Lily's "introduction." Confronted by a member of the opposite sex, Lily is for the first time made aware of her sex and thus of her difference, understood as inferiority: "high towers, solemn bells, flats built every brick of them by men's toil, parliaments too; and even the criss-cross of telegraph wires. . . . What had she to oppose to this massive masculine achievement? An essay on the character of Dean Swift!"[38] Just as Lord Derby reads the face of Fräulein von Sternheim as a signifier for her body, Lily replaces her body with the text of her essay: "what could she do but lay her essay, oh and the whole of her being, on the floor as a cloak for him to trample on, as a rose for him to rifle."[39] In each case the metonymic displacement from text to body places the (male) reader in a position of power which elides the female subject as author of her text, whether the text is read as the virginity which has been preserved or the essay on Swift which has been produced. By embodying her work, rather than authoring it, Lily deprives herself of the possibility of symbolic representation and thus places herself in a position of powerlessness.

Lily's position comes to be defined metaphorically, rather than structurally, as in the case of the eighteenth-century heroine. She neither exists "in direct line from Shakespeare," like Bob Brinsley, nor circulates as an object of exchange, like Fräulein von Sternheim. She comes to recognize "this frail and beautiful creature, this limited and circumscribed creature who could not do what she liked, this butterfly with a thousand facets to its eyes, and delicate fine plumage, and difficulties and sensibilities and sadnesses innumerable: a woman,"[40] as herself.

If Lily in her resemblance to a butterfly recognizes her function as spectacle, at the same time she participates in the story's single event as spectator: Bob Brinsley's dismemberment of a fly. The similarity between fly and butterfly is morphemic; the difference lies in the degree of ornamentation. Lily is made to realize that her trajectory from caterpillar into butterfly may result in the fatal lot of a common fly. Lily's fall, like Eve's, stems from the acquisition of knowledge, not from the loss of virtue. Lily unmasks man, a gendered being, as corrupt, his civilization exposed as constructed on physical violence. Such a recognition leads her not to reinstate virtue through marriage (which makes of a single man the exception) but to acquire a sense of responsibility for "this [male] civilization," which by allowing her to write essays has assigned her the role of accomplice.

An intertextual reading of *To the Lighthouse* and *The Quest for Christa T.* reveals a dialogue with "an/other woman" which takes place within the context of another text. The other text, authored by the other woman—

either Woolf as previous subjectivity or La Roche as literary precursor—
introduces another female subjectivity as historical precedent. This pre-
cedence allows for the rewriting of the female fictional subject as the
producer of texts to be read by the woman writer, thereby inscribing the
female subject as intelligible rather than as inferior.

Lily Briscoe and Christa T., besides being female figures constituted
as specular subjects, appear as successors to a previous figuration. This
figure functions as historical precursor by suggesting that the relation to
the other woman both follows and precedes the relation to the masculine.[41]
Lily Everit represents the figure of Lily Briscoe as adolescent, a prior
moment in female psychological development; Sophie La Roche and Sophie
von Sternheim predate by two centuries Christa Wolf and Christa T.
Again the insufficiency of the female artist as social and sexual subject is
rewritten not as deficiency but as dialogized, in this case not intra- but
intertextually.

THE LOOKING GLASS:
A DISPLACEMENT

Whereas the precursor text provides a specular subject as precedent, the
process of specularization in the looking glass inscribes the female subject
intertextually and re-produces her as visual image. The relationship between the specular and female subjectivity can best be illustrated through
an allegorical reading of Woolf's short story, "The Lady in the Looking-
Glass: A Reflection."[42] There Woolf constructs the female subject as specular image while unveiling her as empty subjectivity. Isabella Tyson represents a doubly unpresentable protagonist, the fictional subject as
decentered subject and as spinster. Isabella Tyson offers "nothing to see"
because she represents the feminine as the sign of signification as such; at
the same time she is made invisible by the very metaphors which are meant
to foreground her visibility. Neither her letters nor her image in the looking glass allow the spectator to get at the "truth" of Isabella Tyson, just
as conventional tropes will not allow the woman writer to arrive at a
different truth about the female fictional subject.

The story begins in a room, likened to a nocturnal bestiary, where
Woolf juxtaposes the gaze of the naturalist as voyeur to the gaze of the
novelist as ravisher. The naturalist, who has disguised himself with cam-

ouflage, observes his environs by becoming indistinguishable from it: "covered with grass and leaves, [he] lie[s] watching the shyest animals— badgers, otters, kingfishers—moving about freely, themselves unseen."[43] The novelist, caught in the difference between intention and representation, seizes the thing he fails to see: "one must prize her open with the first tool that came to hand—the imagination. One must fix one's mind upon her at that very moment. One must fasten her down there" (p. 91). The naturalist studies the room by becoming like his surroundings; the novelist seeks to know Isabella Tyson by making her like the flora she gleans in the garden. To arrive at the truth, the naturalist places himself in the position of the object, while the novelist violates the object in order to arrive at its essence. In each case the structure of metaphoric meaning presupposes a hierarchical relation between the subject and object of discourse.

This metaphoric structure likens Isabella's mind to the room, both unstable, both indecipherable. The things in the room serve as substitutes for the female object who remains unknowable to the male (novelistic) subject: "she was full of locked drawers, stuffed with letters, like her cabinets" (p. 92). The letters, concealed and sealed like regions of the body, once again serve as metonymic displacements of the female subject. Even if "purloined," their secrets would reveal themselves as unreadable, since the letter as metaphor fails to circulate as material object.

In contrast to the similes, the facts about Isabella Tyson are "that she was a spinster; that she was rich; that she had bought this house and collected with her own hands . . . the rugs, the chairs, the cabinets which now lived their nocturnal life before one's eyes" (p. 89). But facts have nothing to do with truth. The truth about Isabella Tyson lies neither in the room, constantly shifting, nor in the garden, where flora provide metaphors for the feminine: "such comparisons are worse than idle and superficial—they are cruel even, for they come like the convolvulus itself trembling between one's eyes and the truth" (pp. 88–89). Truth is likened to a wall, impenetrable and vacant. What, then, is the truth about Isabella Tyson?

The looking glass, in contrast to the letters, produces images which are openly visible and therefore seemingly legible. The only action in the story takes place when the mail (male) arrives, leaving letters scattered in front of the mirror: "A large black form loomed into the looking-glass; blotted out everything, strewed the table with a packet of marble tablets veined with pink and grey, and was gone" (p. 90). The event disrupts the image in the mirror by temporarily erasing it, leaving letters, which like the naturalist take on the appearance of their surroundings. These letters appear neither as metaphors nor as elements of a casual correspondence, but as "marble tablets" inscribed with eternal truth. Unlike an epistle, these tablets cannot be "prized open," thus offering even less in-sight into the female subject. The unreadability of the written text leaves the visual image, the reflection in the mirror, as the only possible source of truth.[44]

Isabella enters the room and thus the looking glass, joining the objects in the mirror rather than effacing them: "Here was the woman herself. She stood naked in that pitiless light. And there was nothing, Isabella was perfectly empty. She had no thoughts. She had no friends. She cared for nobody. As for her letters, they were all bills" (p. 93). Truth is unveiled as absence, while the only presence is that of the aging body: "She stood there, old and angular, veined and lined, with her high nose and her wrinkled neck" (p. 93). The female body, revealed as temporal, can no longer provide a figure for truth; the female character, revealed as empty, cannot provide an essential female subjectivity. The letters that have become bills are less than empty: they insert the female subject into a different economy. What remains are the traces left by conversation: "She was thinking, perhaps, that she must order a new net for the strawberries; that she must send flowers to Johnson's widow; that it was time she drove over to see the Hippesleys in their new house. Those were the things she talked about at dinner certainly" (p. 91). Not the facts, not the metaphors, not even the image in the mirror reveals what there is to know, for there is nothing to know about Isabella Tyson except the text of her everyday words.

Woolf's story deconstructs the fictional as well as the female subject as metaphysical presence. The heroine reveals nothing, just as her life "had led to nothing—that is, she had never married" (p. 89). As allegory the story depicts the position of the modern woman writer who, in constructing the female fictional subject as decentered subject and as spinster, must rewrite both subjectivity as identity and female subjectivity as wife and/or mother. Unable to appropriate the anachronistic tropes of the traditional novelist, she refuses to know the feminine either metaphorically, by establishing her superficial similarity to flowers, or metonymically, by penetrating the recesses of her mail. Nor does she name the feminine by constituting it in the mirror as anything other than a reflection, a reflection of the body as gendered and a reflection on the inscription of that body within novelistic discourse.

Lily and Christa T. are both constructed and deconstructed as visual objects in the displaced looking glass—the canvas and the precursor text. Lily sees both her unrepresentability as spinster and her absence from art history as female artist in the empty canvas, which eventually represents the other woman, Mrs. Ramsay; she in turn is observed by Mr. Bankes who watches her while she paints. Christa T. cannot be seen as the historical figure she impersonates at the costume ball because she appears without a costume, simply stating who she is. Thus only the narrator is able to "see" her because she as reader is familiar with the precursor text from which the historical figure is taken.

In *To the Lighthouse* the oil canvas replaces Isabella Tyson's looking glass as the site of female self-reflection. Mrs. Ramsay fears Lily will never marry not because of her age but because of her tenuous beauty: "Lily's charm was her Chinese eyes, aslant in her white, puckered little face, but it would take a clever man to see it" (p. 42). Since Lily cannot hide her face behind a mask, she can only efface it by displacing her status as visual object onto her role as visual artist. She transfers her inadequacy as icon to her painting, which, like herself, may never be seen: "It would be hung in the servant's bedrooms. It would be rolled up and stuffed under a sofa" (p. 237). While painting is viewed as inferior to writing, which remains the exclusive domain of men in the novel, it specularizes the female subject not by reproducing her in "an/other woman" but by problematizing her position as spectacle for the male gaze.

The whiteness of Lily's canvas provides a visual sign of her name as well as an emblem of her sexual lack; at the same time its blankness signifies the possibility of participating in a radically different aesthetic tradition. Just as Isabella Tyson sees nothing when she looks into the mirror, the canvas fails to reflect the artist. Lily's position as a painter is still inscribed in her physical presence, as she sets up her easel on the Ramsays' stage-like lawn, from where she observes and is observed. She observes the other woman, Mrs. Ramsay, who sees in women only their potential for marriage, and is observed by Mr. Bankes, who seeks only verisimilitude in art.

As a postimpressionist, Lily uses a purple triangle to represent Mrs. Ramsay sitting in the window reading to her son James.[45] Mr. Bankes, a scientist and Lily's suitor, attempts to read the painting, which to him is legible but unintelligible: "Mother and child then—objects of universal veneration, and in this case the mother was famous for her beauty—might be reduced, he pondered, to a purple shadow without irreverence" (p. 81). By rejecting realistic representation, Lily divests the madonna and child of the aesthetic, religious, and political connotations that continually undermine her role as female artist. By emptying the portrait of its anthropomorphism, she eliminates the gender of the generic male child, whose place repeatedly usurps the position of the daughter in the oedipal triangle. She also disempowers the mother of her role as mirror by subverting the mimetic function of art through abstraction. Mr. Bankes questions the sanctity of an art that reads reality as a system of abstract signs, while Lily guarantees her cultural inscription as female artist by dispensing with a form of representation that would code her as a visual object and judge her as lacking in relation to the mother.

The scene in which William Bankes scrutinizes Lily Briscoe's painting rewrites the scene in which Lily Everit feels physically threatened by Bob Brinsley's dismemberment of the fly: "he had put on his spectacles. He had stepped back. He had raised his hand. He had slightly narrowed his clear blue eyes, when Lily, rousing herself, saw what he was at, and winced like a dog who sees a hand raised to strike it" (p. 80). He puts on his glasses to stand back, gain distance, acquire objectivity, while at the same time approaching the canvas to analyze, dissect, dismember: "Taking out a pen-knife, Mr. Bankes tapped the canvas with a bone handle. What did she wish to indicate by the triangular purple shape 'just there'? he asked" (p. 81). Lily's position on the lawn makes her physically vulnerable and therefore psychologically defenseless against the critical judgment which she reads as an act of violation. She fears that the violence in the hand Mr. Bankes raises to point at the canvas is actually meant for her.

Once again the painting, like the essay, serves as a metonymic displacement of the female artist whose artistic achievement is as threatened by the censorship of the educated male as was the virginity of the eighteenth-century heroine by the rake. By functioning as self-reflecting surface, the painting reinforces the lack of separation between the body of the artist and her body of work. So too the penknife serves as an extension of Mr. Bankes's spectacles, the instrument of the male gaze which deciphers the image by threatening to violate it. As scientist Mr. Bankes fails to read

Lily's painting because as male viewer he remains unable to place the female painter within an artistic tradition where woman produces beauty, rather than embodies it.

Christa T.'s moment of visualization takes place at a costume ball, where the artistic precursor is once again La Roche's epistolary novel. The event prefigures Christa T.'s marriage to Justus, the "right" man, who fails to read her disguise as the impersonation of the "wrong" woman. Christa T. does not appear in costume; rather, she simply declares her disguise, thereby subverting her status as image by making her assumed identity invisible. Her role is legible only to the female reader (the narrator) familiar with this noncanonical female text: "the fate of La Roche! An over-ardent and rather sentimental dreamer, chained to a life in the country against her will, so that she pours all her ungratified longing into an invented character . . ." (p. 118). Even worse, she has chosen to play La Roche's protagonist, Fräulein von Sternheim. The narrator summarizes the plot, in the event that the other woman has forgotten it: "Seduction? Intrigue? A false marriage with this rogue Derby? A mournful country life in the English provinces? And, for God's sake, virtue?!" (p. 119). Her choice of disguise makes her role as future wife doubly unintelligible by tracing its source to both an anachronistic historical subject, La Roche, and an artificially constructed subjectivity, von Sternheim.

Christa T.'s costume as verbal mask not only unmasks her life as romance plot: "Christa T. must have reminded her husband that every good love story comes to an end in marriage" (pp. 127–28); it also unmasks the status of the fictional subject as novelistic heroine by insisting on its fictionality. As Helen Fehervary suggests:

> The literary character Christa T.—the name implies a personal yet collective identity—is thus herself a composite of masks. She signifies the accumulation of authorial presence, of a collective tradition, of literary history. One of her many forms, or masks, is given a name in the novel: Sophie La Roche, the first acknowledged woman novelist of the German Enlightenment. While "playing" her at a costume party, Christa T. need not wear a mask because, like Sophie La Roche in her day, she *is* the mask.[46]

If Christa T. *is* a mask, then there is no authentic subjectivity to be deciphered behind the mask. Like Isabella Tyson who sees nothing when she looks into the looking glass, Christa T. is nothing at the costume ball, neither the reflection of a real person (La Roche), nor the re-presentation of a literary persona (von Sternheim). Once again the use of a visual metaphor, this time to reenact history, suggests that reading relies on forms of "seeing," which in the case of the female subject leaves the spectator with "nothing to see." In this case invisibility does not connote sexual lack but the future possibility of a different inscription as subject.

The role of the historical subject as lack beneath a costume is taken a step further when Wolf historicizes even contemporary roles by placing them on the stage of the future:

> In a hundred years, no in fifty, we too shall be historical figures standing on a stage. Why wait so long? Why, since after all it's inevitable, why not take a few strides and jump on the stage oneself, try out a few of the roles, before one defines oneself, rejecting this one or that as too tall an order, finding others already occupied and feeling secretly envious of their occupants: but finally to accept one role in which everything depends on how you play it, depends thus on you and you alone. (p. 120)

Unlike the "stage presence" imposed on Lily by her easel, which leaves her vulnerable in her role as artistic forerunner, Wolf's stage becomes a metaphor for the roles one might adopt before they become assigned by history. In both cases, historical roles have been rejected: just as Lily resists the definition of the female artist—"women can't write, women can't paint"—Christa T. resists any fixity as woman, novelistic heroine or socialist subject. Yet unlike Lily who rejects the gendered role written for her by history, Wolf suggests that every subject position becomes historical when "seen" from somewhere other than the present. The stage roles allow for myriad versions of the self as "other," just as Lily's abstract painting allows for innumerable readings of "an/other woman."

The looking glass as the site of female specularization is displaced onto the site of female artistic production: the canvas and the precursor text. There the other woman appears as "nothing to see": Mrs. Ramsay has no decipherable face and Christa T. has no discernible dress. At the same time each site inscribes the female subject as specular image by constructing her as spectator of the other woman: Lily observes Mrs. Ramsay in order to paint her; Wolf's narrator imagines Christa T. in order to "see" her. The female artist deconstructs the other woman as visual image by inscribing her not as visible but as representable. Woolf makes the representation of the other woman possible by eliminating gender in the dissolution of the portrait through abstract expressionism; Wolf makes the specular subject readable by inserting her into a female plot already provided by literary history. Once again Woolf subscribes to anonymity and Wolf to female specificity in the construction of "an/other woman."

In both novels the act of seeing allows for distance, either geographical or historical, which promotes a more adequate reading of the female subject by subverting femininity as "presence-to-itself," created by the confusion between body and symbolic embodiment. The elegy distances the content of the autobiographical narrative by reconstructing the plot after the death of its protagonist, thereby insuring that the story will be the other woman's. But from what position does one speak for or about that other woman?[47] How does one "see" her without inheriting the gaze, without falsifying the image that can be written only as discursive fiction? By making her visible after she has become invisible, by postponing the completion of her vision, for Woolf until the end of the novel, for Wolf until the transformation of social conditions.

The power over the dead and thus over the fictional subject is not inherited without indebtedness: "She owed it all to her" (p. 241), Lily says of Mrs. Ramsay, just as the narrator says of Christa T.: "She doesn't need us . . . but it seems we need her" (p. 5). Nor is it acquired without a sense of dread. The "anxiety of authorship" stems not from "a radical fear that she cannot create"[48] but from the knowledge that she now has authority over her creation. For Lily the recognition of her power over the mother becomes a moment of triumph: "oh, the dead! she murmured, one pitied them, one brushed them aside, one had even a little contempt for them. They are at our mercy. Mrs. Ramsay has faded and gone, she thought. We can over-ride her wishes, improve away her limited, old-fashioned ideas" (p. 260). With the death of the mother comes the possibility of the daughter's insertion into a radically different history. For *Christa T.*'s narrator losing a female friend becomes a loss accompanied by an overabundance of power: "I can still see her. Worse, I can do what I like with her. I can summon her up quite easily with a quotation, more than I could do for most living people. She moves, if I want her to. Effortlessly she walks before me, yes. That's her long stride, her shambling walk" (p. 4). A different history will require more then the abandonment of a past; it will require cooperation in the preparation for an alternative future. In either case the process of mourning involves the gain of power as well as personal loss.

The elegy dialogizes the contradiction between the deconstruction of the subject and the construction of a female subject by constructing a narrative which inscribes the female fictional subject as loss, as absence whose presence must and can only be reconstructed by "an/other woman." The artist reconstructs the other woman as absent presence, as elegiac heroine, as incompleted subjectivity. She mourns both the individual death and the disappearance of a female figure who remains central to a given social structure: the mother as mediator between sexual differences within the structure of the family, and the nonexemplary heroine as the position of marginality from which to critique the socialist system. Without the mother, the daughter must succumb to the wishes of the father; without the dissident, the citizen must conform to the dictates of the state. But Lily does not succumb to Mrs. Ramsay's pleas, and Wolf's narrator tells her story in spite of possible censorship. The loss of the female subject does not imply a loss of self or of an essential femininity; it implies the gain of a discourse which inscribes the female subject differently, as specular fiction, as intertextual dialogue, as dialogized discourse.

CHAPTER FOUR

LITERARY HISTORY
A Dialogue

To take one's life is to force others to read one's death.
—MARGARET HIGGONET

I

*I*f, as Foucault tells us, "man is an invention of recent date,"[1] then woman is of an even more recent one; if "history is a process without a *telos* or a subject,"[2] as Althusser suggests, then what becomes of the author as subject in literary history? Is the female author—no longer a subject but always already gendered—a recent innovation or already an anachronism? The female subject as literary precursor, like the epistolary addressee and the female fictional subject, appears in Woolf and Wolf as absent presence. In this case the absence is experienced as a missing presence, lost only after it has already been recovered from history. In the female literary history the specular subject as autobiographical is replaced by the inscription of "an/other woman" as biographical subject (the biography of the literary precursor); and the "other woman" functions not as the literary production of the modern woman writer (in the form of a novelistic character), but as a historical figure which prefigures the author's own entrance into literary history.

Bakhtin suggests that "the subject as such cannot be perceived or studied as if it were a thing, since it cannot remain a subject if it is voiceless; consequently, there is no knowledge of the subject but *dialogical*."[3] His statement encodes two elements equally characteristic of a female literary history: the female literary precursor as subject whose voice has been lost to history, and the construction of her subjectivity through a dialogical relation with the modern woman writer. Like the "other woman" in the elegy, the literary foremother acquires her presence as the figuration of an absence. And yet, rather than the premature and accidental death of the novelistic heroine, it is the mnemotic erasure of a literary precursor who dies too soon which brings closure to the narrative. The precursor in both Woolf and Wolf takes her own life and is forgotten until the woman writer (i.e., the author) reinscribes her as literary heroine in the form of biographical subject reinstated in literary history. The literary precursors, Judith Shakespeare in Woolf's *A Room of One's Own* (1929) and Karoline von Günderrode in Wolf's "Der Schatten eines Traumes: Karoline von Günderrode—Ein Entwurf" (1978) [The Shadow of a Dream: Karoline von Günderrode—A Sketch"] have names; but unlike the elegiac heroines, their lack is not inscribed in their names. Rather it is written in the epitaph on their tombstones.

Specifically, the relation to the other woman takes the form of the author-as-critic's (Woolf's and Wolf's) relation to the female historical subject-as-precursor (Judith Shakespeare and Karoline von Günderrode). The construction of the second subject as dialogic double serves not to unveil the abuses of political power, as in the epistolary essay, nor the potential misuses of authorial power, as in the elegiac novel, but to expose the authority of a historical tradition which determines what lives will enter the official emplotment of the past. No one mourns the death of the historical subject because death is a given of historicity; yet the suicidal death of the female historical precursor calls for bereavement on the part of a female successor. The tragedy of such a death forces us to read the life retrospectively as significant in a feminist rereading of the past, to produce not a specular subject predicated on a visual distancing of the other woman but a historical subject whose temporal remoteness is brought into proximity by means of a spatial signifier. The room and the tomb as signifiers of an absent presence guarantee the literary precursor's future accessibility as the author of her own texts by naming the space of her exclusion.

The dialogic reveals itself in literary history both as the relation between the authorial and the historical subject and as the relation between two discourses, the literary and the historical. Literary history attempts to reconcile what Alice Jardine has called "two times: historical time ('reality') and written time ('elsewhere'),"[4] an antagonism which mirrors the relation of the feminine as "elsewhere" to the masculine as "real." The historical itself has been split by the post-structuralists between its status as text—the realm of the historicists or critical theorists—and its status as the "real"—the terrain of the practitioners of history. Given the choice, as proposed by Jardine, "between (1) addressing/rediscovering what women-subjects have always said about that history from within it and (2) investigating what has functioned within that history as 'the feminine,'"[5] female literary theorists will examine the latter, feminist historians the former.

THEORY VS. HISTORY

For Kristeva, a critical theorist, women as subjects have been absent from historical narratives because female subjectivity, in its embodiment of cyclical and monumental time, provides the necessary atemporality by which a teleological conception of history defines itself. In "Women's Time" Kristeva differentiates between cyclical time, which is marked by repetition and bears witness to the eternally recurring (the reproductive destiny of the mother); and monumental time, which refers to the infinite space of eternity (the immortality of the Virgin). Kristeva argues that neither female identification with male power, which results in conformism, nor the construction of a fetishistic female counterpower, which becomes nothing more than an imitation of the contested power, will dissolve the violence of difference.

Kristeva further suggests that the sociosymbolic contract between the sexes has been experienced by women as a sacrificial one, that is as "an essentially sacrificial relationship of separation and articulation of differences."[6] This relationship stems from a notion of the feminine as sacrificial victim or scapegoat. The nature of such a relationship can be challenged only through "the *interiorization of the founding separation of the sociosymbolic contract*" where "interiorization" means the recognition of "the potentialities of *victim-executioner* which characterize each identity, each subject, each sex,"[7] rather than the relation between the sexes. The violence of difference will disintegrate when we acknowledge the relativity of the symbolic as well as the biological, which requires relinquishing the myth of a gendered subject.

For historians, however, women as subjects will continue to be excluded from history unless sexual difference is reexamined in terms of the historical experiences of a specific social group, which for women has been governed by their social status, their place and power within particular social structures. Through such ahistorical concepts as "woman," "patriarchy," and "oppression" historical movement is placed outside the process which constructs the female subject according to "changes in the multiplicity of women's roles over time and across class, race, and ethnic lines, and movement of women as a group toward consciousness of their common condition."[8] If history is imagined as an external process, women once again become its objects; if the subject remains ungendered, women will continue to be deprived of a past.

Feminist historians view woman not as a condition of history; rather they see the changing status of women as moments within history. Sex becomes a social category fundamental to all historical analysis, while gender becomes as historically constructed as any other category. The historian views woman as a subject split between roles, group identities, and symbolic inscriptions, all gender-specific and historically determined. In summary, the female theorist advocates changing the speaking subject by eliminating gender, by relegating it to the metaphysical; while the historian insists on gender as a way of recovering lost subjects and giving them access to speech.

PLOT VS. CHARACTER

Women as subjects within history have been excluded because they have been deprived of political power; at the same time they have been included because of their sexual and reproductive roles. They also have been both absent from and present within historical texts on the basis of traditional functions of the feminine within the paradigms of literary plot and character. Narrations of history resemble literary plots by relying on forms of periodization, dividing a chronological sequence into discrete units of time based on the significance attributed to events.[9] Significance is allocated according to an event's impact on the members of a hegemonic group, defined by sex, class, and race. Periodization, based on political events understood in terms of military developments, necessarily omits women, who historically have been "the one group in history longest excluded from political power"[10] because of their exclusion from military decision-making. At the same time, it has never been possible to exclude women as completely as other marginal groups "because of women's vital importance in the fulfillment of men's needs for pleasure and procreation."[11] By questioning one of the fundamental paradigms of historical writing—periodization—historians have found an explanation for women's exclusion in the very process of structuring the past. They have discovered that women experience the greatest loss in social status during periods of progressive social change (e.g., during the Renaissance),[12] and make the greatest gains in status during periods of social dysfunction, such as war.[13]

The absence of women from historical narratives has led feminist historians to insert "the exceptional woman," modeled on the paradigm of the literary heroine, into an otherwise unaltered chronology. Natalie Zemon Davis has called this activity the compilation of "Women Worthies," the biographies of women who exert power indirectly by influencing notable men, or who imitate men by adopting public roles in social organizations. The exceptional woman, similar to woman as ahistorical category, has once again been removed from the historical process. The solution, Davis suggests, is to study gender groups rather than individual women, and to regard sex roles themselves as unstable: "Our goal is to explain why sex roles were sometimes tightly prescribed and sometimes fluid, sometimes markedly asymmetrical and sometimes more even."[14] Joan Scott in "Gender: A Useful Category of Historical Analysis" takes this idea one step further by questioning gender as an analytic category. She objects to the undue emphasis placed on the "question of the subject" (even a gendered subject), which tends to universalize the categories and relationship of male and female instead of seeing their opposition as historically specific and variable. She writes: "'man' and 'woman' are at once empty and overflowing categories. Empty because they have no ultimate transcendent meaning. Overflowing because even when they appear to be fixed, they still contain within them alternative, denied, or suppressed definitions."[15] Gender no longer refers exclusively to the relation between the sexes, too often depicted as timeless antagonism; rather it becomes a primary way of signifying relationships of power. Thus Scott seeks to link women's history with political history, moving beyond an examination of women's experience to a reading of gender as "one of the recurrent references by which political power has been conceived, legitimized, and criticized."[16]

When the categories of masculine and feminine become unstable the theoretical subject gives way to the historical subject. Gender, in this case, does not perpetuate an anthropomorphic identity or anticipate its dissolution; rather it allows for the interrogation of the subject as historical category. The historian historicizes gender because she recognizes that examining the subordination of women as a sex does not entail leaving the idea of natural sex roles unchallenged. For the literary historian, the instability of gender roles reveals itself in the construction of a female subjectivity as fiction, marked, on the one hand, by an internal splitting—often between masculine and feminine—and on the other hand, by the subject's inscription in a story—self-consciously structured as narrative fiction.[17]

AUTHOR VS. READER

Literary history has borrowed periodization from history as a way of organizing the feats not of heroes but of authors. The search for causes in the past to explain the present is replaced by the search for an originating subject to explain the presence of a literary text. As Foucault suggests: "It would be just as wrong to equate the author with the real writer as to equate him with the fictitious speaker; the author-function is carried out and operates in the scission itself, in this division and this distance."[18] The author-function indicates the status of a text within a particular context by suggesting that some texts have authors, while others only have signatures. But doesn't the status of the author also circumscribe the circulation of texts? If, as Foucault further suggests, "The author is therefore the ideological figure by which one marks the manner in which we fear the proliferation of meaning,"[19] then the female author both proliferates meaning and does so transgressively, by endowing the gender-neutral author-function with a sexual signature.

Barthes announces "the death of the author" by introducing the role of the reader, which takes us back to the epistle: "a text's unity lies not in its origin but in its destination."[20] Like the author, the reader also exists "without history, biography, psychology"; that is, genderless. The reader serves to explain the possibility of producing textual meaning, and returns the literary text to its status as event rather than empirical entity. Yet Barthes's reader, unlike Foucault's author-function, exists outside any context. To posit the reader as ahistorical rather than as gendered subject is to disregard the temporal shifts in her social construction; to rely solely on the reader's participation in the production of meaning is to ignore the power of the author-function in the legislation of what is read.[21]

When Bakhtin argues against the notion of "the image of the author" as the traces of the author discernible in the text, he places the emphasis on "image": "the term 'image of the author' seems to me unfortunate: all that in the work has become image, and that, therefore, enters into its chronotopes, is product, not producer."[22] "Image" in the case of the female author does not refer to a trace but an absence: the image of the author not in her text but in history, either as not there or as eccentric character. Woolf and Wolf retrieve the female author from and for another literary history by deconstructing her male-authored image: either as the nonexistent genius (Judith Shakespeare) or as the suicidal Romantic (Günderrode). At the same time they self-consciously reconstruct her as imagined, as necessary fiction rather than as real author. The female author, lost as the producer of texts, can be retrieved only as the product of a dialogic relation between author-as-critic and literary precursor.

LITERATURE VS. HISTORY

Inserting the female author into literary history reintroduces the concepts "subject" and "history" at a historical moment when any notion of the subject raises questions about further subjection and history has become purely textual. Paul de Man suggests that the contradiction between "literature" and "history" arises when literary history becomes the history of texts rather than interpretations: "a positivistic history of literature, treating it as if it were a collection of empirical data, can only be a history of what literature is not. . . . On the other hand, the intrinsic interpretation of literature claims to be anti- or a-historical."[23] For a female literary history, however, the tension does not lie between a "real" history of experience and the ahistoricity of textual readings; it lies between a history in which it has been virtually impossible for women to write and be read and the texts produced as a form of resistance against particular historical conditions.[24] The construction of the latter requires both the retrieval of an inaccessible past and its inscription in a narrative which has never been told before; that is, a novel fiction. Thus a historical analysis of discourse would take the form of a different kind of "archeology": a study not of formal transformations and not of the conditions of possibility, as Foucault would have it, but of the conditions of the historical impossibility of female literary discourse.

I I

Unlike the epistolary essay, which dialogizes a private and a public discourse in the dialogue between sender and receiver, a female literary history creates a dialogic relationship between the fictions of literature and the "real" of history. This dialogue produces a literary precursor who is both discovered (the handiwork of history) and invented (the creature of literature). Like the subject of the elegy, she enters the text as insufficient subjectivity, as unsuccessful artist, and is recovered not as dead but as forgotten. Just as women have been the authors of epistles rather than essays, women have entered history as the fictional constructs of male authors rather than as autonomous historical agents. For Woolf, woman as fictional construct means woman as character in the fictions (which pass for history) written by men; for Wolf, it means a misreading of history in which women are remembered primarily as fictional characters in the lives of significant men.

Woman as literary precursor rather than as novelistic heroine provides "an/other woman" in the form of a historical figure, who will guarantee the modern woman writer's own inscription into literary history by offering a specifically female precedent. The precursor is both an example from the past and a prefiguring of the future. This time it is the "other woman" herself who is constructed as split subjectivity: split as specular subject—as multiple configurations of the first person pronoun; and as transvestite—as the split between masculine and feminine. The transvestite is another figure for the contradiction between public and private, providing the possibility of entering the public sphere dressed as a man—dressed in his name (Judith Shakespeare) or dressed in his military uniform (Günderrode).

The dialogic relation between literature and history will take the form of an actual dialogue, between Woolf, who creates the literary precursor as fiction, and Wolf, who recreates her as historical figure. The dialogue makes no attempt to imitate the voice of the named speaker; on the contrary, it insists on its status as dialogized discourse. The role of feminist critic is mine.

WOOLF VS. WOLF

Woolf: In *A Room of One's Own* I imagine the product of the division between history and fiction as "a very queer, composite being":

> Imaginatively she is of the highest importance; practically she is completely insignificant. She pervades poetry from cover to cover; she is all but absent from history. She dominates the lives of kings and conquerors in fiction; in fact she was the slave of any boy whose parents forced a ring upon her finger. Some of the most inspired words, some of the most profound thoughts in literature fell from her lips; in real life she could hardly read, could scarcely spell, and was the property of her husband.[25]

Stymied by this dichotomy, I introduce what our feminist critic would call a third term, in the form of a supplementary fiction, Mrs. Martin. Decidedly one of the essay's minor characters, Mrs. Martin represents the middle-class, middle-aged woman who has never appeared in either fiction or history. Though a historical "fact," she also functions as an ideological "fiction," which I create to counteract the "monstrosities" produced by a male-dominated literature and history. In spite of the meticulously detailed portrait I give of Mrs. Martin—her age, marital state, and dress— she develops into a paradox, a historical figure who loses her historicity because of her exceptional position as a woman who is not a "woman worthy."

Wolf: The focus of my essay, "Der Schatten eines Traumes" [The Shadow of a Dream] is not the monstrous produced by the antithetical notions of literature and history but the marginal, the result of an antagonism between literature and life. I wrote this essay in order to introduce contemporary readers to selected "poems, prose, letters, and testimonies of contemporaries" of a forgotten female Romantic, Karoline von Günderrode. I did not attempt to reconcile the dichotomy between fact and fiction by creating a fictional character; rather, I wanted to reconstruct the plot of a historical figure's life:

Marked by an incurable split, talented, so that she expresses the
inadequacy she feels in herself and the world, she lives a short life,
poor in experience but rich in emotional turmoil; she rejects any
compromise, initiates her own death, mourned by few friends,
barely known; she leaves behind, to a large extent unpublished, a
small body of work: poems, prose pieces, dramatic attempts; she
slips into obscurity, is rediscovered decades, a century later by ad-
mirers of her poetry who undertake to preserve her memory and
her posthumous work, saved by a hair's breadth.[26]

The gulf between literature and history takes place in the realm of fact,
not fiction: Günderrode is the member of a German generation (post-
revolutionary, prerestoration, "the young people of 1800") when women
for the first time entered history as writers, yet were not to be remembered except as literary heroines. I make reference to the conventions of
fiction—the epistolary novel and the dramatic tragedy—by rejecting them
as obvious yet insufficient paradigms for the "emplotment" of Günderrode's life.[27] The split between literature and history exists not simply
between literary texts (Günderrode's own writings) and history (previous
biographies of her) but in my own essay. In fact, I attempt to rewrite
history knowing that all I can do is produce another reading. Unlike you,
I do not create the middle-class woman who has never appeared as fiction
in either literature or history; rather, I introduce Günderrode as fact, as
the suppressed writer of an official GDR literary history.

[THE LACK OF a historical representation of female subjectivity, figured
by Woolf as the monstrosity of the feminine ("a worm winged like an
eagle," p. 46) and by Wolf as the silencing of an entire literary generation
("enthusiasts without reverberation, exclaimers without an echo,"
p. 228), raises questions about constructing a female literary history when
(1) there are no historical precedents and (2) the subject itself has been
defined in exclusively masculine terms, that is, through the subjection of
the feminine. Both Woolf and Wolf posit authors as literary precursors by
naming them either as fiction (Judith Shakespeare) or as historical fact
(Günderrode), while at the same time suggesting that the difference between fact and fiction is undecidable. They could, however, decide on a
mode for constructing their subjects which would involve the deconstruction of a unified subjectivity based, as it has been, on the historical certainty of the male subject. In Woolf's essay the decentering of the subject

takes the form of a first-person narrative voice which both refers to and resists an autobiographical referent; in Wolf's case the essay's biographical subject is constituted as a series of splittings: Günderrode as woman who, on several occasions, adopts the name and dress of a man.]

MALE VS. FEMALE SUBJECT

The Female "I"

Woolf: In capitalizing on the inevitable and quite convenient sense of indeterminacy attached to the referent of the first-person pronoun, "I," as the narrator of *A Room of One's Own,* can be read either as a purely fictional character or as the historical subject we call the author, in this case, Virginia Woolf—me. I nevertheless encourage you to read the narrator as discursive subject position rather than as the signifier of an autobiographical referent: " 'I' is only a convenient term for somebody who has no real being" (p. 4). This statement might mean that pronouns serve only as linguistic functions—signifiers of a discursive fiction—or that I as author have no authorial being—no authority as a female speaking subject. Historically condemned to anonymity by madness and male pseudonyms, the female speaking subject in my essay freely chooses to be unidentifiable. This she does to avoid embodying the subject as identity, a product of the male imagination predicated on the subjection of the feminine.

The male "I" finds its most explicit representation in the novel of Mr. A.: "in the shadow of the letter 'I' all is shapeless as mist. Is that a tree? No, it is a woman. But . . . she has not a bone in her body, I thought, watching Phoebe, for that was her name coming across the beach. Then Alan got up and the shadow of Alan at once obliterated Phoebe" (p. 104). Even in abbreviating the author's name, I cannot mask the referential relationship between the author, Mr. A., and his character, Alan. The feminine, Phoebe, exists only insofar as she is necessary to constitute the masculine, Alan; she does not exist as a woman unto herself, as decipherable subjectivity. Named by a male author, Phoebe's physical presence at first disappears into the natural objects around her, then disintegrates as the male subject draws near. For the female reader, the male writing "I" has constituted itself by eliminating the female body, leaving only a specter from which to construct her own subjectivity. And further, the female writer is left with either a specter or a male subjectivity from which to construct her female fictional subjects.

Wolf: Günderrode, as woman writer, inscribes the female "I" in a discursive splitting which retains the female body as corpse. In a letter [1803?] to Clemens Brentano, the brother of her friend Bettina and the first of three suitors, she writes:

> It seems odd to me that I listen to how I speak and my own words appear stranger to me than those of strangers. Even the most truthful letters are in my opinion only corpses; they describe a previous life which still inhabits them, and even though they resemble the living, the purpose of their existence has already past: that is why it appears to me (when I read what I wrote a short while ago), as though I were seeing myself lying in a coffin and my two 'I's were staring at each other in amazement.[28]

It is not the female body but the letter (both epistolary and linguistic) which inscribes the body, which is dead. The letter functions as coffin for the female subject who no more easily recognizes herself in her own discourse than in that of the male author. The "I" comes into existence by obliterating the self as unified subjectivity. The specular splitting—the seeing of oneself—described by our feminist critic as characteristic of the elegy, duplicates rather than annihilates the female subject. Yet because this doubling takes place within the writer as historical subject and not within the writer's text, it must take the form of a literal, not figurative death—Günderrode's suicide. Once again the female "I" has no real being: she exists only discursively and even then only as other, the "other woman" not as fictional subject but as corpse.

To me this splitting is the product of historical conditions, and to view it as specifically female is not to essentialize it but to historicize the gendered subject. One could even go so far as to read the specular splitting as inscribing within it the division of sexual difference, which is what I do in my essay: "The schism of the times goes through her. She divides herself into various people, one of them a man. 'That is why it appears to me as though I were seeing myself in a coffin and my two "I"'s were staring at each other in amazement'" (p. 281). As I see it, the emergence of the female subject coincides historically with the disappearance of a male subjectivity usurped by the use and exchange values demanded by commodity capitalism. The female poet—who has access to an education, not an occupation—stands in as strict an opposition to the (female) bour-geoise as she does to the male intellectual, who himself must conform to the restrictions imposed by the increasing professionalization of middle-class life.[29] Günderrode's two other suitors, Carl von Savigny, a jurist who becomes the Prussian Minister of Justice, and Friedrich Creuzer, professor of classics at the University of Heidelberg, regard their vows in marriage and to the state as equally sacrosanct. Such an institutional devotion allows them to deny Günderrode's subjectivity, even though they recognize it as intellectually superior, by disregarding the emotional implications of their admiration and affection for her. For Günderrode to find fulfillment through love is as impossible as finding it through work. All she can have from her suitors is "the shadow of a dream": not the obliterating shadow of a male "I" but the shadow which will objectify her as unrequited lover, the most banal of female roles. Obliteration will come later, in the form of self-annihilation.

Historical Naming

Wolf: In addition to splitting the "I," Günderrode splits herself between a literal and figurative gender position by adopting the epistolary role of "der Freund" toward her two suitors, Savigny and Creuzer. In German "Freund" signifies friend, but only in the masculine; "Freundin," its feminine form, implies sexual intimacy. Thus the relation between male and female intellectuals as it emerged for the first time among the German Romantics has no name, no signifier. Günderrode changes her sex, then addresses herself in the third person; "Freund" thus refers to both herself and her male addressee. In 1806 she writes to Creuzer:

> My friend was just with me; he was very lively, and an unusual red burned on his cheek. He says he dreamed of Eusebio [the name Günderrode gives Creuzer] in his morning slumber, how he was completely united with him and wandered with him through charming valleys and wooded hills in blessed love and freedom. Is such a dream not worth much more than a year of my life? If only for months I could be as happy and as innocently happy as in this dream, how willingly and with what thankfulness toward the gods would I die.[30]

Günderrode eroticizes her relationship to Creuzer by imagining a scene between two men, who themselves appear behind the masks of pseudonyms. In later letters, Creuzer and Günderrode address each other with nicknames coded in Greek: Günderrode "die Poesie"; Creuzer "der Fromme" [the pious one]. Just as the erotic becomes legitimate only through the "hommo"-erotic whereby the woman adopts a male persona, Günderrode can become an author only by appropriating a male pseudonym, Tian. Yet behind the male disguise lies Günderrode's female body. Her literal, gendered being leads Creuzer to suppress her final collection of poems, *Melete* (which appears in print only in 1906), and leads her to drown the body which in discourse or in dress can pass for a man, but not in love.

Woolf: In my text the precariousness of the female subject causes names to proliferate without multiplying personae. The narrator elaborates on the identity of her "I" parenthetically: "Here then was I (call me Mary Beton, Mary Seton, Mary Carmichael or by any name you please— it is not a matter of any importance)" (p. 5). Rather than adopting a male pseudonym, the narrator chooses the names of several women, the repetition of the first name implying an interchangeability of female identities. The "Marys" refer to three of the four Marys who appear in an anonymous ballad entitled "Mary Hamilton," whose various versions will be found (after my time) from the *Norton Anthology of Poetry* to a Joan Baez album from the 1960s. The last stanza reads:

> *Last night there was four Maries,*
> *The night there'll be but three;*
> *There was Marie Seton, and Marie Beton,*
> *And Marie Carmichael, and me.*[31]

The first person, this time in the objective case, remains nameless, just as I as historical author fail to name Mary Hamilton, fail to give her any "real being" as a discursive subject. In the ballad, Mary Hamilton literally ceases to be when the queen has her sent to the gallows for bearing the king's child and shipping it out to sea. The other ladies-in-waiting enter my text not as subordinates and rivals of a queen who must privilege her relation to the king but as participants in the construction of a female subject who breaks her complicity with forms of male dominance: Mary Seton the science teacher provides her female college students with a technical education; Mary Beton the aunt leaves her niece a financial legacy which will enable her to write; and Mary Carmichael the contemporary novelist will write both for and about a future female audience. Together they transform the "I" who has no "real being" into a "multiple individual" rather than a split subjectivity.

It is not the failed attempt of the woman writer (your Günderrode) to create a "hommo-sexual" couple but the suppression of the name of the last Mary, the fourth term, which marks the disappearance of a female historical subject in my text. The fact that historians remain divided and undecided over the place of the real Mary Hamilton (not knowing whether the events of her life took place at Mary Stuart's court in the sixteenth century or at the eighteenth-century court of Peter the Great) secures Mary Hamilton's status as a legendary folk figure. But her status as absent figure comes not only from her undecidable status as historical subject; it also results from a historically gendered and denigrated position which condemns to death those who circumvent paternity, the legitimizing fiction.

Cross-Dressing

Woolf: To resolve this dilemma and rid myself of the absent female presence, I transcribe Mary Hamilton's historical irretrievability into a retrievable fiction—that of Judith Shakespeare. Judith internalizes the consequences of female transgression, signified by her illegitimate child, by inducing her own death. Judith commits suicide following the splitting of the female subject not in the "letter" but through literal conception. I create the fiction of Shakespeare's sister in response to a bishop's assertion that "women cannot write the plays of Shakespeare" (p. 48), thus attempting to historicize the absence of women in literary history by providing reasons for the absent playwright in the sixteenth century. Here I think we would find ourselves in complete agreement: the absence of women in literary history is the result of the limitations imposed on them by historical conditions, not of their literary inferiority:

> Let me imagine, since facts are so hard to come by, what would
> have happened had Shakespeare had a wonderfully gifted sister,
> called Judith, let us say. . . . She had the quickest fancy, a gift like
> her brother's, for the tune of words. Like him, she had a taste for
> the theatre. She stood at the stage door; she wanted to act, she said.
> . . . At last—for she was very young, oddly like Shakespeare the
> poet in her face, with the same grey eyes and rounded brows—at

last Nick Greene the actor-manager took pity on her; she found herself with child by that gentleman. (pp. 49–50)

Thus I construct my narrative, which in spite of its historical specificity reads like a generic female biography, by reversing the sex of the biographical subject.[32] The gift, the adventurous spirit, youth—these traits the siblings have in common; formal education, marital expectations, and employment opportunities are what they do not share. Youth serves to erase obvious differences in physical appearance, but eventually their unequivocally opposite relations to reproduction leads to a different relation to literary production: William writes and Judith does not. Judith, the victim of the oldest female profession, receives neither monetary nor marital compensation and is thus herself made illegitimate and excluded from her chosen profession, writing. By coding gender differences in the form of a sibling relationship, I attempted to locate the origin of sexual inequality in the city rather than in the family. What I failed to realize then was that the family both produces differences through biological reproduction and reproduces the significance of those differences by insisting on the legitimizing function of paternity.

Wolf: The circumstances of Günderrode's life in the nineteenth century, scarcely different from those of Judith in the sixteenth, suggests that any notion of the "feminine" is based more in "timeless" plots borrowed from literature than in the historical emplotments of actual events. In Günderrode's case the splitting between masculine and feminine exists within the female subject herself. I open my essay with a quotation which translates this schism into the exclusion from military participation, the stuff of traditional history. In 1801 Günderrode writes to Gunda, the sister of Clemens and Bettina Brentano:

I have often had the unfeminine wish of throwing myself into, of dying in a wild melée. Why wasn't I born a man! I have no sense for feminine virtues, for female felicity. I like only the wild, the enormous, the brilliant. It is an unfortunate but incorrigible disparity in my soul; and it will and must remain so, for I am a woman, and have the longings of a man, without the vigor. That is why I am so changeable, and so at odds with myself. (p. 225)

Günderrode imagines not a different life but a different death—a military hero's final moment—rather than the suicide of a literary heroine. In this sense, the internalization of the conflict between genders can be resolved only through death, just as the nature and means of death itself is determined by sexual difference.

Günderrode pursues this logic even further when she suggests dressing as a man in order to follow Creuzer into battle. In 1805 she writes:

> The friend has told me that if this war becomes dangerous for him or his wishes, that he would like to, beknown to you, put on his dress, make his escape and become your servant. You cannot send him away and he will have such a fine disguise that one will not be able to recognize him. At your convenience he wanted to make this all comprehensible. If still you do not accept him because of public opinion, then he will seek his death.[33]

Again addressing herself in the third person as "der Freund," she attempts to literalize the discursive persona by means of cross-dressing. Later, when Creuzer is called to the University of Moscow she imagines disguising herself as his student in order to accompany him. Again their relationship is conceivable only as the relationship between two men, in which she adopts the masculine role. When this seems impossible, Günderrode proposes moving into Creuzer's household as its third member, with Creuzer's wife as housekeeper and maternal friend of the two lovers. Lisette Nees, perhaps the most gifted of the female Romantics, is the harshest critic of Günderrode's attempt to transform her dream into reality: "Your fantasy would take its revenge . . . because you wanted to transpose it to bourgeois conditions" (p. 268).

Literary History

Wolf: In spite of Günderrode's isolation and eventual suicide, her emergence as historical subject becomes conceivable only within the context of a literary circle which for the first time in German intellectual history included women:

> As little as Günderrode allows herself to be classified according to one of the categories of literary history—"early Romanticism," "Classicism"—so too is she unthinkable without the intellectual contact with those who around the turn of the century in Jena amount to a new literary tendency—the Schlegels, Tieck, Novalis, Clemens Brentano, Schelling, scholars such as Savigny, Friedrich

Creuzer, Christian Nees von Esenbeck; in addition the women—sisters, friends, lovers, wives, and for the first time, colleagues of these men, even if they, like Dorothea Schlegel, conceal their contribution to the Shakespeare translation, their participation in the work of the men. The names of those who became famous—such as Caroline Schlegel-Schelling, Bettina Brentano, Sophie Mereau-Brentano, Rahel Varnhagen—stand for others, similarly educated, similarly restless, similarly searching: the correspondence of Günderrode is evidence of women who manage to reflect on their own situation. . . . (pp. 235–36)

I begin my literary history at the end of the eighteenth century, when women in Germany for the first time appear as names in history, although they still remain hesitant to attach their names to literary contributions. Günderrode represents one of the many forgotten women writers for whom the canonized ones serve as tropes, canonized because the men they were associated with became more famous. Originally Günderrode's significance lay in the tragedy of a life whose accomplishments were almost immediately interred with her, but the singularity of her death—brought to my attention by Anna Seghers[34]—led me to reinvestigate the historical circumstances of Günderrode's life and time. The result: my introductory essay which facilitated the reissue of her literary work. The Romantic circle both produced translators of Shakespeare and gave birth to his sister Judith, in Günderrode—the first female lyric poet in Germany. In fulfillment of your prophecy that the future female poets will put on the literal body of Judith Shakespeare, I have attempted to recover the figurative body of Günderrode's work.

I chose the genre of the literary biography for this process of recovery because it allows me to reconstruct the literary precursor as historical figure while I deconstruct her as literary heroine. By self-consciously emplotting Günderrode's life as "bürgerliches Trauerspiel" [bourgeois tragedy], I suggest that the plot's outcome lies less in the overwrought sensibility of an individual psyche than in the narratives we have available for refamiliarizing ourselves with the female lives forgotten by history. Once Günderrode adopts the lead role, that of tragic heroine, in the drama where she has always played the third term in someone else's conjugal plot, death becomes a matter not of individual choice but of historical inevitability. Günderrode, a figure who has been absent from history, can only acquire historical prominence by becoming legible to readers in the present moment. The Women's Movement of the 1970s made this a possibility, both for myself and younger generations of women in Germany, by encouraging us to reread our own historical circumstances through the figures of the past.

Woolf: The fact that many readers have actually mistaken Judith Shakespeare for a historical figure, reading her as a long lost "sister," rather than as a "convenient" fiction, suggests that the fictive construction and the historical reconstruction of the female subject are what our feminist critic would call dialogical activities. I also begin my female literary history (in chapter 4 of *A Room of One's Own*) in the eighteenth century, not when women first appear as named writers but when, as writers, for the first time they earn a living: "Thus towards the end of the eighteenth century a change came about which, if I were rewriting history, I should describe more fully and think of greater importance than the Crusades or the Wars of the Roses. The middle-class woman began to write" (p. 68). For me the collectivity which makes possible individual literary production is not a community of women but of the masses: "masterpieces are not single and solitary births; they are the outcome of many years of thinking in common, of thinking by the body of the people, so that the experience of the mass is behind the single voice" (pp. 68–69). By insisting on "the voice of anon,"[35] I seek to undermine the formation of a literary canon which singles out the solitary author by disembodying its voice from history.

Within a specifically female literary tradition marked by brevity, scarcity, and massive disjunctions, I would choose Jane Austen (1775–1817) as the female author who comes closest to Shakespeare in embodying "the voice of anon." As with Shakespeare, the lack of biographical information surrounding Austen's life prevents us from knowing her except as the signature we associate with her texts. Unlike the works of Charlotte Brontë (or Günderrode), they do not reveal an author whose gift failed to match her gendered circumstances, disrupting artistic integrity through anger, ignorance, and fear, as in the passage I quote from *Jane Eyre:* "It is vain to say human beings ought to be satisfied with tranquillity; they must have action; and they will make it if they cannot find it. Millions are condemned to a stiller doom than mine, and millions are in silent revolt gainst their lot" (p. 72). For me the disjunction between gender and art lies in the difference between the author as fiction, Shakespeare's sister (where I emphasize Judith's historical circumstances because she failed to produce any art) and Austen, a kind of Shakespeare, because her art will not allow us to learn anything about her circumstances.

[WOOLF RETRIEVES THE historical female subject via the legendary Mary Hamilton who was sent to the gallows, the fictive Judith Shakespeare who took her own life, and the figure of Jane Austen about whose life we know very little. Wolf focuses on the life of Günderrode, reveals it as a story, reads it as a fiction, and in the process retrieves a moment in history which saw the beginnings of a female literary community. Woolf's diachronic approach to an alternative literary history emphasizes an exclusively female genealogy as supplement to the male literary canon, while Wolf's synchronicity focuses on gender roles as they functioned during the early 1800s when women emerged as intellectual equals, even as the emergence of a solidified middle class required stricter gender roles. Wolf attempts to reinsert the individual subject into a GDR literary history that has sought to invalidate individual subjectivity (particularly as practiced by the Romantics) by reconstructing the biography of a forgotten precursor; Woolf seeks to deemphasize a reified subjectivity by privileging those writers about whom we possess almost no biographical information. In both cases the female literary historical subject is not only the product of a discourse which consciously deconstructs the masculine subject but also the product of a dialogic relation between literature and history, between critic and precursor, between the figurative and the literal death of the forgotten foremother.]

ROOM VS. TOMB

[THE DIFFICULTY OF retrieving a female tradition in temporal terms leads to its configuration in spatial forms, in an "elsewhere" which substitutes for another time. "Elsewhere" for both Woolf and Wolf lies in the room and the tomb: the room as a figure for the female imagination, both secluded and excluded, and the tomb as "nowhere," the place of the female literary precursor.

The female subject's relation to the room as a figure for a masculine tradition raises the issue of whether it is more desirable to be locked in or locked out. Kamuf reads the exclusively male library at Oxbridge in *A Room of One's Own* as the metaphoric "locked room of history": "That is, since women's history cannot be studied in the library, it will have to be read into the scene of its own exclusion. It has, in other words, to be invented—both discovered and made up."[36] Günderrode, whom Wolf recovers, is locked into her "Stiftszimmer" as an impoverished gentlewoman; and Judith, whom Woolf invents, is locked out of the theater which prohibits women from acting. Finally, the tombstone which marks their respective suicides becomes a signifier for what has been called a woman's ultimate room of her own—the grave.]

Woolf: Not only do I split the female subject into a multiplicity of names, such as the "Marys" of the narrator; I also place her in myriad rooms, from the common sitting room to the room of one's own, from the laboratory to the "vast chamber where nobody has yet been" (p. 88) of female intimacy. On the one hand, the history of women has taken place almost exclusively in the seclusion of interiors; on the other hand, those rooms have been neither private nor part of the public record. They have been the site of scenes of interruption, freely entered into like the female body, offering room only for the imagination because there has been no historical documentation:

> One goes into the room—but the resources of the English language would be much put to the stretch, and whole flights of words would need to wing their way illegitimately into existence before a woman could say what happens when she goes into a room. The rooms differ so completely; they are calm or thunderous; open on to the sea, or, on the contrary, give on to a prison yard; are hung with washing; or alive with opals and silks; are hard as horse hair or soft as feathers—one has only to go into any room in any street for the whole of that extremely complex force of femininity to fly in one's face. (p. 91)

Rooms become the places where the undifferentiated subjectivities of obscure women are subsumed under an abstract notion of the feminine. The only sign of the differences between women lies in the material conditions of the rooms as indicators of social class. The room can be "a room of one's own" where the middle-class woman begins to write, or the place where the working-class woman cannot write until she has finished the washing. For a voice to seep out of these rooms one would need to hear a different language. This language would "see" the women who have always been there rather than insisting on the fact that they never existed.

Wolf: Locked into her "Stiftszimmer," Günderrode retreats from history to study the historical texts Bettina thinks will help to ground Günderrode's overactive imagination. I too resort to the spatial enclosure as a way of articulating the constraints of gender and class:

> Since she was nineteen she has lived as canoness in the aristocratic Cronstetten Evangelical Sisterhood—which one must not at all imagine as a convent, but as a quiet, retiring place for the custody of unmarried daughters from the penniless nobility. The regulations, which require a minimum age of thirty for admittance, are altered for Gründerrode—this may intimate a hard-pressed situation. She is not intent on amusements—the canonesses should avoid the theater and balls as much as possible. We know of a visit Günderrode made to the theater, and shortly before her death an anonymous correspondent is said to have seen her as silent pilgrim at a costume ball; the rule not to receive men alone is not strictly enforced; she can move without restriction in the vicinity; for trips of greater distance she needs a permit which is easily come by. Now and again she excuses herself with friends: she cannot make a requested visit because she remains tied down. (pp. 233–34)

Like Judith, Günderrode is warned to avoid the theater, although as spectator, not as actress. Her avoidance of secular pleasures nevertheless does not lead to religious devotion. Instead, Günderrode finds an outlet for her imagination on paper, in her reading, her writing, and the maps she draws with Bettina as a substitute for geographical displacement. After Günderrode's death, Bettina writes: "We made travel plans, we invented routes and adventures, we wrote everything down, we mapped everything out, our imagination was so active that we could not have experienced it better in real life."[37] The room does not signify a space which has never been entered but one which cannot be escaped; it is the place of figurative rather than literal (i.e., insignificant) experience. This experience is read as having nothing to do with reality—the experiences of men—or as too close to reality—Creuzer withdraws Günderrode's poems from publication because they might implicate him. Günderrode, as a single subject confined to a solitary room, becomes the sign of a whole generation caught between a changing class structure and shifting gender roles (this generation could also be mine).

[THE ROOM AS BOTH sanctuary and exile from a masculine culture marks the space where the female literary precursor comes into conflict with historical conditions. Historical conditions, such as those that prevent women from appearing on stage or that finally allow middle-class women to receive an education, are nevertheless invalidated in the biography of the female historical subject by ahistorical sexual categories. For Judith an illegitimate pregnancy and for Günderrode unrequited love are the alleged reasons for their suicides, not the impossibility of becoming writers. In an essay on women's suicide, Margaret Higonnet suggests:

> Suicide, like woman and truth, is both fetish and taboo. A symbolic gesture, it is doubly so for women who inscribe on their own bodies cultural reflections and projections, affirmation and negation. . . . To embrace death is at the same time to read one's own life. The act is a self-barred signature; its destructive narcissism seems to some particularly feminine.[38]

Suicide eliminates the body that has never been inscribed in culture by turning it into a text. It forces one to read a life which would otherwise remain illegible; yet that life becomes intelligible only as a result of the woman writer-as-critic who recovers the death of the literary precursor not as suicide but as historical elision. Death as a form of closure is differently inscribed in historical and novelistic discourses because, rather than beginning a story with the end of a life, the ending of a life produces a story which tells a different literary history; it inscribes death as a historical text to be rewritten. Judith's death offers a self-explanatory text for why there are no female Shakespeares; Günderrode, who had already written her epigraph at the time of her death, writes it in the form of an allegory—the form repeatedly chosen by Wolf herself.

Higonnet suggests further that myths of female suicide tend to focus on two themes: defeated love and chastity, the motives attributed to the suicides of Günderrode and Judith Shakespeare, respectively.[39] Both Woolf and Wolf suggest, however, that these motives allow only for the historical inscription of the female writing subject and thus do not provide an explanation for the act based on historical circumstances. Such an inscription relies on literary paradigms which emplot the female historical subject as novelistic heroine; yet the literary-historical inscription of Judith and Günderrode relies on very different motives: the impossibility of becoming an author. The female writer, because of the incompatibility between the body and the text, can be constructed only as bodiless, and thus becomes inscribed in the epitaph rather than in history.]

Woolf: For Judith there is no final text in the form of an inscription on a tombstone. She "lies buried at some cross-roads where the omnibuses now stop outside the Elephant and Castle" (p. 50), beneath the flow of London traffic, a victim of "the traffic in women." The omnibus stop marks a presence that is not hers, a visible sign that cannot mark her as a female literary precursor.[40] Even as a fiction Judith must rely on the patronym of her brother; had she been a historical figure, her anonymity would have been written in her pseudonym rather than on her tombstone.

Wolf: Günderrode's grave (which I have visited), lies marked in the cemetery at Winkel-am-Rhein. Her body washed up on the river's shore the day after she stabbed herself with her brother's dagger. [THE INSTRUMENT FOR ending rather than entering life is once again owed to the fraternal relation.] In contrast to the unmarked grave situated at the busy intersection of a European metropolis, Günderrode marks her pastoral grave by writing her own inscription. She bases it on an East Indian lyric she finds while reading Gottfried Herder (1744–1803):

> Earth, my mother, and my nourisher, breath of air
> Holy fire, friend of mine, and you, o brother, mountain stream.
> And you my father, ether, I tell you all with reverence
> Many thanks; with you I have lived
> And I go to the other world, leaving you gladly.
> Farewell, brother and friend, father and mother, farewell. (p. 275)

In equating kinship terms with natural elements, Günderrode omits the nonmaternal female functions of the sister and the female friend. Even in writing her epitaph, she inscribes her own elision: a sign of her belatedness as literary precursor and a prefiguring of the second death she died when her work was withheld from publication. Unlike Judith who will be reborn in the body of an as yet unborn woman writer, Günderrode's anonymity finally has been converted into the legibility of a literary text through my search for a historical precursor.

[THE LOSS OF chastity which results in Judith's suicide and the anonymity of the marker which designates her grave are the elements of a fiction which Woolf reproduces in her version of a female literary history; the unrequited love of Günderrode and the rewriting of a traditional lyric as epitaph are facts which symbolically structure Wolf's alternative literary history. Woolf attempts to deconstruct the canonized literary male subject by positing Judith as the missing precursor and Austen as the precursor without an identifiable subjectivity. Both have names, yet retain their anonymity, Judith because she is a fiction and dies too soon, and Austen because her fiction makes it impossible to decipher biographical facts. Wolf reconstructs the literary historical subject by reinstating subjectivity within history in a female form, posited as the site of conflict between the masculine and the feminine. Günderrode loses her anonymity through Wolf's biographical essay, which focuses on the many pseudonyms she used during her lifetime.

The female literary precursor exists both as fact and as fiction; a female literary history attempts to historicize the feminine by placing the precursor in time, which can be figured only by temporarily suspending it in space. The dialogic relation between space and time, literature and history, author and precursor makes possible the re-presentation of an absent female literary tradition.]

CHAPTER FIVE

HISTORICAL FICTIONS
The Portrait

The "difficulty of saying 'I'" is ultimately the desire not to say "I."
—HELEN FEHERVARY

Of reading history, Catherine Morland, the heroine of Jane Austen's *Northanger Abbey*, says:

> But history, real solemn history, I cannot be interested in . . . I wish I were too. I read it a little as a duty, but it tells me nothing that does not either vex or weary me. The quarrels of popes and kings, with wars or pestilences, in every page; the men all so good for nothing, and hardly any women at all—it is very tiresome: and yet I often think it odd that it should be so dull, for a great deal of it must be invention. The speeches that are put into the heroes' mouths, their thoughts and designs—the chief of all this must be invention, and invention is what delights me in other books.[1]

This statement follows a discussion of Mrs. Radcliffe's *The Mysteries of Udolpho* between Catherine and Henry Tilney, Austen's hero, and his sister, Eleanor. Catherine assumes that men find novels less appealing than other books because they must judge them to be less clever. Henry confesses that men read nearly as many novels as women do, leading to Catherine's lament that history has no appeal for her. Eleanor admits that she too enjoys reading history, since if a speech is interesting it matters little if written by a novelist or a historian, thus implying that an appreciation for historical writing has much to do with training and little to do with gender. Catherine at that point realizes that historians have voluntary readers, as well as the involuntary audience of schoolchildren who must subject themselves to torment at the hands of historical tomes. Henry suggests that historians cannot be held responsible for the difficulty one might have in literally learning to read—conflating literacy with the untrained readership of women. Without knowing how to read one would not even be able to read Gothic fiction, he argues, thus closing this particular topic of conversation.

Catherine's comment about the nature of historical writing carries with it assumptions about the gendered subject, the presence of men and the absence of women in history, the role of fiction-making in the retelling of facts—all previously discussed in conjunction with literary history. History holds little interest for her because in it there are no women, no female subjects with whom to identify; this in turn suggests that, failing to exist as historical facts, women enter only those texts considered fictions. And yet, she concludes, most of the past must be imagined and therefore cannot be qualitatively different from the inventions of novels. She even realizes that the textual hierarchy of "truthfulness" which places history above fiction is not a product of content but of readership, since as long as men read history and women fiction, history will be perceived as superior. Henry convinces her that men gain equal pleasure from the suspenseful plot of *Udolpho,* while Eleanor persuades her that she is as fond of history as any man. Does this then invalidate Catherine's claim?

Her argument, which correctly traces the origins of textual hierarchy to the reader, fails to recognize that the gendered reader is constituted by linguistic usage, not by the text. Sexual difference is decipherable in how and not what people read, and in how they speak about what they have read. Henry reprimands Catherine for describing Radcliffe's novel as "nice," which to him means "neat" and can only refer to the binding, and for using "to instruct" and "to torment" synonymously in her discussion of how children learn to read. In spite of her literacy, Catherine has not yet "learned" to read history, because, in contrast to Eleanor, the difference between fact and fiction still matters to her; nor is she a "good" reader of fiction because she has not yet learned to say more about a novel than whether or not it is good. As Terry Eagleton has written: "Literature presents itself as threat, mystery, challenge and insult to those who, able to read, can nonetheless not 'read.' To be able to decipher the signs and yet remain ignorant: it is in this contradiction that the tyranny of Literature is revealed."[2] The tyrant in this case takes the form of Henry Tilney, who functions as representative of a "masculine," therefore privileged relation to language. Catherine nevertheless forms an opinion about what she reads, even if her word choice betrays an ignorance attributed to her sex. The adjective she uses to describe the book is the very attribute one might use to describe her—"nice." Thus the act of reading becomes a form of specularization in which the female reader "sees" no more than herself, that is, as she has been read by the masculine subject.

The next topic of conversation revolves around a discussion of the view:

> They were viewing the country with the eyes of persons accustomed to drawing, and decided on its capability of being formed into pictures, with all the eagerness of real taste. Here Catherine was quite lost. She knew nothing of drawing—nothing of taste:—and she listened to them with an attention which brought her little profit, for they talked in phrases which conveyed scarcely any idea to her.[3]

In a literate culture, reading is an assumed skill while drawing becomes an accomplishment practiced by a privileged few. Catherine has learned to read and to express herself verbally, if inexactly by male standards, but she has not yet learned to "read" nature in order to reproduce it as landscape: "It seemed as if a good view were no longer to be taken from the top of an high hill, and that a clear blue sky was no longer a proof of a fine day."[4] Here again her reading is characterized by "literalness"; not as literacy, the ability to recognize signs, but as the inability to reproduce signs which would transform nature into landscape through the conventions of art. The view leaves her doubly silenced: she neither possesses the language with which to make the scene speak nor recognizes the advantages of a silence which marks her desirability as marriage partner. The landscape, itself mute, fails to supply Catherine with the proper discourse, obliging Austen's narrative voice to speak for her: "Where people wish to attach, they should always be ignorant. . . . A woman especially, if she have the misfortune of knowing any thing, should conceal it as well as she can."[5] As female subject, even if she had access to words, she must learn not to speak them out loud. Catherine in her innocence confesses her ignorance and immediately receives instruction in discerning natural beauty from Henry. A gifted pupil, she successfully acquires the "correct" way of looking by reproducing her suitor's linguistic competence. The conversation continues its natural course until it arrives at politics, of interest only to men, where it once again stumbles on silence.

Catherine prefers reading fiction to reading history and learns to read nature as landscape, implying that the constitution of the female reader relies on the privatization of two public discourses, language and visual art. At the same time reading in the novel is not just a private experience but openly discussed in discursive acts which appear between quotation marks. The undecidability of history as fact or fiction—already encountered in the construction of a literary history—enters Austen's novel as a topic of conversation; at the same time, conversation as actual dialogue begins to resemble a dramatic or public performance. Catherine's discourse is nevertheless devalorized as "feminine" or dictated to her by a male mentor; in either case, the narrative voice counsels silence, if she wishes to inscribe herself not as reader but as wife.

Woolf's *Between the Acts* (1941) and Wolf's *No Place on Earth* (1979) can be read as fictions which rewrite the dialogic relation between literature and history as historical fiction. The fiction does not take the form of a novel narrative, a story never before told; it appears as an interpolated history—the rewriting of prior texts. Historical fictions stage literary history as dramatic performance, thus dramatizing history as well as discursive acts. The dramatic dialogue takes the form, on one level, of private conversations at an afternoon tea gathering, and on another level, of intertextual dialogues produced by the interpolation of historical discourses.

In Woolf's novel the performance takes place at an outdoor pageant which reenacts scenes from English literary history, interpolated in the novel as dramatic event. These scenes are witnessed by the characters who play the role of audience and read by the reader in the form of a script which interrupts the narrative proper. In Wolf a single scene—the encounter between two Romantics, Karoline von Günderrode (1790–1806) and Heinrich von Kleist (1777–1811)—takes the form of a novella which consists almost exclusively of dialogue and interior monologues. Wolf does not divide the dialogue into passages attributed to specific speakers; rather she includes excerpts taken from historical writings, such as the private letters of the protagonists, without the use of quotation marks. By interpolating texts from literary history as drama, Woolf and Wolf interrogate the texts of the literary canon as well as the role of the female speaking subject in history.

Those who legislate the dialogues are no longer the Henry Tilneys—the individual male mentors—but the female dramatists, Woolf's Miss La Trobe and Wolf's Günderrode. The possibility of the woman writer as historical subject has no historical precedent and thus exists only in the present, the moment of the dramatic performance. La Trobe writes the script for a publicly performed pageant which consists almost exclusively of parodic rewritings of Elizabethan, Restoration, and Victorian drama; Günderrode, a published poet who mentions that she is working on a play, becomes a performer in Wolf's script, which is largely based on Günderrode's private writings. In each case the dramatist engages dialogically with a male-authored text: La Trobe parodies the texts of British male literary dramatists; Günderrode becomes the reader and critic of Kleist's historical drama, *Guiscard*.

The other woman within the text of the historical fiction is not "an/other woman" as fictional subject but the very category "woman" as defined by the authors of a masculinist culture. Woman as "the feminine" appears in each text in the form of a portrait which silences the female speaking subject through her containment as image. Against this image of "the feminine" produced by sexual difference, Woolf and Wolf rewrite the female fictional subject as sexually different. La Trobe and Günderrode enter history as historical anomalies: female subjects in the body of a woman seeking to inscribe themselves as writers, which is read a priori as "manly." In order to differentiate the "other woman" in the historical fiction from her appearance in the elegiac novel, the female protagonist appears as successful (even if less successful than the author herself) and as solitary. La Trobe's pageant is performed (in spite of the weather), unlike Lily's paintings which she believes will never be seen; yet she lives alone and retires by herself into the smoke-filled corner of a pub after the performance of her play. Günderrode's writings will be published under her own name, in contrast to those of Christa T.; yet she encounters Kleist without passion (her love for Creuzer and Savigny unrequited), and departs from the tea gathering never to see him again. At stake is not the quality of the art but the sexual identity of the female artist, understood in terms of the contradiction between masculine and feminine.

The novelistic heroine as dramatist represents the most specular of the female fictional subjects encountered thus far, in that she most closely represents the author herself, as woman writer who must read the place assigned to her by history and inscribe herself within it. The novelty of the woman writer in history becomes rewritten as the precariousness of history. La Trobe and Günderrode write themselves into history at the very moment when they are forced to contemplate its end: for La Trobe the end of history is prefigured by the preparations made for war; for Günderrode the end is marked by the end of her life, terminated by the suicide she commits shortly after her encounter with Kleist. The woman writer as simultaneously successful and solitary rewrites each author's position as female but as marginal: Woolf a sexual outcast because of her lesbianism and Wolf a political outsider, a critic of the GDR who has chosen not to leave it.

The visual component of the specular enters the historical fiction as portrait—the historical silencing of the feminine—and as dramatic performance—the appearance of the female subject on the stage of history. The female dramatist subverts "the feminine" as visual image by concealing herself offstage, leaving center stage to the male subject, who talks too much and in the process fails to produce any meaning. La Trobe, hiding in the bushes, speaks to the anonymous audience through a megaphone, leaving the act of interpreting the play, and its practical appeal (raising money for the church), to the minister; Günderrode speaks to the public through her poetry by using male pseudonyms, while Kleist monopolizes the conversation at the tea gathering with autobiographical anecdotes introduced to illuminate his plays. Yet the voice of the historical fiction belongs not to the individual speaker (of either gender) but to the audience (a transcription of Austen's reader). The female subject who is seen as an anomaly (as both masculine and feminine), and speaks without being seen, disappears in the voice of a "we."

For both authors the "we" represents a collapse of the distinction between author and audience—audience as the spectators of La Trobe's pageant and the readers of Wolf's novella. Within the text itself, the "we" takes the form of Woolf's fragmented audience which cannot agree on the meaning of the play and Wolf's heterosexual couple which cannot transcend uncertainty with reciprocity. On the one hand, the "we" represents the loss of the individual subject for the greater social good—the threat of totalitarianism as well as the promise of socialism. On the other hand, it represents the possibility of a community which no longer discriminates between subjects on the basis of gender. The "we" comes to figure the utopian ideal of an ungendered subjectivity. Thus the dialogic in the historical fiction is rewritten not just as specularity but as alterity, as the possibility of a nonhierarchical sexual difference.

HISTORY

The dialogized discourse in *Between the Acts* and *No Place on Earth* makes its appearance both in the interpolation of historical texts written by literary historical figures and in the rewriting of a previously written text. History enters the historical fiction not as the reanimation of past occurrences (as in the historical novel of the realist tradition) but as the rewriting of an essay in novel form: *Between the Acts* rewrites *Three Guineas* and *No Place on Earth* rewrites "The Shadow of a Dream." The past reenacted by this intertextual dialogue is a historical text, which by providing the specificity of a women's history makes possible the writing of a female-authored historical fiction.[6] Thus a history which inscribes the female subject as historical subject—the necessary precondition for a historical fiction—can only be found in a previous text, authored by the writer herself. The essay requires revision because of its status as supplementary history—a text primarily written for the female reader. When the female subject becomes inscribed in a historical fiction, the history loses its separatism and becomes instead a history of sexual differences.

Between the Acts returns to *Three Guineas*, which is about (among other things) the entrance of English middle-class women into the professions. Woolf rewrites the essay by expanding upon the relation between the familial patriarch and the political dictator to include the connection between the battle of the sexes and conflicts on the battlefield. Not female oppression in the domestic sphere but the repression of illegitimate sexual desires (such as adultery or homosexuality) produces the physical violence which finds its most extreme form in war. Similarly, Wolf in *No Place on Earth* rewrites "The Shadow of a Dream," which returns to the moment when women first appeared as writers in nineteenth-century Germany and replaces the individual female biography with an encounter between a male and a female literary figure. Kleist and Günderrode meet for the first time shortly before each commits suicide, yet the historical contradictions which lead to their respective deaths are gender specific: for Kleist it is work, for Günderrode it is love which cannot be reconciled with artistic production. Both novels, in contrast to the essays, uncover how men and women have been restricted by gender roles, even if in historically different ways.[7]

Each of the rewritten essays focuses on a historical moment which grants women entrance into the public sphere, only to place them in structurally subordinate positions. The novels, in contrast, construct women who have entered the public realm successfully, which means becoming "like a man": La Trobe and Günderrode are both masculinized by means of their clothing. Thus women who leave the private sphere, rather than causing a shift in the social structure, shift from one gender identity to another. Whereas the essay, through its logical structure, argues against the oppression of women in history, the novel, through dramatic performance, stages history as the conflict between gendered positions.

History in Woolf's novel appears as literary history, as a series of plays performed at an annual pageant on an English estate. Scenes from English drama rewritten by Miss La Trobe and performed by the villagers are presented in parodic form. According to Bakhtin, parody, the most concrete form of the dialogic, is the scene of conflict between a represented and a representing discourse: "The intentions of the representing discourse are at odds with the intentions of the represented discourse; they fight against them, they depict a real world of objects not by using the represented language as a productive point of view, but rather by using it as an exposé to destroy the represented language."[8] In *Between the Acts* the represented discourse takes the form of the canon of English literature, and the representing discourse speaks with the voice of the pageant's producer: Miss La Trobe as artist, suspected foreigner, and probable lesbian.

The pageant provides an "outline of history" (a reference to H. G. Wells' monolithic and "authoritative" *Outline of History* as well as G. M. Trevelyan's *A Shortened History of England*) by focusing on what has been omitted, thus raising questions about what it is that history traditionally includes. History as discourse not only resides in books and returns as reenactments on stage; it also serves as the topic of conversation during one of the pageant's many intervals. At the opening of the "Nineteenth Century," Colonel Mayhew turns to his wife and says: "Why leave out the British Army? What's history without the army, eh?"[9] The question takes us back to those raised by feminist historians concerning the dichotomy between political and social history, yet does so by foregrounding the question's status as discursive act: the military enters the conversation "between the acts" and does so only as question, not as historical fact.

Wolf in her text constructs only one scene: the imaginary encounter between two German Romantics, Karoline von Günderrode and Heinrich von Kleist in an art patron's house on the Rhine. She imposes elements of the dramatic on the imagined discourse of two literary figures, presented as if they were stage actors playing historical roles.[10] Unlike Woolf, who rewrites the past as parody, seeking to lighten the burden of history, Wolf rewrites it as parable, enabling the past to serve as metaphor for present conditions. The novel's dialogized discourse takes the form of an interpolation which is textually less visible. The novel borrows heavily from Wolf's own "The Shadow of a Dream"—as well as from the letters of Günderrode, Kleist, and other Romantics—while the essay produces a historical and self-referential dialogue which does not use quotation marks to distinguish typographically between the fiction and its historical sources.

The question in Wolf's novel is thus not whether history should include the army but whether it is capable of representing nonmilitary historical conflicts. Günderrode and Kleist's conversation leads to a discussion of Kleist's historical drama, *Guiscard,* a play which attempts to address the problem of conflicting loyalties which govern Kleist's, as well as Günderrode's, life.[11] Rather than discussing the history presented on stage, Kleist and Günderrode attempt to dramatize their individual conflicts—those between thought and action, art and vocation, the masculine and the feminine—as historically determined. History as discursive act rewrites the past as fiction by re-presenting a historical event which never happened.

Between the Acts and *No Place on Earth* are not historical novels as defined by the realist tradition—since in Woolf history is parodied and in Wolf the "historical event" never took place. Yet they emerge from the same impulse which, according to Lukács, governs the appearance of the historical novel as a separate literary subgenre. In *The Historical Novel,* Lukács writes: "The question of the historical novel as an independent genre only ever arises if for some reason or other the proper and adequate connection with a correct understanding of the present is lacking, if it is either *not yet* or *no longer* present."[12] Thus the historical novel evolves from an inability to understand the present. The "present" in both novels is marked by shifts in gender relations, and is also highly precarious, threatened by the possibility of annihilation. For Woolf and Wolf, women's exclusion from economic and cultural production is *no longer,* while their collaboration in military decision-making is *not yet.* The past enters the present not as the historical conditions which prohibit female literary production (as in the case of a female literary history) but as history's textual trace, interpolated in order to transform the discourses of both history and fiction. Historical fiction rewrites history to include the female subject as historical contradiction, positioned "in between" the past and the future, a masculine and feminine subject position.

THE PLACE

If the unknowability of the present leads to a reliance upon the past, then the literary form which makes the historical past most present is drama. Lukács makes a sharp distinction between the historical novel and historical drama by suggesting that in historical drama we experience the past "as if" it were taking place in the present, while in the historical novel we experience the past as our own prehistory.[13] Thus the novel is more "historical" than drama because it informs our historical present rather than reenacting history in the present moment of the dramatic performance. The extent to which the past can be known depends on the accessibility of the present as a historicized present, but above all it depends on the ability of the audience to know itself. Thus Woolf ends her pageant in the present moment, forcing her audience to examine itself directly reflected in mirrors rather than displaced into the past and onto the stage; Wolf writes a parable placed in the past which allows her audience "to see" the present by reenacting it from a temporal distance. The interpolation of the dramatic into the novel breaks down any opposition between the two genres, in turn producing a dialogized discourse which reenacts the past "as if" it were in the present (thus allowing the female dramatist to enter history), and reenacts it as the present's prehistory (thus allowing her to write her historical exclusion). Such a historical fiction collapses the distinction between past and present to suggest that the past exists only as a rereading of the present, whose sole function is to alter the course of the future.

In spite of its dramatized dialogue, Bakhtin considers drama the most monologic of literary forms: "drama is by its very nature alien to genuine polyphony; drama may be multi-leveled, but it cannot contain *multiple worlds;* it permits only one, and not several, systems of measurement."[14] For Bakhtin the difference between the novel and drama is not a temporal but a discursive one. Unlike Lukács, he does not juxtapose the unity of drama as the essence of historicism with the concrete historicism provided by an abundance of novelistic detail. Rather, he juxtaposes the unity of history to a multiplicity of worlds produced through the collision of simultaneous discourses. Yet, although dramatic action is purely monologic, the multileveled interaction between author, producer, and audience against the background of such a unified world produces dialogic oppositions. Woolf and Wolf dramatize these oppositions in their historical fictions by staging the interaction between female dramatist, the production of her work, and the audience's reception of it against the unity of a canonized literary history. Thus the real drama does not take place in a historical past but in the production and reception of the dramatic performance in the present moment.

"Between the acts" refers to the pageant inserted into the novel's plot, to the intermission between the acts of the pageant, and to the decades between the two world wars.[15] "Between the acts" of history lie the unrecorded lives of the obscure; "between the acts" of the play lie the repressed desires of the novel's protagonists. "Between the acts" of language lie the sounds of prehistory[16] and those that could bring it to an end. Breaks between historical periods, the wind scattering the words of the actors, and a malfunctioning gramophone produce discursive gaps filled by the bellowing of cows and airplanes flying overhead. As Europe prepares itself for another war, Woolf fears the disappearance of the writing "I" who is in the process of losing its audience. In her diary she writes: "the writing 'I' has vanished. No audience. No echo. That's part of one's death."[17] Miss La Trobe as writer and producer disappears behind the bushes, leaving the meaning of the play to be deciphered by the audience (just as Woolf herself disappears by drowning, leaving her text unrevised).

"No place on earth" inexactly translates the original German title, *Kein Ort. Nirgends,* or "no place. nowhere," itself a translation of "utopia" from the Greek "ou" + "topos" or "no where." Wolf's novella stages a scene from German literary history as "erwünschte Legende" [a wished-for legend], in order to retrieve the literary precursors' echoes. The imagined encounter between Kleist and Günderrode also takes place on the eve of their destruction, from suicide, which they both commit before reaching the age of thirty. The title itself refers to the homelessness each feels as the inhabitant of a particular set of social and historical circumstances. Günderrode: "Oh, this innate bad habit of always existing in places where I do not live, or in a time which is past or is yet to come" (p. 27) and Kleist: "Happiness is the place where I am not" (p. 4). The title's utopian ideal would enable each individual "to act and at the same time to remain ourselves" (p. 113), which Kleist and Günderrode can find only through writing (not considered a form of action) and through death (interpreted as a subject lost by the German state). The spatial signifier "nowhere" also refers to the suppression of the Romantics within GDR literary history, following Goethe's dictum that Classicism implies health and Romanticism illness. The writing "I" disappears in the dialogue of the heterosexual couple where the individual voice becomes undecipherable (just as it does when suppressed by political censorship).

The place of the present moment is the "in between" and the "nowhere" of historical fiction. In contrast to the signifiers of literary history (the room and the tomb) which mark an absence in history with a spatial signifier, the markers of historical fiction signify the temporally unrepresentable present as the impossibility of a place from which to speak. The present is not just the moment which cannot exist because it is always already past; it is also the moment which will cease to exist if aborted by a cataclysmic future. Thus the lack of a locus for the speaking subject marks both the absence of a female historical subject and the potential loss of any subject to military conflict. This lack is inscribed in the title of each novel as the homelessness of the historical subject who fails to become a speaking subject even in the present moment. Woolf resurrects the past as parody—the "in between" as gap, fissure, fiction—because its continuation cannot be guaranteed beyond the present; Wolf rewrites it as parable because it must offer a "no where," the possibility of a different future.

THE TIME

The absence of a "place" from which to speak suggests the possibility of a different subjectivity as a kind of "placelessness." In historical fiction, such a place takes the form of a suspension in time: the single afternoon staged as dramatic event. The dramatic event belongs both to the present moment and to public life. Thus the exclusion of women from history as the record of public life offers a parallel to the lack of female participation in drama as public event (and correlatively, the association between actresses and prostitutes as the only female professionals in the public sphere). In fact, just as the epistolary dialogue can be read as receiving a "literal" representation in the literary salon, so too can the salon be posited as a kind of figurative "drama."

Helen Fehervary suggests calling the German salon of the late eighteenth and early nineteenth centuries

> a new kind of "theater" in which there was no need for an audience, for this theater was not the representation of life but its verbal enactment. . . . The form of the salon demanded subjectivity—as intersubjectivity—on everyone's part. In the salon, subjectivity and Otherness were two sides of the same persona, because no one was able to speak alone or *for* others. The art of conversation assumed the human presence of a literary partner, an active listener, a real "reader."[18]

If conversation allows for a kind of authentic presence which privileges speech over writing, then the salon, like the theater, undermines the illusion of an original presence by distributing roles whose existence depend upon scripts which have already been written. The dramatic as reenactment unmasks the subject as dramatic persona, as theatrical role governed by gender and class which depend as much on a change in costume as on historical changes. Conversation foregrounds the construction of the subject as subject position by representing discourse as a material presence, arbitrarily constituting the subject in the same way clothes do.

Fehervary's description of the salon shares certain similarities with Bakhtin's notion of the carnival, translated into the bourgeois setting of the afternoon tea party:

> Carnival is a pageant without footlights and without a division into performers and spectators. In carnival everyone is an active participant, everyone communes in the carnival act. Carnival is not contemplated and, strictly speaking, not even performed; its participants *live* in it, they live by its laws as long as those laws are in effect; that is, they live a *carnivalistic life*.[19]

The tea party, like the carnival, blurs the distinction between actor and audience. But unlike the carnival, which temporarily destabilizes the social order by reversing its hierarchical oppositions (high/low, birth/death, male/female), the tea party stages these oppositions as the antagonisms which require the suppression of one of their terms in order to maintain an illusory social stability. Woolf and Wolf locate their subjects in the public institution of the private gathering in order to unveil private passions as the repressed origin of historical conflict.

Both novels stage history as the present moment and constitute the public event as a tea gathering. The time: a single day in June. In Woolf's text the year is 1939, just before Hitler declares war; in Wolf's it is 1804, just after Napoleon has been declared emperor. The place: a rural manor. Formerly the seat of the aristocracy, it now serves as secondary residence for the middle-class. Woolf's Pointz Hall, possessed by the Olivers for a hundred years, is presently owned by Bartholomew Oliver, a retired Indian civil servant with a country gentleman's library. Wolf's tea party takes place in Winkel-am-Rhein at the residence of Joseph Merten, "wholesale dealer in foodstuffs and perfume in Frankfurt am Main. Amateur of the arts and sciences" (p. 40).

As a social event, gathering for tea represents a moment outside time which vacillates between spoken discourse and the silence of private thoughts.[20] At the same time it constitutes a historical moment governed by a particular mode of production: industrial capitalism's dependence on imperialism. The appropriated wealth of foreign goods provides not only the tea and "foodstuffs" but the capital and leisure time which make artistic patronage possible. The topos of the leisured retreat harks back to the Renaissance, the age of discovery, when the garden provided both a spatial and a temporal haven from political activity and social obligation.[21] History and politics, fields of activity formerly of interest only to men, have been transformed into topics of conversation.

THE VIEW

The dramatic event belongs to the realm of the visual as well as to the present and to public life. In this instance, the visual does not refer to "seeing" as a form of knowing (as in the elegy) but to the silence of the image as the underside of speech. Just as the historian freezes past events in scenes or "tableaux"[22] and the historical novelist frames history as staged scene, the audience of Woolf's pageant and the actors in Wolf's drama see nature framed as view. In Woolf the view from the terrace provides both something to see "between" the scenes of the pageant and nothing to see because nothing happens in nature; in Wolf the view of the Rhine through the window provides an "elsewhere" to the confines of an interior and a silence against which to measure the meaninglessness of talk. Unlike the landscape in Austen's novel—a text to be written out loud—the landscape in these two novels represents the silencing of dialogue through the interior monologue. The landscape, as backdrop to the present moment, provides the repetition of cyclical time (marked by the changing position of the sun) against which discourse inscribes historical change.

Bakhtin associates the inception of the landscape with drawing-room rhetoric, whose most significant form is the letter (once again connecting the epistolary, the salon, and the dramatic as dialogic activities). The landscape privatizes nature, which no longer exists as autonomous force and thus must come into being as discourse, just as the epistle, as discourse, marks the privatization of public life:

> "Landscape" is born, that is, nature conceived as horizon (what a man sees) and as the environment (the background, the setting) for a completely private, singular individual who does not interact with it. . . . Nature enters the drawing-room world of private individuals only as picturesque "remnants," while they are taking a walk, or relaxing or glancing randomly at the surrounding view. . . . These picturesque remnants can exist only in the isolation created by closed verbal landscapes that surround them.[23]

In the historical fiction the landscape exists only as verbal construct, like the historical moment for which it serves as setting. It provides the muted (back)ground which foregrounds historical change as well as unutterable desires—adulterous, incestuous, and homoerotic—which fail to enter the conversations between historical subjects. For Woolf and Wolf the landscape also privatizes speech, replacing dialogue with interior monologues. The view, a product of discourse, yet mute, foregrounds the repressed side of speech, which is silence: silence, in turn, represents the repressed side of history, which includes the unrequited desires produced by sexual difference.

Woolf associates the view with the absence of speech in the attendant
audience during one of the pageant's many intervals:

> They were silent. They stared at the view, as if something might
> happen in one of those fields to relieve them of the intolerable burden
> of sitting silent, doing nothing, in company. Their minds and bodies
> were too close, yet not close enough. We aren't free, each one of
> them felt separately, to feel or think separately, nor yet to fall asleep.
> We're too close; but not close enough. (p. 65)

Unlike the salon which requires speech, the dramatic performance makes
a request for silence, thus erasing the speaking subject in order to guarantee his or her inclusion in the audience. La Trobe's dramatic performance
fails to meet the expectations of the audience because it is unable to provide
a seamless production. The interval displaces the silence from the spectators onto the stage, revealing the audience as incapable of replacing the
actors as speakers, no longer anonymous enough to avoid speech, yet not
autonomous enough to engage in conversation. Rather than filling the
silence with talk, the spectators would like to dispense with talk by filling
it with the silence of the view. The view is unpredictable: during another
interval it offers "something to see" in the form of a rainshower. In spite
of the silence there is still a community, indicated by the final "we"
produced by a shared view, even if the view offers nothing to see.[24]

In Wolf's novel the view enters as landscape painting rather than dramatic backdrop. Here the problematic nature of the view lies in its inability to represent the silence still present when two people are talking.
Walking with Günderrode, Kleist paints the following scene:

> He sees himself and her from a long distance away as if, at the same
> time that he is walking beside her, he were standing at some obser-
> vation post high above them, and saw them as droll figures on the
> banks of the Rhine. Not a bad subject for a watercolor. But would
> a painter be able to capture on paper the separation of each figure
> from itself, from the other, and from the natural world? (pp. 101–
> 2)

Unlike the spectators who have nothing to see, here the viewer paints
something he cannot see—himself from a distance. The question becomes
not how to break the silence by making the audience speak but how to
represent the silence which exists in the midst of speaking. Like Günder-

rode (who sees the otherness of her own subjectivity lying in a coffin), Kleist splits himself between the subject and the object of the gaze. Kleist and Günderrode are neither actors who have left the stage, leaving it silent, nor members of the audience who remain silent because it is not their turn to speak. Rather, they represent the division within the individual subject (a division created by language and history)—the split between viewer and viewed—which can be represented only by silence. Kleist imagines that Günderrode sees the landscape differently (unlike Catherine, who has learned to see it like Henry); yet in that difference lies the burden of being able to look behind the scenes. Once again the division between viewers, or within the viewer, marks the difference between Woolf and Wolf's inscription of the subject: Woolf seeks a collectivity of anonymous subjects; Wolf seeks to insert the subject whole into a social collective.

Rather than, as Bakhtin does, mourn the retreat of the subject into a privacy heralded by the appearance of the landscape in literature, the woman writer locates her fictional subjects in the public space of the private gathering in order to unveil sexual passions as the repressed origin of historical conflicts. The female subject in historical fiction appears both as portrait, a figure as silent as the landscape, and as dramatist who, by rewriting the view that associates the muteness of the landscape with "the feminine," rewrites the category "woman." The dramatist displaces the female artist as the object of the gaze constituted in the elegy, by standing in the wings from where she speaks without being seen (Miss La Trobe) or by standing on a metaphoric stage where her thoughts, rather than her body, acquire visibility (Günderrode).[25] The dramatist as producer (La Trobe) or as product (Günderrode) of history does not participate in retrieving a missing past in a supplementary history but in tracing the origins of a threatened future in the fissures of historical time: the unacted parts, the plays without an audience, the plots not yet written.

The female subject writes herself into speech as part of a collective "we." For Woolf the "we" lies in the audience, fragmented but temporarily united by the pageant; for Wolf it lies in the couple, disunited, the figure of a future union. The "we" no longer stands for the separatist collectivity of a female literary history; it stands for the collective concern about the possible end of history. The discursive fissures between speakers find their roots neither in open conflict nor in silence but in sexual difference; in fact, they dramatize conflicting relations to discursive and visual forms of representation, as depicted in the difference between

Catherine's and Henry's reading of the landscape. Male and female subjects are thus equally but differently inscribed in institutionalized forms of sexual repression and political oppression. The woman in man's clothing (La Trobe and Günderrode) has been joined by the "half-man," the male homosexual (William Dodge) or the man who loves his sister (Kleist).

THE PORTRAIT

"The feminine" which cannot speak finds its most vivid representation in the portrait. There the silenced image is spoken for most loudly by the voice of the male subject, who insists either on being painted himself or on painting the picture which for him represents "woman." It is against both the muteness of "the feminine" and masculine speech that the female subject-as-dramatist must learn to speak. The portrait in Wolf's novel remains a figure in the mind (like the landscape painting), painted in silence by Kleist; in Woolf's novel the portrait is a painting, hanging on the wall of Pointz Hall, a recent purchase of Bartholomew Oliver.

In each case the picture, although mute, is characterized by movement: the movement not of historical time marked by change but of an aesthetic reinscription marked by repetition. The painting in *Between the Acts* appears at several intervals in the novel, each time accompanied by a different description; in *No Place on Earth* the portrait is constructed as infinite regression, the product of a single reproducible image. Unlike the "tableau," which attempts to arrest historical time in the present moment, the painting seeks to put into motion "the feminine" which has been arrested by the spectator as view.

In Woolf's novel the painting purchased by Mr. Oliver hangs next to the portrait of an ancestor:

> Two pictures hung opposite the window. In real life they had never met, the long lady and the man holding his horse by the rein. The lady was a picture, bought by Oliver because he liked the picture; the man was an ancestor. He had a name. . . . He was a talk producer, that ancestor. But the lady was a picture. (p. 36)

The ancestor and the lady had never met (like Kleist and Günderrode); thus their spatial contiguity is a necessary fiction. Unlike the man who is inscribed historically because he speaks and can be named, the woman is simply a picture: mute, nameless, a monetary rather than a patrimonial acquisition. Her position on the wall is allowed because of her beauty as a "lady," a product of the social class indicated by her dress: "A length of yellow brocade was visible halfway up; and, as one reached the top, a small powdered face, a great headdress slung with pearls, came into view" (p. 7). Ascending the principal staircase becomes analogous to climbing a summit, with the portrait replacing the landscape as the reward in the form of a view. Nature and "the feminine" fall prey to framings provided by the viewer.

Whether or not a different portrait from the one hanging in the staircase, the painting opposite the window also portrays a woman in yellow. In this incarnation she is "in her yellow robe, leaning, with a pillar to support her, a silver arrow in her hand, and a feather in her hair, she led the eye up, down, from the curve to the straight, through glades of greenery and shades of silver, dun and rose into silence" (p. 36). Here she represents not the nameless ancestress but the timeless feminine, Diana, the goddess of chastity and the hunt. She acquires the status of the nonfeminine as virgin, never to be coupled with a man, and as hunter, man at his most virile; and thus she steers the gaze away from herself into silence, into prehistory, into a time prior to sexual difference.

Bartholomew's sister, Mrs. Swithin, standing in front of the cracked canvas, reveals that the lady is not even an ancestress: "'But we claim her because we've known her—, ever so many years. Who was she?' she gazed. 'Who painted her?' She shook her head" (p. 68). For Mrs. Swithin history refers as legitimately to cyclical as to monumental time, represented by the portrait which is hung out of habit and a need for symmetry, rather than acquired as part of an inheritance. Here the female subject is constituted by the female spectator, who inscribes her not in silence but in the interrogative. The unanswerability of Lucy's questions evokes the muteness of anonymity, in contrast to the demands of ancestry which privilege lower-class men and dogs over women: "'I always feel,' Lucy broke the silence, 'he's saying: "Paint my dog"'" (p. 49). Since the questions about the past can never be answered, the female subject once again exists only in the present: "I like her best in the moonlight" (p. 68) says Mrs. Swithin. Rather than insisting on what she is, "a picture," or what she is not, "an ancestress," the female viewer focuses on the portrait's effect. Unlike the female viewer who leaves the portrait inscribed in silence, the female dramatist must break the silence which associates her with the muteness of "the feminine."

In *No Place on Earth* Kleist's imaginary portrait represents the feminine as equally silenced, as a group of women who will be remembered as the wives of famous men. Rather than representing the opposition between the loquacious masculine and the silent feminine, the wives serve as setting to a scene which places women in the background in order to leave center stage to male literary figures. In response to Bettina von Arnim's spirited behavior at the clavichord, Kleist paints the following picture:

> Admittedly he prefers women who remain inconspicuously in the background, like this Gunda, this Lisette, Savigny's and Esenbeck's wives, who have seated themselves on the narrow couch directly beneath the big oil painting which, by the most scrupulous treatment of all the gradations of green, has conferred on a simple landscape an incredible articulation, brilliance, and depth. A curious notion: a second painter, should he see the canvas, could apply himself to fashioning a second painting based on this new theme—the image of the first picture, with the little couch and the very dissimilar young women sitting there—designed to hang above the gentle arc of the chest of drawers on the narrow side of the room opposite him, thus forming yet another group which in its turn might serve as a suitable subject for a painting. In this way the process would go on and on, and would also introduce a certain forward movement into the art of painting. (pp. 15–16)

To translate "im Rahmen bleiben" [to remain in the frame, i.e., the proper parameters] as "to remain inconspicuously in the background" fails to capture a notion of framing which applies both to the landscape and to the women seated under a literal picture. Kleist characterizes Bettina's behavior at the clavichord, where she has improvised after confessing her inability to read music, as falling "ausserhalb dem Rahmen" (outside the frame, i.e., the boundaries of social convention—a phrase which easily could apply to Günderrode).

In contrast to the oil painting, which confers on the landscape "an incredible articulation, brilliance, and depth," Kleist's attempt to achieve a similar effect in the representation of his female subjects produces instead an infinite regression; that is, an illusion of depth based on the repetition of a single image (similar to the portrait of the lady who is multiply inscribed as picture). Thus the women who now serve as backdrop, dissimilar from each other even in their similar "background" positions as wives, would recede into invisibility masked as a sign of progression. The painting within the painting sets up "a chain of increasing fictionality"[26] in which the spectator becomes more and more removed from the object of representation.[27] Wolf's critique of such a diminishing perspective unmasks an illusory notion of historical change.[28] What Kleist imagines to be a spatially forward movement is actually an ideologically—and historically—regressive one: regression in one painting will not lead to progress in the history of painting. Innovation in representation requires a new subject matter, a notion of "the feminine" which resists the status of a "suitable subject for a painting."

Günderrode paints a picture in which the feminine does not recede into the background like a landscape; rather the female subject perceives the landscape as a specular reflection of herself:

> Nothing, she says, could be more solid and more beautiful and more real than this landscape, which often seems to her like the extension of herself. And yet in the blink of an eye it could change into a painted canvas stretched over a frame, for no other reason than to mock her. And she was afraid, but at the same time she also desired, that the canvas would tear asunder. When she was sleeping, she would suddenly start up, and she could often hear the sound of the tearing. And what we would see then, Kleist, if we looked through the rents into the abyss behind the beauty: that would turn us mute.
>
> (p. 96)

Once again the female subject inscribes "the feminine" in discourse as a question whose answer lies in silence. In contrast to Kleist's controlled look, which appropriates more and more human subjects for a landscape painting, Günderrode's vision is characterized by unpredictability: of the landscape's transformation into a painted canvas; of the canvas's ability to serve as a screen. Like Lily in *To the Lighthouse,* whose canvas is threatened by the pen knife of Mr. Bankes, Günderrode both desires and fears the tearing of a veil which would expose nature as her own human nature—masculine passions imprisoned in a female body. Here the muteness of the female subject stems not from the lack of a name, as in the portrait of the "lady," but from an inability to name what no one has ever seen; that is, illicit desires.

The silent feminine which, like the landscape, is mute because it cannot name itself (Woolf) or is made mute so as to serve only as backdrop (Wolf), also inscribes the other side of "the feminine," historical women, speaking either anonymously (Woolf) or from the margins (Wolf). For Woolf silence also means the possibility of a different history for women who will not repeat the platitudes mouthed by male ancestors; for Wolf "the feminine," contained within a single frame, cannot nullify the possibility of falling outside the frame, through improvisation (Bettina) or intellect (Günderrode). The portrait nevertheless secures "woman," as static image (eternal) or as recurring category (cyclical). In spite of its multiple inscriptions within the novels, the image is reinscribed repeatedly as the static picture, the ahistorical "feminine." The historical fiction, however, rewrites the picture in terms of the name: what does one call a woman who enters history in the role of a man?

THE NAME

Like the female portrait which must be spoken for, the female dramatist is spoken about before she makes actors speak on stage. The difficulty other characters have in speaking to or about her lies in their lack of knowledge about her history. Unlike the elegiac heroine whose name inscribes her lack, and unlike the literary precursor whose name must be "discovered" or "invented," the female writer enters history as a subject whose position has not yet been named. La Trobe's name, of undecidable origin, inscribes the unknowability of her personal history as well as the undecidability of her sexuality. Kleist fails to find an appropriate form for addressing Günderrode because history has never before produced a woman in what he considers to be a man's role, a writer. Like the women in the portrait, the female dramatist comes into being through someone else's discursive inscription. Yet the inscription does not attempt to speak for "the feminine"; rather, it writes woman into history through speech.

Woolf introduces Miss La Trobe as follows:

> She was always all agog to get things up. But where did she spring from? With that name she wasn't presumably pure English. From the Channel Islands perhaps? Only her eyes and something about her always made Mrs. Bingham suspect that she had Russian blood

in her. 'Those deep-set eyes; that very square jaw' reminded her—
not that she had been to Russia—of the Tartars. Rumour said that
she had kept a tea shop at Winchester; that had failed. She had been
an actress. That had failed. She had bought a four-roomed cottage
and shared it with an actress. They had quarrelled. Very little was
actually known about her. (pp. 57–58)

Like the lady who is a picture, Miss La Trobe or "Miss Whatshername"
springs from uncertain origins, but she is constituted from rumor, not
habit or necessity. Unlike the predictable familiarity of a portrait which
produces silence, the unfamiliarity of her name leads to gossip about her
origins.[29] In contrast to the male ancestor, whose speech continues to
assault the viewer in spite of the portrait's silence, Miss La Trobe's silence
produces talk about her past. Her story takes the form of a minimal
narrative sequence marked both by repetition, reminiscent of the pageant,
and by a failure to sustain emotion—mourned by the playwright at each
interval in the performance. Unlike the words of the ancestor who continues to be quoted, the words in quotation marks are those of the female
spectator, Mrs. Bingham, who attempts to fill historical gaps with speculation.

Like Lily Briscoe, whose marginality as woman and as artist is read by
Mrs. Ramsay in her Chinese eyes, Mrs. Bingham reads La Trobe's difference in her resemblance to a Tartar, an inhabitant of the outer reaches
of Siberia, or Hades. The figure of the Tartar stands in opposition to that
of the "lady" and yet, like the lady in the portrait who appears both in
an evening gown and in the robe of a huntress, Miss La Trobe wears a
frock, the sign of the feminine, while carrying the accessories of the
masculine:

> Outwardly she was swarthy, sturdy and thick set; strode about the
> fields in a smock frock; sometimes with a cigarette in her mouth;
> often with a whip in her hand; and used rather strong language—
> perhaps, then, she wasn't altogether a lady? At any rate, she had a
> passion for getting things up. (p. 58)

Her "passion for getting things up" betrays a masculinity which in turn
finds expression in metaphors of despotism, marked by the nickname
"Bossy." Unlike the male ancestor whose social status remains undisput-
ably upper class in spite of his speech (for instance, when he asks to have

both dogs in the portrait: "Ain't there room for Colin as well as Buster?" (p. 36), La Trobe's "rather strong language" casts doubt over the designation "lady" as an indicator of both gender and class. Her status as a lesbian unites attributes of the masculine and the feminine but fails to fuse them: the feminine remains a mystery and the masculine suggests tyranny.

In contrast to the assurance with which Mrs. Bingham speaks about La Trobe's Russian origin, Kleist hesitates to speak to Günderrode, because he is uncertain about the proper mode of address. The facts surrounding Günderrode are common knowledge, including the fact that she has just been discovered publishing poetry under a pseudonym. Her marital status (single) and her social class (noble) make it clear that "the correct way to address her would be Fräulein, or, if that would not do, Demoiselle" (p. 18). Here "Demoiselle" functions as a form of *politesse* rather than as a sign of foreignness:

> "Fräulein" seems to him in some way unsuitable. He cannot dispose of something for which he cannot find the proper word. Naturally, as often as expediency allows, Bettine calls to Lina to come over to her, while the latter listens attentively but without any real responsiveness to Clemens, who standing there beside her assumes the guise of a suppliant. The other young women call her Karoline. But this, too, would be an inappropriate form of address for him to use. Obviously, less appropriate still would be Savigny's term of endearment, which appears to give Günderrode unwarranted pleasure: Günderrode my pet. (pp. 18–19)

Like the series of failures that constitutes La Trobe's biography, Kleist runs through a series of possible names, all of them ill-fitting. Unlike La Trobe's masculinizing nickname "Bossy," Günderrode's nicknames diminish her status as a public/published literary figure. Bettina, her closest female friend, shortens her given name to Lina, while Savigny, her unrequited lover, adds the diminutive ending to her patronym, creating "Günderrödchen," translated as "Günderrode my pet." Those who would not use terms of endearment call her by her first name, an intimacy allowed only to the female sex and therefore equally unsuitable for Kleist.

This lack of designation leads to speculations about the forms of experience these designations attempt to name:

> The way she stands there, not imposing herself, not expressly with-

drawing. Highborn lady [*Dame*]. Girl. Female. Woman. All designations glide away from her again. Virgin: absurd, even insulting; later I'll think why. Youth-maiden [*Jünglingin*]. Curious notion; enough of that. Kleist suppresses the word which seems to him suitable. He does not inquire into the roots of his antipathy to the hermaphroditic. (p. 19)

Unlike Bettina—who takes center stage—and unlike the wives of the prominent men—who recede into the background—Günderrode's circumstances have "no place on earth," signified by the fact that the most appropriate name for her still needs to be invented. "Jünglingin" replaces the term that Kleist suppresses because it comes too close to the appropriate designation, "Dichterin" or "woman writer." Both neologisms add the feminine ending to a masculine noun, thereby stressing the ontological status of the subject as masculine and the need for the female subject to play the role of a male speaking subject if she is to relinquish her silence. In Günderrode's case the hermaphroditic does not suppress a deviant sexuality which must not be spoken but an entrance into history which cannot yet be named.

The problem of naming the female dramatist lies in the suppression of the female subject, given her status as a public figure (which in itself puts into question her sexual identity). "Lesbian" and "Dichterin" are the linguistic signifiers which the texts repress, designating an undecidable gender which arises when women enter into a male-defined and dominated history. The question remains: do they enter as women or as men? Woolf in her depiction of the lesbian emphasizes the masculine and thus women's lack of immunity against tyranny; Wolf emphasizes the feminine in her juxtaposition of the "masculine" woman and the "feminized" man, by endowing Günderrode with a greater knowledge of Kleist, both as psychological subject and as writer, than Kleist has of Günderrode. In either case the notion of an unnameable subject resulting in an unstable sexual identity suggests that gender definitions require a cultural rewriting of the body.

THE COSTUME

The dramatist reinscribes the body by placing it on stage in order to emphasize clothes as the site of sexual difference, the sign of a potentially different sexual identity. The woman writer stages the possibility of gender as undecidable by disjoining the correspondence between actor and character. If sexual identity is a function of costume, the dramatist questions gender as role, defined by the clothes we can put on and take off. In *Orlando* Woolf writes: "There is much to support the view that it is clothes that wear us and not we them; we make them take the mould of arm or breast, but they mould our hearts, our brains, our tongues to their liking."[30] If clothes function as costume, then we adopt the part they allot to us, implying that we are all taking on roles. The extent to which those parts are already assigned, temporarily or for life, will determine the extent to which clothes determine gender roles.

Sandra Gilbert has suggested that the male modernists saw clothing as true and costume as false, whereas the female modernists saw all clothing as costume and all costume as false.[31] For both Woolf and Wolf "nakedness" refers to what lies beneath the clothes, similar to what lies behind the scenes on stage—not the real but the repressed. Woolf thinks of clothes in terms of the theatrical nature of clothing itself, and of costumes as linked to the dramatic, to the roles appointed to the subject, both on and off stage; Wolf focuses on the uniform, suggesting that subjectivity is less a matter of choice than of subjection, while transvestism offers a way of transforming one's role in history through clothes. Is history a matter of costume change, behind which we stay the same, as Woolf surmises; or do the costumes construct the subject who will determine his or her own exit from history if it proves too constrictive, as Wolf suggests?

In *Between the Acts* the blurring between actor and audience leads one of the protagonists to conclude that being a member of the audience is a part to be played, as important as any on stage. Thus the clothes that are not considered costumes (the gray suit, the tennis shoes, the military uniform) more successfully sustain an illusion—most often of power—than those the actors wear, because they do it more "naturally." The clothes that Miss La Trobe has available, "cardboard crowns, swords made of silver paper, turbans that were sixpenny dishclothes" (p. 62) fail to deceive the audience into thinking that the kings and queens of English literary history are anyone other than the villagers. Instead, the birds and the butterflies are deceived into thinking that the silver paper and purple dresses strewn on the grass are elements of nature. Mrs. Manresa, the "wild child of nature" who is "over-sexed, over-dressed for a picnic" (p. 41), is the least exposable member of the audience because her dress and behavior remain the most artificial. By playing the role of the *femme fatale,* the most "feminine" of female postures, she exposes femininity for what it is, mere role-playing.

The distinction between "dressing up" for a social occasion and "getting into costume" for the next appearance on stage is raised in connection with history, when someone in the audience asks: "D'you think people change? Their clothes, of course. . . . But I meant ourselves. . . . Clearing out a cupboard, I found my father's old top hat. . . . But ourselves—do we change?" (pp. 120–21). An item of clothing that appears in the street during one historical era will appear only on stage the next. If human nature is perceived as unalterable, then history becomes a mere change in costume, the present as parody of the past. According to Lukács, the gravest travesty against the historical novel lies in "the mannerism of bringing past and present together by clothing individual allusion to contemporary phenomena in historical costume, although the characters, despite their costume, retain modern sensibilities."[32] Woolf brings past and present together not in order to mask history but in order to make us see that even those in everyday dress are affecting its future course. The present already has become a part of the past by the time it reaches the stage; yet if left unreflected, the present will not enter history but bring it to an end.

The present differs from the past because it does not require a costume, and because the spectacle takes place in the audience, not on stage. Rather than displacing the emotions that govern any plot—"love, hate and peace"—onto history, Woolf's audience is forced to look at itself in mirrors without a chance to dress up: "To snap us as we are, before we've had time to assume. . . . And only, too, in parts. . . ." (p. 184). Because only Mrs. Manresa looks at herself (even if to powder her nose) while the rest try to avoid the reflecting objects, an anonymous voice with a megaphone tells them what to see: "*consider the gun slayers, bomb droppers here or there. They do openly what we do slyly. Take for example . . . Mr. M's bungalow. A view spoilt for ever. That's murder. . . .*" (p. 187). The gramophone continues to play "dispersed are we," leading the audience to wonder whether they as subjects consist of the "scraps, orts and fragments" seen in the mirrors and heard in the words, or whether the anonymous voice which unites them through the megaphone is theirs. The "we" of the fragmented audience stands in opposition to both the "I" of the dramatist—who retains her anonymity by hiding in the bushes—and the "they" of the fascists—who are exposed as being no more prone to tyranny than members of the audience. Like the historical subjects who remain the same except for their costumes, the spectators act different roles but ultimately resemble each other. And yet their play has not yet been written: "Each still acted the unacted part conferred on them by their clothes" (p. 195).

Whereas Woolf emphasizes the theatrical nature of clothing to reveal subjectivity as a role, Wolf focuses on clothes as uniforms used to assign a single historical part. As Sandra Gilbert states: "until the middle of the late nineteenth century most people wore what were essentially uniforms: garments denoting the one form or simple shape to which each individual's life was confined by birth, by circumstance, by costume, by decree."[33] For Kleist this condition requires the hazardous mobility of a soldier; for Günderrode, the oppressive quiescence of a deaconess. In Wolf's essay we learn that Günderrode proposed several times to increase her mobility as a woman by dressing as a man, one of many desires that never passed beyond "the shadow of a dream." In No Place on Earth, Günderrode learns that Kleist's sister realized this dream, which leads her to wish she could make the sister's acquaintance rather than his.

Günderrode introduces the subject by relying on rumor: "Your sister, I hear, is an enterprising lady?" (p. 91) and "Your sister, they say, accompanied you to Paris in man's clothing" (p. 92). Kleist reluctantly tells the tale, assuming that Günderrode wishes to view Ulrike as an eccentric, rather than as a reflection of herself. If she is revealed as not quite a woman, in turn he might be revealed as not quite the man he is. He nevertheless recounts the anecdote:

> How, when she was in Paris, where no one else perceived that this person dressed in man's clothing was really a woman, she was addressed as "Madame" by a blind musician whom she had complimented on his artistry, and had then had to leave the salon with Kleist as if they were fleeing for their lives. (p. 92)

A woman dresses as a man to mask her sexual identity, and is subsequently unmasked by a blind man, an "impotent" spectator. Here the feminine is not the exaggerated femininity of a Mrs. Manresa, who knows she is playing a role, but the trace left by the voice of a woman who seeks to change her gender. For Wolf the body determines the subject's place in history, and clothes can only temporarily disguise it.

Günderrode is less interested in the man than in the woman who plays a man, because only women remain to fill the position of a different subjectivity left by men who have become too fragmented by professional responsibilities: "We women are looking for a whole human being, and we cannot find him" (p. 93). Kleist misreads Günderrode's interest in his sister as an eroticized rather than a historically motivated one, leading him to question Ulrike's sexuality. Unlike Miss La Trobe, who seeks out other women, Kleist's sister remains satisfied with only her brother; but the impulse stems from a similar source. Lesbianism and incest (neither specifically named) offer "a kinship which mitigates one's incomprehension of that alien sex to which one cannot surrender oneself" (p. 95).

Rather than asking whether we are all the same, apart from our clothes, Wolf imagines how Kleist and Günderrode might become more similar in spite of the military uniform and the religious habit: "One must first be beside oneself in order to know the longing to tear off one's clothing and roll around in this meadow" (p. 98). They strip not the body but the gaze, so that each becomes both spectator and spectacle:

> They examine each other candidly, without reserve. Naked gazes.
> Self-abandonment, a tentative experiment. . . . Don't come too
> close. Don't stay too far away. Conceal yourself. Reveal yourself.
> Forget what you know. Remember it. Masks fall away, superincrus-
> tations, scabs, varnish. The bare skin. Undisguised features. So
> that's my face. This is yours. Different down to the ground, alike
> from the ground up. Woman. Man. Untenable words. We two, each
> imprisoned in his sex. That touching we desire so infinitely does
> not exist. It was killed along with us. We should have to invent it.
> . . . We remain unknowable to each other, unapproachable, craving
> disguises. The names of strangers in which we wrap ourselves. . . .
> I am not I. You are not you. Who is "we"? (pp. 108–9)

Rather than having the audience look at itself in a literal mirror, Kleist and Günderrode become mirrors for each other in which they see only sexual difference, an audible silence speaking of desires so repressed that their loss cannot be mourned. The opposites remain dialogized because there is no third term, no third sex, not even the woman who passes as a man.

The "we" becomes a figure for a nonhierarchical difference which can realize itself only in death. In spite of the protagonist's imaginary unmasking, the answer to the question, "who is 'we'?" is not one that says "we are all the same," but one that knows our part has already been written: "We are very alone. Insane diagrams which send us onto that eccentric path. Following the man one loves dressed in man's clothing. To practice a trade: a form of camouflage, first of all a camouflage from ourselves" (p. 109). The costume becomes a metaphor for the construction of a subjectivity which sends men and women in opposite directions: Günderrode would dress as a man to follow her lover; Kleist pursues his profession in order to avoid the opposite sex. Women can dress as men because femininity is a role which can be changed through dress, but not exchanged for the role of the male historical subject. Language functions to unmask sexual difference not as an equal or different constriction but as another form of disguise. The "we" which stands in opposition to an "I" and a "you" is not dispersed, as in Woolf, but dissolved. To the question "who is speaking?" (NP 4, 113) Wolf provides no answer from the bushes.

History, to Woolf, is the eternal repetition of the heterosexual act which fails to distinguish between nature and culture; for Wolf it is a single imaginary moment which fails to bridge sexual difference with even a physical gesture. Both these scenes of history (at the end of each novel) take place in silence, prefiguring the historical silencing of the female subject through suicide: Woolf's death through drowning in the River Ruse, Günderrode's in the Rhine. If, as Isa predicts, it is time "someone invented a new plot, or that the author came out from the bushes . . ." (BA 215), that time is still to come. Yet the historical fiction, because it is about the present and cannot know the end of history, provides no closure. The very last lines in both novels: "Then the curtain rose. They spoke" (BA 219) and "We know what is coming" (NP 119) anticipate a future about to come, but one which is still unspoken.

In the historical fiction the portrait inscribes the silent "feminine" as a function of sexual difference, while the costume signifies the sexual undecidability of a genderless "we." The female subject fails to see itself reflected in the image of "the feminine," and thus enters the stage of history as writer. Her discursive inscription begins not with what she writes but with how she is written—the name for a woman who adopts the role of a man. The way she is written depends on her dress, not as an image suitable for framing but as a body occupying both historical and a gendered position. As dramatist she exposes the historical and a gendered roles predicated on signs which inscribe us all in oppressive social relations. For Woolf, clothes have become merely arbitrary—gender and historical differences are no longer inscribed on the body, because underneath we are all the same; for Wolf clothes determine everything—historical roles (in terms of how and when we die) are assigned to us and are largely determined by gender. If the burden of history and gender were lifted, we would finally be able to say "we," a figure for the possibility of alterity as a nongendered subjectivity. The historical fiction stages a prehistory of the present, but also a different history, a history of an altered inscription of the subject in visual and verbal systems of representation.

CONCLUSION

_____

*T*he contradictory position of "woman" in feminist critical theory—
the construction of a specifically female subjectivity or the deconstruction of subjectivity as such—poses itself as a historical and not a
theoretical question for Woolf and Wolf. In using the term "historical" I
mean to contextualize each author in her own time and place—Woolf in
England between the two world wars, Wolf in the GDR during its first
decades—without proposing a historical reading. The term also refers to
each author's view of history and the meaning of the "historical": for
Woolf subjectivity transcends history, which ultimately amounts to
changes in costume; for Wolf each subject must assume the role conferred
on it by history. For these two women writers, "women" exist both as
authors and as characters, so that it becomes a matter not of naming
"woman" as theoretical fiction but of inscribing her as fictional subject
within both history and discourse. In turn, the discursive inscription of
the female subject is determined by the historical specificity of the gendered subject and by the position of the subject under specific forms of
historical domination.

Thus the theoretical question which counters a female subject against
subjecthood itself might be rephrased: how does one represent the female
subject position as gender-specific while exposing gender as an arbitrary

and artificial construct? Both Woolf and Wolf construct the female subject through a rewriting of sexual difference as a nonhierarchical difference between two subjects who engage in dialogue. "Dialogue" suggests a discursive struggle between two subjects rather than the construction of another subjectivity based on a recognition of the other as object, already silenced and spoken for. In Woolf and Wolf the subject is both dialogized (i.e., in a discursive relation to another subject within a social context), and constructed as specular subject (i.e., as a female subject which must first assure its representability before it can inscribe itself in history).

The specular subject constitutes itself as split subject not in the Lacanian mirror but through "an/other woman," as historical, fictional, and self-reflexive female subject. The specular subject which neither assimilates nor annihilates the other ensures the possibility of a female subjectivity and makes possible a differently constructed subject position. Woolf and Wolf imagine a subject based not on the pseudo-difference of sexual difference but on alterity as the possibility of a radically different subjectivity, one free of domination—for Woolf the anonymous self, for Wolf the female "I" represent utopian visions of an alternative subject position. Subjectivity predicated on alterity would both guarantee the inscription of a female historical subject and perpetuate the history of a culturally specific subject against the forces of annihilation—fascism or nuclear war.

If, as Irigaray suggests, "any theory of the subject has already been appropriated by the masculine," then the feminine becomes the object of male desire, figured by male discourse and the male gaze. The dialogic inscribes difference not as the theoretical relation between "masculine" and "feminine" but as the discursive relation between author and character. On the one hand, the dialogic undermines the hierarchy of sexual difference by positing the relation between author and character as one between two subjects; on the other hand, the character remains inscribed in the author's discourse (the object of her "gaze") and cannot exist as another ontological speaking subject. The dialogic relation between author and character might alter the discourse of the novel through a different inscription of the character; yet how might such an inscription of the character affect the historical inscription of the author? What happens when the woman writer inscribes her character and herself as the possibility of a female subjectivity in these self-consciously dialogized texts?

Initially the female author must differentiate both herself and her character from the "feminine" (i.e., the position of the object), as the marked term in the binary opposition of sexual difference. Yet to create a character, even if it is constructed dialogically, implies creating a discursive object; it requires participating in a process of objectification. Thus the female author who writes a dialogized text constructs her character as subject and also foregrounds the process of textual production. She rewrites Bakhtin's dialogic by positing the subject as gendered and exposes the discursive process as one predicated on an unequal power relation between author and character. The dialogic relation between female author and female character becomes a specular one, in which the author can "see" herself as historical subject only through her self-authored fictional subjects.

Given the female subject's historical and theoretical position as other (i.e., as object), the specular relation between female author and character also involves the historical relation between woman and her representability. The relation between two female subjects requires the discursive inscription of a subject which, on the one hand, has no history, and on the other, writes itself into history for the first time: in Woolf's case a woman writes for the women of her social class who for the first time are able to work in the male professions, acquiring gainful employment other than through writing; in Wolf's case a woman writer in the GDR for the first time writes critically of its socialist system not as Marxist revisionist but as feminist. The character represents a female fictional subject and the possibility of a female subject as author, writing herself into history simultaneously as author and as character.

The dialogic as social practice does not refer to a harmonious dialogue based on amiable disagreement; rather it refers to the struggle between antagonistic discourses. Because alterity as the absolute reciprocity between two subjects remains a utopian ideal and a discursive impossibility, the struggle between author and character must necessarily result in the silencing of one or the other: Woolf silences herself, Wolf her character. Woolf leaves *Between the Acts* completed but unrevised before writing her final text, a suicide note; Wolf, after completing *No Place on Earth*, an extended suicide note for Günderrode, writes *Cassandra*, the first-person preamble to an even more heinous death. Woolf ultimately loses the struggle to her characters because she attempts to subvert the importance of the subject, privileging the multiple discursive inscriptions of her fictional subjects over her own inscription as a woman in history. Woolf could not realize in herself the androgyne, and was overcome. Wolf, on the other hand, requires a subject in order to combat the repression of the individual by the socialist state; her characters lose the struggle because the utopia of a universally undecidable subjectivity is no more a historical possibility than Woolf's androgynous being.

How, then, does one construct a subject which is recognizably feminine, while deconstructing gender as a category? Woolf and Wolf both construct the female subject as "an/other woman," as a fictional and/or biographical presence predicated on a historical absence. The epistolary addressee, the elegiac heroine, the literary precursor, and the female dramatist all fail as subjects within their cultures not because they are fictions but because as female subjects they have no precedent, no name or appropriate costume. They are predicated on absence, elision, death. Woolf and Wolf would disagree over the most appropriate means of deconstructing gender, either by dissolving the subject or by rewriting gender distinctions. Woolf advocated erasing the historical subject through androgyny or anonymity, thereby eliminating once and for all the problem of gender; Wolf advocates retaining the subject by foregrounding its construction as gendered in order to resolve the contradictions of a subject's historical position.

The explanation for each answer is not the function of a theoretical choice but the product of historical conditions. Woolf diminishes the importance of the subject because the subject has been defined historically as masculine. A rewriting of the subject as feminine would entail perpetuating the domination of the subject as such. Yet in constructing the female subject as anonymous, Woolf also constitutes an ungendered subject; and in constructing the ideal subject as androgynous, she cannot include a historical subject that is always initially inscribed as biologically male or female. Wolf, in contrast, reintroduces the importance of the subject in terms of an individual identity jeopardized in its relation to the state—the state not as a collectivity but as the instrument of a collective repression of subjectivity. The recovery of subjectivity entails retrieving it in history and rewriting it as gendered; that is, as female. Wolf represents the undecidability of gender not as an ideal but as a historical contradiction which can be resolved only on an individual level: the "womanly" man and the "manly" woman are not exemplary models but victims of suicide because they do not fit into a culture which requires distinct and ahistorical inscriptions of gender.

These two positions thus articulate themselves dialogically and "historically." Woolf, in suggesting that we are all the same, regardless of gender or historical circumstance, implies that we can escape history just as we can escape our gendered position through androgyny. Wolf, by suggesting that our position as subjects has already been assigned, and above all has always already been gendered, implies that gender contradictions can only be acted out individually, in history. The implications of these two positions write themselves out of the text and into the lives of each author: Woolf literally escapes history by committing suicide, thus literalizing the elimination of the subject; Wolf eliminates the undecidability of gender by having her characters kill themselves, while she continues to write in the hope of transforming GDR history. By advocating the abolition of the subject, Woolf avoids her own historical inscription as female subject, which remains unescapable except through death. (Ironically, of course, she becomes one of the most famous women in modern history.) Wolf, by retaining the subject, suggests that only historical subjects can determine the course of history. In killing herself, Woolf privileges the fictional existence of her characters and prolongs her utopian ideal of androgyny; by having her characters kill themselves, Wolf encourages us to alter the historical conditions which have produced contradictions whose resolution has too often been found in the self-imposed death of the individual.

In both cases the logical inconsistency of the double bind, whether to rewrite the subject or to deconstruct it, is resolved by an illogical suicide. The historical circumstances which produce these deaths have once again been rewritten as theoretical debate; clearly, Woolf and Wolf are historical subjects who in this text function as metaphors for the two positions which constitute the "double bind" within feminist critical theory. Whether these two positions resolve themselves as contradiction, or will later be rewritten as a different question, cannot be decided by any text but that of a still unwritten history.

NOTES

----••••----

INTRODUCTION

1. Christa Wolf, now living in East Berlin, was born in Landsberg/Warthe (now part of Poland), where she attended school until her family fled from the Allies to Mecklenburg in 1945. In 1949 (the year of the GDR's founding), she completed her "Abitur" in Bad Frankenhausen/Kylhäuser and became a member of the Communist party (SED). In 1951, after completing her "Diplomarbeit" under Hans Mayer, she married a colleague, Gerhard Wolf, with whom she has collaborated on several works, and now has two daughters. She moved to Halle in 1953, where she worked in a factory and later as editor at the Mitteldeutschen Verlag. In 1962, after the first of her many literary prizes, she became a freelance writer. Because of her controversial politics, her name was removed from the list of candidates for the Central Committee of the SED in 1967; and in 1976 she was dropped from the Board of Directors of the Berlin chapter of the "Schriftsteller Verband" because she was one of twelve writers to protest Wolf Biermann's exile. She has made two visits to the United States, to Oberlin College as writer-in-residence in 1974 and to Ohio State University in Columbus as visiting professor in 1983.

2. Wolf's literary tradition, which is as well the literary history of the GDR, actually begins in her own lifetime with a writer of her own sex, Anna Seghers, whom she finds and cultivates as literary precursor. This brief but prolific female literary tradition has certain elements in common with the current emergence of an Afro-American female literary tradition, so that the relationship between

Christa Wolf and Anna Seghers becomes not unlike the one between Alice Walker and Zora Neale Hurston.

3. Alice Jardine, *Gynesis: Configurations of Woman and Modernity.*

4. The term "dialogic" is that of M. M. Bakhtin, best known as the author of *Problems of Dostoevsky's Poetics* and *Rabelais and His World.*

5. A reference to the title of Toril Moi's *Sexual/Textual Politics: Feminist Literary Theory,* which offers the first complete overview of the Anglo-American/French debate in feminist critical theory.

6. One of the most eloquent formulations of this question can be found in Domna Stanton, "Autogynography: Is the Subject Different?" in Stanton, ed., *The Female Autograph,* pp. 3–20.

7. See Jardine, *Gynesis.*

8. See Jane Gallop, *The Daughter's Seduction: Feminism and Psychoanalysis.*

9. See Elaine Scarry, *The Body in Pain: The Making and Unmaking of the World.*

10. See Luce Irigaray, *Speculum of the Other Woman.*

11. For works of Wolf for which translations were not yet available, I provide an English rendition of the title in brackets. Subsequent references to those works appear only in German.

CHAPTER ONE

THE FEMALE DIALOGIC: A Self-Interview

1. Katerina Clark and Michael Holquist, *Mikhail Bakhtin,* p. 277. This critical biography provides the best introduction to Bakhtin's life and work.

2. The texts in question are V. N. Volosinov, *Freudianism: A Marxist Critique* and *Marxism and the Philosophy of Language,* and P. N. Medvedev/M. M. Bakhtin, *The Formal Method in Literary Scholarship: A Critical Introduction to Sociological Poetics.* For an analysis of the differences in the discourse used by all three authors, which thus argues against a single authorship, see Nina Perlina, "Bakhtin-Medvedev-Volosinov: An Apple of Discourse."

3. See, for instance, Michel Foucault, "What Is an Author?" in Josué Harari, ed., *Textual Strategies: Perspectives in Post-Structuralist Criticism,* pp. 141–60, and Roland Barthes, "The Death of the Author" in *Image, Music, Text,* pp. 142–48.

4. See Clark and Holquist, *Mikhail Bakhtin,* p. 15, and Michael Holquist, "The Politics of Representation" in Stephen J. Greenblatt, ed., *Allegory and Representation: Selected Papers from the English Institute, 1979–1980,* p. 174.

5. For a more radical view of ventriloquism, where the ventriloquist's voice is not privileged over the voice of his dummies, see David Carroll, "The Alterity of Discourse: Form, History, and the Question of the Political in M. M. Bakhtin," pp. 73–74.

6. Tzvetan Todorov, *Mikhail Bakhtin: The Dialogical Principle,* p. 11. In his chapter on Bakhtin in *Critique de la critique,* pp. 83–103, Todorov begins by suggesting that it is the diversity of Bakhtin's thought which makes it difficult to

imagine him as always one and the same person. A somewhat altered version of this chapter appeared as Tzvetan Todorov, "A Dialogic Criticism?"

7. Caryl Emerson, "The Tolstoy Connection in Bakhtin," p. 70.

8. Michael Holquist, "Answering as Authoring: Mikhail Bakhtin's Trans-Linguistics" in Gary Saul Morson, ed., *Bakhtin: Essays and Dialogues on His Work*, p. 67.

9. Volosinov, *Marxism and the Philosophy of Language*, p. 86.

10. See Todorov, *Mikhail Bakhtin*, p. 39.

11. Tzvetan Todorov, *The Conquest of America: The Question of the Other*, pp. 42–43.

12. Ibid., p. 132.

13. Ken Hirschkop, "A Response to the Forum on Mikhail Bakhtin" in Morson, *Bakhtin*, p. 74.

14. Bakhtin, *Problems of Dostoevsky's Poetics*, p. 184.

15. The dialogic in the novel is discussed most extensively in ibid. and in Bakhtin, *The Dialogic Imagination: Four Essays*. For a provocative review of the latter see Hadyn White, "The Authoritative Lie." See also Don Bialostosky, "Booth's Rhetoric, Bakhtin's Dialogics, and the Future of Novel Criticism."

16. As Todorov succinctly puts it: "A dialogue is not the addition of two monologues, whatever else it may be." *The Conquest of America*, p. 239.

17. For a discussion of the dialogic in its relation to both rhetoric and dialectic as self-conscious, discursive practices, see Bialostosky, "Dialogics as an Art of Discourse in Literary Criticism."

18. Julia Kristeva, "Une Poétique ruinée."

19. The work which focuses most explicitly on the carnival is Bakhtin's *Rabelais and His World*. See also Dominick La Capra, "Bakhtin, Marxism, and the Carnivalesque" in *Rethinking Intellectual History: Text, Contexts, Language*, pp. 291–324.

20. Carroll, "The Alterity of Discourse," p. 81.

21. See Robert Young, "Back to Bakhtin," pp. 76–79 for the most complete review of Marxist appropriations of Bakhtin. See Terry Eagleton, "Wittgenstein's Friends" in *Against the Grain: Selected Essays*, pp. 118, 129 for the most provocative discussion of the carnival. See also Graham Pechey, "Bakhtin, Marxism, and Post-Structuralism" in Francis Barker et al., eds., *Literature, Politics, and Theory: Papers from the Essex Conference, 1976–1984*, pp. 104–25.

22. Bakhtin, *Dostoevsky's Poetics*, p. 63. See also Nina Perlina, "Mikhail Bakhtin and Martin Buber: Problems of Dialogic Imagination."

23. Julia Kristeva, "Word, Dialogue, and Novel" in *Desire in Language: A Semiotic Approach to Literature and Art*, pp. 86–87.

24. See Volosinov, *Freudianism*, p. 88. See also Jacques Lacan, "The Mirror Stage as Formative of the Function of the I" in *Ecrits: A Selection*, pp. 1–7, and "Of the Gaze as *Objet Petit a*" in *Four Fundamental Concepts of Psycho-Analysis*, pp. 67–122.

25. See Jacques Lacan, "The Agency of the Letter in the Unconscious or Reason

Since Freud" in *Ecrits: A Selection,* p. 151. For a feminist reading of this image see Jacqueline Rose, "Introduction—II," in Juliet Mitchell and Jacqueline Rose, eds., *Feminine Sexuality: Jacques Lacan and the "Ecole Freudienne,"* pp. 41–42.

26. Caryl Emerson, "The Outer Word and Inner Speech: Bakhtin, Vygotsky, and the Internalization of Language" in Morson, *Bakhtin,* p. 32.

27. This has been done most explicitly by Irigaray in *Speculum of the Other Woman,* pp. 13–129.

28. For a discussion of the semiotic, see Julia Kristeva, "From One Identity to an Other" in *Desire in Language,* pp. 124–47.

29. For a more general discussion of the maternal, see Julia Kristeva, "Stabat Mater" in *The Kristeva Reader,* pp. 160–86.

30. Julia Kristeva, "Unes femmes," p. 26.

31. Julia Kristeva, *About Chinese Women,* pp. 39–41.

32. "For the subject is 'questionable' (in the legal sense) as to its identity, and the process it undergoes is 'unsettling' as to its place within the semiotic or symbolic disposition." Leon Roudiez, "Introduction" to Kristeva, *Desire in Language,* p. 17.

33. Alice Jardine, "Theories of the Feminine: Kristeva," p. 13.

34. Toril Moi in *Sexual/Textual Politics* concludes: "Kristeva's romanticizing of the marginal is an anti-*bourgeois,* but not necessarily anti-*capitalist,* form of libertarianism" (p. 172).

35. Kristeva, "Lutte des femmes," p. 99. Translation mine.

36. See, for instance, Fredric Jameson, *The Political Unconscious: Narrative as a Socially Symbolic Act,* p. 84.

37. Volosinov, *Marxism and the Philosophy of Language,* p. 97.

38. See *penetration* under Glossary, Bakhtin, *The Dialogic Imagination,* p. 431.

39. See "Editor's Preface," Bakhtin, *Dostoevsky's Poetics,* pp. xxxvii–xxxviii.

40. Except Barbara Johnson; see her "Gender Theory and the Yale School" in Robert Con Davis and Ronald Schleifer, eds., *Rhetoric and Form: Deconstruction at Yale,* pp. 101–12, in which she renames the Yale School the Male School and reveals "an implicit theory of the relations between gender and criticism" in its manifesto, *Deconstruction and Criticism* by Harold Bloom, Paul de Man, Jacques Derrida, Geoffrey Hartman, and J. Hillis Miller (New York: Seabury Press, 1979).

41. Wayne Booth, "Freedom of Interpretation: Bakhtin and the Challenge of Feminist Criticism" in Morson, *Bakhtin,* p. 165.

42. Nancy Chodorow, *The Reproduction of Mothering: Psychoanalysis and the Sociology of Gender,* p. 207. For an application of Chodorow's object relations theory to the portrayal of female friendships in several women's novels, including Wolf's *The Quest for Christa T.,* see Elizabeth Abel, "(E)merging Identities: The Dynamics of Female Friendship in Contemporary Fiction by Women."

43. Michèle Barrett, *Women's Oppression Today: Problems in Marxist Feminist Analysis,* p. 139.

44. Elaine Showalter, "Feminist Criticism in the Wilderness" in Showalter, ed., *The New Feminist Criticism: Essays on Women, Literature, and Theory,* p. 263.

45. Rachel Blau DuPlessis in *Writing Beyond the Ending: Narrative Strategies of Twentieth-Century Women Writers*, in her reading of the romance "as a trope for the sex-gender system," introduces the categories of "the multiple individual and the collective protagonist," but "dialogic" continues to refer to the position of the female subject as "critical inheritor"—i.e., "with one economic foot in and one ethical foot out of the dominant ethos" (p. 170)—embodied most explicitly in Virginia Woolf's figure of the "outsider." DuPlessis further defines the dialogic position of Woolf's "anonymous" "I" as: "probably a resolution of the contradiction between individualism, voluntarily allowing itself not to be known, and the mass that must be rejected" (p. 171). Patricia Yaeger, the only critic to apply the dialogic directly to a female-authored text, again articulates the dialogic conflict as one between "feminocentric" and dominant ideologies, and further seeks to reduce the "conflict" to a "dialogue"; see Patricia Yaeger, " 'Because Fire Was in My Head': Eudora Welty and the Dialogic Imagination."

46. The only other articulation of the dialogic inscription of the "other" woman can be found in Sigrid Weigel's " 'Woman Begins Relating to Herself': Contemporary German Women's Literature (Part One)," p. 91, where she writes of "the writing of the self-duplicating woman," to be encountered above all in the novels of Christa Wolf. Weigel borrows this term from Elisabeth Lenk's "The Self-Reflecting Woman," where Lenk bases her concept of self-duplication on visual art and specifically on the figuring of woman in the mirror. In the second part of Weigel's essay, "Overcoming Absence: Contemporary German Women's Literature (Part Two)," Weigel describes further Wolf's notion of "radical subjectivity," most concretely in the "I" of Wolf's female protagonists, "as the aggressive elimination of the consciously logical subject and as the formation of its nonuniformity in textual incoherence" (p. 9). For an earlier discussion of "radical subjectivity" as epistemological model, see Sara Lennox, "Trends in Literary Theory: The Female Aesthetic and German Women's Writing."

47. Monique Wittig, "Author's Note" to *The Lesbian Body*, pp. 10–11.

48. Luce Irigaray, *This Sex Which Is Not One*, p. 74. For the best introduction to her work see Irigaray, "Women's Exile: Interview with Luce Irigaray." See also Carolyn Burke, "Irigaray Through the Looking-Glass."

49. Irigaray, *This Sex*, p. 171.

50. Ibid., p. 80.

51. Irigaray, *Speculum of the Other Woman*, p. 43.

52. Irigaray, *This Sex*, p. 155.

53. For a detailed discussion of the difference between literal and figurative language as gendered and the process of literalization engaged in by nineteenth-century women writers, see Margaret Homans, *Bearing the Word: Language and Female Experience in Nineteenth-Century Women's Writing*.

54. Jane Gallop, "*Quand nos lèvres s'écrivent*: Irigaray's Body Politic," p. 83.

55. Irigaray, *This Sex*, p. 135.

56. See Luce Irigaray, *Amante Marine: De Friedrich Nietzsche* and *L'Oubli de l'air: Chez Martin Heidegger.*

57. See Luce Irigaray, "When Our Lips Speak Together" in *This Sex*, pp. 205–18; "And the One Doesn't Stir Without the Other"; and *Passions élémentaires*.

58. Irigaray, *This Sex*, p. 216.

59. Irigaray, *Speculum*, p. 133.

60. Irigaray, *This Sex*, p. 28.

61. Sigmund Freud, "On Narcissism: An Introduction (1914)" in *General Psychological Theory: Papers on Metapsychology*, p. 70.

62. Irigaray, *Speculum*, p. 87.

63. For a discussion of "difference" within feminist critical theory, see Elizabeth A. Meese, *Crossing the Double Cross: The Practice of Feminist Criticism*, pp. 69–87.

64. For a reading of the "other woman" as the woman in the mirror who is of a different social class from the woman writing the letter, see Jane Gallop, "Annie Leclerc Writing a Letter, with Vermeer."

65. Anthony Wilden, *System and Structure: Essays in Communication and Exchange*, p. 486.

66. John Berger, *Ways of Seeing*, p. 51.

67. Ibid., p. 47.

68. See Laura Mulvey, "Visual Pleasure and Narrative Cinema." For the most important contributions to feminist film theory, see Annette Kuhn, *Women's Pictures: Feminism and Cinema*; E. Ann Kaplan, *Women and Film: Both Sides of the Camera*; Teresa de Lauretis, *Alice Doesn't: Feminism, Semiotics, Cinema*; and Mary Ann Doane, *The Desire to Desire: The Woman's Film of the 1940s*.

69. Mary Ann Doane, "Film and the Masquerade: Theorising the Female Spectator," pp. 81–82.

70. Gayatri Shakravorty Spivak, "Displacement and the Discourse of Woman" in Mark Krupnick, ed., *Displacement: Derrida and After*, pp. 185–86.

CHAPTER TWO
THE EPISTOLARY ESSAY: A Letter

1. Danna Blesser, "The Relationship Between Epistolary History and Edith Wharton's Fiction."

2. Ibid., p. 9.

3. Ibid., p. 27.

4. Virginia Woolf wrote volumes of letters herself, edited and reviewed collections of other people's letters, and made statements about the relation of her own age to the great age of letter writing. See the collection edited by Nigel Nicolson and Joanne Trautman: *The Letters of Virginia Woolf*, 6 vols. Wolf's published correspondence consists of an exchange between herself and Gerti Tezner, a member of the younger generation of GDR writers, in an anthology entitled *Was zählt, ist die Wahrheit: Briefe von Schriftstellern der DDR* [What Counts Is the Truth: Letters from Writers in the GDR], pp. 9–33. Tezner is the author of *Karen W.*, which from its title indicates an indebtedness to Wolf's *The Quest for Christa T.*

5. Jacques Lacan, "Seminar on 'The Purloined Letter.'"
6. Jacques Derrida, "The Purveyor of Truth," p. 61.
7. Lacan, "Seminar," p. 72.
8. Barbara Johnson, "The Frame of Reference: Poe, Lacan, Derrida" in *The Critical Difference: Essays in the Contemporary Rhetoric of Reading*, p. 141.
9. Ibid., p. 141.
10. Ibid., p. 144. See also Norman N. Holland, "Recovering 'The Purloined Letter': Reading as a Personal Transaction" in Susan R. Suleiman and Inge Crosman, eds., *The Reader in the Text: Essays in Audience and Interpretation*, pp. 350–70, for a reader-response reading of Poe's text.
11. For a discussion of the origin of the *The Letters of a Portuguese Nun* as written by a woman but authored by a man, see Peggy Kamuf, "Writing Like a Woman" in Sally McConnell-Ginet, Ruth Borker, and Nelly Furman, eds., *Woman and Language in Literature and Society*, pp. 284–99. See also Kamuf, *Fictions of Feminine Desire: Disclosures of Heloise*.
12. By describing the single letter as monophonic I am not arguing against its dialogic nature but rather differentiating it from the correspondence, or exchange of letters, as found in the epistolary novel. Linda S. Kauffman in *Discourses of Desire: Gender, Genre, and Epistolary Fictions* has done a superb job of documenting both the dialogic and intertextual structures of the epistolary from the *Heroides* to *The Three Marias: New Portuguese Letters*. To her I am indebted for the discussion of amorous discourse.
13. For a discussion of the "type portugais," the epistle of the solitary lover who fails to establish a veritable dialogue, as a particularly feminine form, see Susan Lee Carrell, *Le Soliloque de la passion féminine ou le dialogue illusoire: Etude d'une formule monophonique de la littérature épistolaire*. François Jost in "Le Roman épistolaire et la technique narrative au XVIIIᵉ siècle" makes the distinction between "passive and static" letters addressed to a friend and "active, cinematic, or dynamic" letters addressed to an antagonist, although he does not examine this opposition in relation to gender.
14. Laclos's *Les Liaisons dangereuses* (1782) represents the culmination of this genre, generating the most varied formalist approaches to the epistolary. For examples of such readings, see Jean Rousset, *Forme et signification*, and Tzvetan Todorov, *Littérature et signification*. For a feminist reading of Laclos, see Nancy K. Miller, *The Heroine's Text: Readings of the French and English Novel, 1722–1782*.
15. Virginia Woolf, *A Room of One's Own*, p. 65.
16. Ruth Perry, *Women, Letters, and the Novel*, p. 17.
17. Lyn Lloyd Irvine, *Ten Letter-Writers*, p. 27.
18. Mikhail Bakhtin, *The Dialogic Imagination*, p. 143.
19. Helen Fehervary, "Christa Wolf's Prose: A Landscape of Masks," p. 79.
20. See Ingeborg Drewitz, *Berliner Salons: Gesellschaft und Literatur zwischen Aufklärung und Industriealter*, and Hannah Arendt, *Rahel Varnhagen: The Life of a Jewish Woman*.
21. Fehervary, "Christa Wolf's Prose," p. 79. Robert Day in *Told in Letters:*

Epistolary Fiction Before Richardson, referring to three women writers of the eighteenth century, states: "It is noteworthy that Mrs. Behn, Mrs. Manley, and Mrs. Haywood alike turned seriously to [epistolary] fiction only after writing for the stage, with its far greater financial rewards, was denied to them" (p. 79). Janet Altman in chapter 2 of *Epistolarity: Approaches to a Form* makes the connection between epistolary confidentiality and the figure of the "confidant," borrowed from the theater.

22. Bakhtin, *Dostoevsky's Poetics,* pp. 195–96.

23. This is not to suggest that letters have not been written with publication in mind, particularly by male authors, but these letters become supplementary texts to the author's literary production. In the case of women writers, letters are perceived as the sign of a lack of formal education, an indication that the writer was unable to make the leap from the "spontaneous" to the "artificial," from the "literal" to the "literary."

24. François Rigolot, "Montaigne's Purloined Letters," p. 160. See also Anthony Wilden, "Par divers moyens on arrive à pareille fin: A Reading of Montaigne."

25. Rigolot, "Montaigne's Purloined Letters," p. 166.

26. Virginia Woolf, "Dorothy Osborne's 'Letters'" in *The Second Common Reader,* p. 52.

27. Virginia Woolf, *Three Guineas.*

28. "Come! Into the Open, Friend!" trans. Maria Gilardan and Myra Love. The complete version was originally published as "Komm! ins Offene, Freund."

29. Virginia Woolf, "A Letter to a Young Poet" in *The Death of the Moth and Other Essays,* pp. 208–26.

30. Christa Wolf, "A Letter, About Unequivocal and Ambiguous Meaning, Definiteness and Indefiniteness; About Ancient Conditions and New View-Scopes; About Objectivity" in *Cassandra,* pp. 272–305. Originally "Vierte Vorlesung: Ein Brief über Eindeutigkeit und Mehrdeutigkeit, Bestimmtheit und Unbestimmtheit; über sehr alte Zustände und neue Seh-Raster; über Objektivität" in *Voraussetzungen einer Erzählung: Kassandra,* pp. 126–55.

31. Virginia Woolf, "Introductory Letter to Margaret Llewelyn Davies" in Margaret Llewelyn Davies, ed., *Life as We Have Known It* by Cooperative Working Women. Reprinted, with minor alterations, as "Memories of a Working Women's Guild" in Virginia Woolf, *The Captain's Deathbed and Other Essays,* pp. 228–48.

32. Christa Wolf, "Nun ja! Das nächste Leben geht aber heute an: Ein Brief über die Bettine" in *Lesen und Schreiben,* pp. 284–318. Originally published as the introduction to Bettina von Arnim's *Die Günderode.*

33. Jacques Derrida, *La Carte postale: de Socrate à Freud et au-delà,* p. 16. See Shari Benstock, "From Letters to Literature: *La Carte Postale* in the Epistolary Genre." See also Sandra M. Gilbert, "What Do Feminist Critics Want: A Postcard from the Volcano" in Showalter, ed., *The New Feminist Criticism,* pp. 29–45.

34. Woolf, *Three Guineas,* p. 11. Further references will be given in the text. Woolf offers her own reply to the responses she received to *Three Guineas* in "Thoughts on Peace in an Air Raid" in *The Death of the Moth and Other Essays.*

35. Woolf's rhetorical strategy is a highly self-conscious one, as evidenced in this passage from her diary: "I had an idea—I wish they'd sleep—while dressing—how to make my war book—to pretend it's all the articles editors have asked me to write during the past few years—on all sorts of subjects—Should women smoke: Short skirts: War etc. This would give me the right to wander; also put me in the position of the one asked. And excuse the method: while giving continuity. And there might be a preface saying this, to give the right tone." Woolf, *A Writer's Diary*, pp. 252–53. For an understanding of the amount of research that went into the writing of *Three Guineas*, see Brenda R. Silver, "*Three Guineas*: Before and After: Further Answers to Correspondents" in Jane Marcus, ed., *Virginia Woolf: A Feminist Slant*, pp. 254–76. For a formalist reading of why Woolf chooses the form of the letter, see Madeline R. Hummel, "From the Common Reader to the Uncommon Critic: *Three Guineas* and the Epistolary Form," and for a political reading of the use of the epistle, see Jane Marcus, " 'No more Horses': Woolf on Art and Propaganda," p. 274. See also Jane Marcus, "Art and Anger," and Berenice A. Carroll, " 'To Crush Him in Our Own Country': The Political Thought of Virginia Woolf."

36. The first reader to notice this connection was Maria-Antonietta Macciocchi in "Female Sexuality in Fascist Ideology."

37. Wolf, "Come! Into the Open, Friend," p. 12. Further references will be given in the text. See also Wolf's "Büchner Preis Rede 1980" in *Lesen und Schreiben*, pp. 319–32 (English trans. Henry J. Schmidt, " 'Shall I Garnish a Metaphor with an Almond Blossom?' ") for another critique of nuclear war and its connection to male domination.

38. See Barbara Johnson's discussion of Derrida's critique of triangularity in "The Frame of Reference," pp. 119–22.

39. Woolf, "Letter to a Young Poet" in *The Death of the Moth and Other Essays*, p. 209. Further references will be given in the text. Apparently Peter Quenell answered this letter in "A Letter to Mrs. Woolf" in *The Hogarth Letters*, pp. 325–46. For this information I am indebted to Catherine R. Stimpson, "The Female Sociograph: The Theater of Virginia Woolf's Letters" in Domna Stanton, ed., *The Female Autograph*, pp. 168–79.

40. Wolf, "A Letter, About Unequivocal and Ambiguous Meaning . . . ," p. 295. Further references will be given in the text.

41. "Notes on the Women's Co-operative Guild, by the Editor" intro. to Davies, ed., *Life as We Have Known It*, p. x.

42. Woolf, "Introductory Letter to Margaret Llewelyn Davies," in Davies, ed., *Life as We Have Known It*, p. xv. Further references will be given in the text.

43. Wolf, "Nun ja! Das nächste Leben geht aber heute an: Ein Brief über die Bettine," p. 284. Further references will be given in the text. All translations mine.

44. See Jonathan Culler's section on "Reading as a Woman" in *On Deconstruction: Theory and Criticism After Structuralism*, pp. 43–63.

45. Bettina nevertheless displayed great sympathy toward the working class,

particularly in her *Armenbuch* [Book of the Poor], a sociological study of the weavers in Schlesien, one of the first books on the poor to appear in Germany.

46. T. W. Adorno, "The Essay as Form," p. 158.

CHAPTER THREE
THE ELEGIAC NOVEL: The Looking Glass

1. For a discussion of Wolf's view of film as a form of memory to be resisted and its implications for women filmmakers, see Judith Mayne, "Female Narration, Women's Cinema: Helke Sander's *The All-Round Reduced Personality/Redupers.*"

2. As quoted in Tzvetan Todorov, *Mikhail Bakhtin*, p. 109.

3. By "antiheroic" I mean "nonexemplary" in a widely accepted social sense, not "unsuccessful" within the confines of the novel.

4. Virginia Woolf, *To the Lighthouse*, p. 32. Further references will be given in the text.

5. Christa Wolf, *The Quest for Christa T.*, p. 137. Originally published as *Nachdenken über Christa T.* Further references will be given in the text.

6. For a reading of Christa T. as embodying "the utopian potential of a historically female subjectivity" and of the relation between Wolf and Christa T. as "the coming-into-being of subjectivity free of domination," see Myra Love, "Christa Wolf and Feminism: Breaking the Patriarchal Connection."

7. This format was frequently chosen by the first popular American women writers of the early 1970s; a good example is Marge Piercy's *Small Changes*.

8. Sula and Nel in Toni Morrison's *Sula* have often been read this way. See, for instance, Barbara Smith, "Towards a Black Feminist Criticism" in Gloria Hull et al., eds., *But Some of Us Are Brave: Black Women's Studies*, pp. 157–75.

9. See Virginia Woolf, "Professions for Women" in *The Death of the Moth and Other Essays*, pp. 235–42 for a description of "the Angel in the House."

10. Bakhtin, *The Dialogic Imagination*, p. 145.

11. Woolf, *A Writer's Diary*, p. 78. For an archetypal reading of this mourning process, see Jane Lilienfeld, " 'The Deceptiveness of Beauty': Mother Love and Mother Hate in *To the Lighthouse.*"

12. Sandra Gilbert and Susan Gubar, *The Madwoman in the Attic: The Woman Writer and the Nineteenth-Century Literary Imagination*, p. 15.

13. For a discussion of the relation of grief to modern literary structures in general, as well as to female ones, see John Mepham, "Mourning and Modernism," in Patricia Clements and Isobel Grundy, eds., *Virginia Woolf: New Critical Essays*, pp. 137–56.

14. For biographical information see Quentin Bell, *Virginia Woolf: A Biography*, Phyllis Rose, *Woman of Letters: A Life of Virginia Woolf*, and Lyndall Gordon, *Virginia Woolf: A Writer's Life*. See also the biography of Frances Spalding, *Vanessa Bell*.

15. Woolf, *A Writer's Diary*, p. 135.

16. Woolf, *The Letters of Virginia Woolf*, 3:572.

17. Woolf, *Moments of Being: Unpublished Autobiographical Writings*, p. 81.

18. Woolf, *Letters*, 3:572.

19. Ibid.

20. Ibid.

21. Ibid., 3:383.

22. Ibid., 3:573.

23. This has been recognized by Ellen Hawkes, who reads Virginia's relation to Vanessa as prefiguring other relationships with women in "Woolf's 'Magical Garden of Women,'" in Jane Marcus, ed., *New Feminist Essays on Virginia Woolf*, pp. 31–60; and also by Gayatri Spivak, who reads the relation between the two sisters as a copula between "artist (Virginia) and material (Vanessa)" in "Unmaking and Making in *To the Lighthouse*" in Sally McConnell-Ginet, Ruth Borker, Nelly Furman, eds., *Women and Literature in Language and Society*, p. 320. Neither Hawkes nor Spivak positions the sister dialogically, however.

24. Woolf, *Moments of Being*, p. 124.

25. Woolf, *Letters*, 3:341.

26. Ibid.

27. See "Vanessa Bell by Virginia Woolf" in S. P. Rosenbaum, ed., *The Bloomsbury Group: A Collection of Memoirs, Commentary, and Criticism*, pp. 169–73, for a discussion of the painter as spared from having to inscribe gender distinctions in her art, in contrast to the novelist.

28. Thomas Beckermann, "Das Abenteuer einer menschenfreundlichen Prosa: Gedanken über den Tod in der sozialistischen Literatur," p. 37. Translation mine. See also Hermann Kähler, "Christa Wolfs Elegie."

29. See Hans Mayer, "Christa Wolf: Nachdenken über Christa T.," *Neue Rundschau* (1970), 81:180–86; quoted in Heinrich Mohr, "Produktive Sehnsucht: Struktur, Thematik und politische Relevanz von Christa Wolfs *Nachdenken über Christa T.*," p. 213, n. 16.

30. Translation mine.

31. It should be noted that the title of the novel in German is *Nachdenken über Christa T.*, suggesting a process of "thinking after" or "remembering" or "ruminating about" the protagonist. The emphasis is much more on the process than on the goal, which already at the very beginning of the novel has been established as impossible.

32. For a discussion of the first-person pronoun as linguistic function, see Emile Benveniste, *Problèmes de linguistique générale*, p. 262. See also Nelly Furman, "The Politics of Language: Beyond the Gender Principle" in Gayle Greene and Coppélia Kahn, eds., *Making a Difference: Feminist Literary Criticism*, pp. 59–80.

33. Christa Wolf, *The Reader and the Writer*, p. 79.

34. Ibid., pp. 76–77.

35. Sophie von La Roche, *Geschichte des Fräuleins von Sternheim: Von einer Freundin derselben aus Original-Papieren und anderen zuverlässigen Quellen gezogen*. See Silvia Bovenschen, *Die imaginierte Weiblichkeit: Exemplarische Untersuchungen zu kulturgeschichtlichen und literarischen Präsentationsformen des Weiblichen*, pp. 190–220 for a discussion of La Roche's novel.

36. La Roche, *Geschichte des Fräuleins,* p. 159. Translation mine.
37. Virginia Woolf, *Mrs. Dalloway's Party,* p. 37.
38. Ibid., p. 40.
39. Ibid., p. 41.
40. Ibid., p. 39.
41. This reading stands in contrast to the Lacanian notion of the Imaginary as the relation to the mother preceding the Symbolic as the relation to the father. For the female subject the movement is from the same sex to sexual difference, rather than from difference to sameness, as it is for the male subject. Thus the return to sexual sameness for the female subject involves a stage which is later, more mature, and often self-consciously political.
42. I am indebted to Susan Squier's "Mirroring and Mothering: Reflections on the Mirror Encounter Metaphor in Virginia Woolf's Works," for bringing this story to my attention. See also R. T. Chapman, *"The Lady in the Looking-Glass:* Modes of Perception in a Short Story by Virginia Woolf."
43. Virginia Woolf, "The Lady in the Looking-Glass: A Reflection," in *A Haunted House and Other Stories,* p. 87. Further references will be given in the text.
44. For a parallel reading of the letter and the mirror as means for the female subject to acquire self-knowledge, see Joan Hinde Stewart, "Colette and the Epistolary Novel" in Erica Mandelson Eisinger and Mari Ward McCarty, eds., *Colette: The Woman, the Writer,* pp. 43–53.
45. Lacan offers a discussion of expressionism and its privileged position in terms of its "direct appeal to the gaze" in "Of the Gaze as *objet petit a"* in *The Four Fundamental Concepts of Psycho-Analysis,* p. 109. For the influence of Roger Fry's aesthetics on Woolf see John Hawley Roberts, "Vision and Design in Virginia Woolf," and Sharon Wood Proudfit, "Lily Briscoe's Painting: A Key to Personal Relationships in *To the Lighthouse."*
46. Fehervary, "Christa Wolf's Prose," p. 72.
47. Shoshana Felman asks this question in "Women and Madness: The Critical Phallacy," p. 10.
48. *The Madwoman in the Attic,* p. 49.

CHAPTER FOUR
LITERARY HISTORY: A Dialogue

1. Michel Foucault, *The Order of Things: An Archeology of the Human Sciences,* p. 387.
2. Louis Althusser, *Réponse à John Lewis* (Paris: Maspéro, 1973), pp. 91–98; quoted in Fredric Jameson, *The Political Unconscious,* p. 29.
3. Mikhail Bakhtin, quoted in Tzvetan Todorov, *Mikhail Bakhtin,* p. 18.
4. Alice Jardine, *Gynesis,* p. 82.
5. Alice Jardine, "Introduction to Julia Kristeva's 'Women's Time,'" p. 9.
6. Julia Kristeva, "Women's Time," p. 23.
7. Ibid., p. 34.

8. Ann D. Gordon, Mari Jo Buhle, and Nancy Schrom Dye, "The Problem of Women's History" in Berenice A. Carroll, ed., *Liberating Women's History*, pp. 88–89. For an overview of work in women's history, see Elizabeth Fox-Genovese, "Placing Women's History in History."

9. For the most interesting discussion of chronology and narrativity, see Hadyn White, "The Value of Narrativity in the Representation of Reality" in W. J. T. Mitchell, ed., *On Narrative*, pp. 1–23. See also J. Hillis Miller, "Narrative and History," and Louis O. Mink, "History and Fiction as Modes of Comprehension" in Ralph Cohen, ed., *New Directions in Literary History*, pp. 107–24.

10. Gerda Lerner, "Placing Women in History: A 1975 Perspective" in Carroll, *Liberating Women's History*, p. 362.

11. Hilda Smith, "Feminism and the Methodology of Women's History" in Carroll, *Liberating Women's History*, p. 374.

12. See Joan Kelly, *Women, History, and Theory*, pp. 19–50.

13. See Smith, "Feminism," in Carroll, *Liberating Women's History*.

14. Natalie Zemon Davis, "'Women's History' in Transition: The European Case," p. 90. See also Davis, *Society and Culture in Early Modern France*.

15. Joan Scott, "Gender: A Useful Category of Historical Analysis," p. 1074.

16. Ibid., p. 1073. See also Joan Scott, "Rewriting History" in Margaret Higonnet et al., eds., *Behind the Lines: Gender and the Two World Wars*, pp. 21–30.

17. In her examination of romances as encoding a notion of history as evolution, Rabine discovers that for the heroines, as opposed to the hero, there is no evolutionary line and that they do not proceed through a teleological development. The heroines "are fragmentary figures, suggesting only potential, as yet unknown, forms of development." Leslie Rabine, *Reading the Romantic Heroine: Text, History, Ideology*, p. 5.

18. Michel Foucault, "What Is an Author?" in Harari, *Textual Strategies*, p. 152.

19. Ibid., p. 159.

20. Roland Barthes, *Image, Music, Text*, p. 148.

21. Nancy K. Miller addresses both these issues surrounding the death of the author in "Changing the Subject: Authorship, Writing, and the Reader," where she reminds us: "Because women have not had the same historical relation of identity to origin, institution, production, that men have had, women have not, I think, (collectively) felt burdened by too much Self, Ego, Cogito, etc. Because the female subject has juridically been excluded from the polis, and hence decentered, "disoriginated," deinstitutionalized, etc., her relation to integrity and textuality, desire and authority, is structurally different" (p. 106).

22. Bakhtin, quoted in Todorov, *Mikhail Bakhtin*, p. 52.

23. Paul de Man, *Blindness and Insight: Essays in the Rhetoric of Contemporary Criticism*, pp. 162–63.

24. For an example of each type of female literary history see Hiltrud Gnüg and Renate Möhrmann, eds., *Schreibende Frauen: Frauenliteraturgeschichte vom Mittelalter bis zur Gegenwart*, and Sandra Gilbert and Susan Gubar, eds., *The Norton Anthology of Literature by Women: The Tradition in English*. The former places women

writers within an international intellectual-historical context, arranged chronologically yet thematically, rather than according to traditional literary periods. The latter attempts to draw the contours of a female literary canon by arranging women writers according to the significant phases of their own tradition. For an interesting review of Gilbert and Gubar's anthology see Lee R. Edwards, "Canons and Countercanons."

25. Virginia Woolf, *A Room of One's Own*, pp. 45–46. Further references will be given in the text.

26. Christa Wolf, "Der Schatten eines Traumes," in *Lesen und Schreiben,* pp. 225–26. Originally printed as the introduction to Karoline von Günderrode, *Der Schatten eines Traumes: Gedichte, Prosa, Briefe, Zeugnisse von Zeitgenossen* [The Shadow of a Dream: Poems, Prose, Letters, Testimonies of Contemporaries], ed. Christa Wolf. All translations mine. Further references will be given in the text.

27. For an introduction to Hadyn White's notion of emplotment see "The Historical Text as Literary Artifact" in *Tropics of Discourse*, pp. 81–100.

28. Günderrode, *Der Schatten eines Traumes*, p. 184.

29. See Gert Mattenklott, "Romantische Frauenkultur: Bettina von Arnim zum Beispiel" in Gnüg and Möhrmann, *Frauenliteraturgeschichte,* pp. 123–43.

30. Günderrode, *Der Schatten eines Traumes*, pp. 235–36.

31. *The Norton Anthology of Poetry* revised, Alexander W. Allison et al., eds. (New York: Norton, 1975), p. 105.

32. See Olive Schreiner, *The Story of an African Farm*, pp. 189–90, for the source of this mode of theorizing about gender.

33. Günderrode, *Der Schatten eines Traumes*, p. 232.

34. Wolf's interest in Günderrode can be traced to several statements about the German Romantics made by Anna Seghers, Wolf's most immediate literary precursor. The following appeared in "Rede auf dem I. Internationalen Schriftstellerkongress zur Verteidigung der Kultur 1935": "Think of the astonishing series of young German writers who after a few extravagant efforts were eliminated. No outsiders and no frail sophists belong to this list, only the best: Hölderlin died in madness, Georg Büchner died of brain disease in exile, Karoline Günderrode died of suicide, Kleist of suicide, Lenz and Bürger of madness. This happened in this country at a time when Stendhal and later Balzac were in France. These German writers write hymns on their country, on whose social wall they rub their foreheads raw. They nevertheless loved their country—they did not know that their continuous, lonely blows were barely audible to their peers. Through these blows they will forever remain the representatives of their fatherland." Anna Seghers, *Über Kunstwerk und Wirklichkeit: Die Tendenz in der reinen Kunst,* pp. 5–6. Translation mine.

35. See Virginia Woolf, " 'Anon' and 'The Reader': Virginia Woolf's Last Essays." See also Maria DiBattista, *Virginia Woolf's Major Novels: The Fables of Anon.*

36. Peggy Kamuf, "Penelope at Work: Interruptions in *A Room of One's Own*," p. 9.

37. Günderrode, *Der Schatten eines Traumes*, p. 259.

38. Margaret Higonnet, "Speaking Silences: Women's Suicide" in Susan Rubin Suleiman, ed., *The Female Body in Western Culture: Contemporary Perspectives,* pp. 68–69.

39. Ibid., p. 73.

40. See Nelly Furman, "*A Room of One's Own:* Reading Absence" in Douglas Butturff and Edmond Epstein, eds., *Women's Language and Style,* pp. 99–105.

CHAPTER FIVE
HISTORICAL FICTIONS: The Portrait

1. Jane Austen, *Northanger Abbey,* p. 123.

2. Terry Eagleton, *Criticism and Ideology: A Study in Marxist Literary Theory,* p. 165.

3. Austen, *Northanger Abbey,* p. 125.

4. Ibid.

5. Ibid.

6. For instance, *No Place on Earth* could not have been written without the history researched by Wolf in preparation for the writing of "The Shadow of a Dream." Wolf, *No Place on Earth,* trans. Jan Van Heurck. Further references will be given in the text. Originally published as *Kein Ort. Nirgends.*

7. Each novel simultaneously retraces the past to provide a prehistory for the historical present and prefigures the end of history in a world threatened by global conflict. Woolf left *Between the Acts* completed but unrevised when she committed suicide in 1941, fearing a return of her own madness, as well as the effects of a potential military madness provoked by the spread of fascism; Wolf used the occasion of her acceptance speech for the Büchner Prize (which she received in 1980 for *No Place on Earth*) to make an explicit anti-nuclear-armament statement, focusing not on the double suicide of two German subjects but on a Germany which might cease to exist altogether.

8. Bakhtin, *The Dialogic Imagination,* p. 364.

9. Virginia Woolf, *Between the Acts,* p. 157. Further references will be given in the text.

10. Günter Kunert in "Zweige vom Selben Stamm (Christa Wolf in Freundschaft)" in Klaus Sauer, ed., *Christa Wolf: Materialienbuch,* p. 16, reads the novel as dramatic form: "Whatever else comes up for discussion, two topics underlie the dialogue (and inner monologues): intellect and power; that is, thought and action as well as (for the practice of art) the individual and society and their respective courses. We see an experiment; actually a performance with divided roles, which, because historicized (without historicizing the problems), brings answers to light, with so much purity and so little dross, to questions we ask daily." Translation mine.

11. "It was prophesied to the historical Guiscard—who died on Corfu—that his life would end in Jerusalem. Too late he learned that here, on Corfu, where he had thought himself safe, there once lay a city called Jerusalem. How cruelly

the prophecy led him astray. So he dies cursing the gods who played their little game with him? Or cursing himself for having trusted them rather than himself alone? Did he frivolously and sacrilegiously impute to their decree ends identical to his own? Was he guilty of presumption? Or did he esteem himself too lightly?" (Wolf, *No Place on Earth*, pp. 115–16).

12. Georg Lukács, *The Historical Novel*, pp. 169–70.

13. Ibid., p. 152.

14. Bakhtin, *Problems of Dostoevsky's Poetics*, p. 34.

15. See Alex Zwerdling, "Between the Acts and the Coming of War," in *Virginia Woolf and the Real World*, pp. 302–23, and Werner J. Deiman, "History, Pattern, and Continuity in Virginia Woolf." See also B. H. Fussell, "Woolf's Peculiar Comic World: Between the Acts" in Ralph Freedman, ed., *Virginia Woolf: Reevaluation and Continuity*, p. 267, for a detailed analysis of the pun on interval.

16. See Gillian Beer, "Virginia Woolf and Pre-History" in Eric Warner, ed., *Virginia Woolf: A Centenary Perspective*, pp. 99–123.

17. Woolf, *A Writer's Diary*, p. 323.

18. Fehervary, "Christa Wolf's Prose," p. 79.

19. Bakhtin, *Problems of Dostoevsky's Poetics*, p. 122. For a more extensive discussion of the carnival see Bakhtin, *Rabelais and His World*.

20. See J. J. Wilson, "A Comparison of Parties, with Discussion of Their Function in Woolf's Fiction."

21. For instance, Thomas More's *Utopia*.

22. For a discussion of the "tableau," see Peter Hughes, "Narrative, Scene, and the Fictions of History" in A. Mortimer, ed., *Contemporary Approaches to Narrative*, pp. 73–87.

23. Bakhtin, *The Dialogic Imagination*, pp. 143–44.

24. For a reading of drama as communal act, see Brenda Silver, "Virginia Woolf and the Concept of Community: The Elizabethan Playhouse."

25. For a discussion of the "not-said" as a way of circumventing the "not-seen" as female lack in historical fiction, see Leslie W. Rabine, *Reading the Romantic Heroine*, pp. 107–33.

26. J. Hillis Miller, *Fiction and Repetition: Seven English Novels*, p. 210.

27. This chain stands in sharp contrast to the play within the play in *Between the Acts*, which finally assimilates the audience into itself to become a moment in the history of England. See Sallie Sears, "Theater of War: Virginia Woolf's *Between the Acts*" in Marcus, *Virginia Woolf*, pp. 212–35.

28. In *The Reader and the Writer*, p. 180, Wolf describes this in terms of a Libby's milk can: "the entire effort of imagination led to nothing, the funnel down which one had forced one's imagination to creep finally ended up in empty space."

29. For speculations about the historical origins of the name La Trobe, see Diane Filby Gillespie, "Virginia Woolf's Miss La Trobe: The Artist's Last Struggle Against Masculine Values," p. 43. Auerbach claims that La Trobe was modeled on Ellen Terry's daughter, Edie, who worked with the Pioneer Players, an experimental theater group in London from 1914 to 1929. This troupe, which special-

ized in the relation of female pageants to history, staged yearly barn productions in memory of Ellen Terry; Nina Auerbach, "Demonic Acting: A Victorian Ophelia's Prophecy." See also "Some Sources for *Between the Acts*." Ingeborg Glier (Yale University), in a personal communication, has suggested that La Trobe might stem from "trobar" or troubadour as metaphor for the poet as "finder" (Fr. *trouver*).

30. Woolf, *Orlando*, p. 188.

31. Sandra Gilbert, "Costumes of the Mind: Transvestism as Metaphor in Modern Literature," p. 393.

32. Lukács, *The Historical Novel*, pp. 71–72.

33. Gilbert, "Costumes of the Mind," p. 392.

BIBLIOGRAPHY

GENERAL AND THEORETICAL WORKS

Adorno, T. W. "The Essay as Form." Trans. Bob Hullot-Kentor and Frederic Will. *New German Critique* (Spring–Summer 1984), 32:151–71.

Altman, Janet Gurkin. *Epistolarity: Approaches to a Form*. Columbus: Ohio State University Press, 1982.

Austen, Jane. *Northanger Abbey*. Harmondsworth: Penguin, 1972.

Barrett, Michèle. *Women's Oppression Today: Problems in Marxist Feminist Analysis*. London: Verso, 1980.

Barthes, Roland. *Image, Music, Text*. Trans. Stephen Heath. New York: Farrar, Straus, and Giroux, 1977.

de Beauvoir, Simone. *The Second Sex*. Trans. H. M. Parsley. New York: Vintage, 1952.

Benstock, Shari. "From Letters to Literature: *La Carte Postale* in the Epistolary Genre." *Genre* (Fall 1985), 18(3):257–95.

Benveniste, Emile. *Problèmes de linguistique générale*. Paris: Gallimard, 1966. Trans. *Problems in General Linguistics*. Miami: University of Miami, 1973.

Berger, John. *Ways of Seeing*. London: BBC and Penguin, 1972.

Blesser, Danna. "The Relationship Between Epistolary History and Edith Wharton's Fiction." Unpublished essay, 1983.

Burke, Carolyn. "Irigaray Through the Looking-Glass." *Feminist Studies* (Summer 1981), 7(2):288–306.

Butturff, Douglas and Edmond Epstein. *Women's Language and Style.* Akron: University of Akron, 1978.

Carrell, Susan Lee. *Le Soliloque de la passion féminine ou le dialogue illusoire: Etude d'une formule monophonique de la littérature épistolaire.* Tübingen: Gunter Narr, 1982.

Carroll, Berenice, ed. *Liberating Women's History: Theoretical and Critical Essays.* Urbana: University of Illinois Press, 1976.

Chodorow, Nancy. *The Reproduction of Mothering: Psychoanalysis and the Sociology of Gender.* Berkeley: University of California Press, 1978.

Cohen, Ralph, ed. *New Directions in Literary History.* Baltimore: Johns Hopkins University Press, 1974.

Culler, Jonathan. *On Deconstruction: Theory and Criticism After Structuralism.* Ithaca: Cornell University Press, 1982.

Davis, Natalie Zemon. *Society and Culture in Early Modern France.* Stanford: Stanford University Press, 1975.

—— " 'Women's History' in Transition: The European Case." *Feminist Studies* (Spring–Summer 1976), 3(3–4):83–103.

Davis, Robert Con and Ronald Schleifer, eds. *Rhetoric and Form: Deconstruction at Yale.* Norman: University of Oklahoma Press, 1985.

Day, Robert Adams. *Told in Letters: Epistolary Fiction Before Richardson.* Ann Arbor: University of Michigan Press, 1966.

Derrida, Jacques. "The Purveyor of Truth." Trans. Willis Domingo, James Hulbert, Moshe Ron, and M.-R. L. *Yale French Studies* (1972), 48:31–113.

—— *La Carte Postale: de Socrate à Freud et au-delà.* Paris: Flammarion, 1980. Trans. Alan Bass. *The Post Card: From Socrates to Freud and Beyond.* Chicago: University of Chicago Press, 1987.

Doane, Mary Ann. "Film and the Masquerade: Theorising the Female Spectator." *Screen* (September–October 1982), 23(3–4):74–87.

—— *The Desire to Desire: The Woman's Film of the 1940s.* Bloomington: Indiana University Press, 1987.

DuPlessis, Rachel Blau. *Writing Beyond the Ending: Narrative Strategies of Twentieth-Century Women Writers.* Bloomington: Indiana University Press, 1985.

Eagleton, Terry. *Criticism and Ideology: A Study in Marxist Literary Theory.* London: Verso, 1978.

Edwards, Lee R. "Canons and Countercanons." *Women's Review of Books* (June 1986), 3(9):16–17.

Eisinger, Erica Mandelson and Mari Ward McCarty. *Colette: The Woman, the Writer.* University Park: Pennsylvania State University Press, 1981.

Felman, Shoshana. "Women and Madness: The Critical Phallacy." *Diacritics* (Winter 1975), 5(4):2–10.

Foucault, Michel. *The Order of Things: An Archeology of the Human Sciences.* New York: Vintage, 1973.

Fox-Genovese, Elizabeth. "Placing Women's History in History." *New Left Review* (May–June 1982), 133:5–29.

Freud, Sigmund. *General Psychological Theory: Papers on Metapsychology*. Ed. Philip Reiff. New York: Macmillan, 1963.

Gallop, Jane. *The Daughter's Seduction: Feminism and Psychoanalysis*. Ithaca: Cornell University Press, 1982.

—— "*Quand nos lèvres s'écrivent:* Irigaray's Body Politic." *Romanic Review* (January 1983), 74(1):77–83. Rpt. as "Lip Service" in Jane Gallop, *Thinking Through the Body*. New York: Columbia University Press, 1988.

—— "Annie Leclerc Writing a Letter, with Vermeer." In Nancy K. Miller, ed. *The Poetics of Gender*. New York: Columbia University Press, 1986. Rpt. as "The Other Woman" in Jane Gallop, *Thinking Through the Body*. New York: Columbia University Press, 1988.

Gilbert, Sandra and Susan Gubar. *The Madwoman in the Attic: The Woman Writer and the Nineteenth-Century Literary Imagination*. New Haven: Yale University Press, 1979.

—— eds. *The Norton Anthology of Literature by Women: The Tradition in English*. New York: Norton, 1985.

Gnüg, Hiltrud and Renate Möhrmann, eds. *Schreibende Frauen: Frauenliteraturgeschichte vom Mittelalter bis zur Gegenwart*. Stuttgart: J. B. Metzler, 1985.

Greene, Gayle and Coppélia Kahn, eds. *Making a Difference: Feminist Literary Criticism*. London: Methuen, 1985.

Harari, Josué, ed. *Textual Strategies: Perspectives in Post-Structuralist Criticism*. Ithaca: Cornell University Press, 1979.

Higonnet, Margaret. "Speaking Silences: Women's Suicide." In Susan Rubin Suleiman, ed., *The Female Body in Western Culture: Contemporary Perspectives*. Cambridge, Mass.: Harvard University Press, 1986.

Higonnet, Margaret, Jane Jenson, Sonya Michel, and Margaret Collins Weitz, eds. *Behind the Lines: Gender and the Two World Wars*. New Haven: Yale University Press, 1987.

Homans, Margaret. *Bearing the Word: Language and Female Experience in Nineteenth-Century Women's Writing*. Chicago: University of Chicago Press, 1986.

Hull, Gloria, Patricia Bell Scott, and Barbara Smith, eds. *But Some of Us Are Brave: Black Women's Studies*. Old Westbury: Feminist Press, 1982.

Irigaray, Luce. "Women's Exile: Interview with Luce Irigaray." With Diana Adlam and Couze Venn. Trans. Couze Venn. *Ideology and Consciousness* (May 1977), 1(1):57–76.

—— *Amante Marine: De Friedrich Nietzsche*. Paris: Minuit, 1980.

—— "And the One Doesn't Stir Without the Other." Trans. Hélène Wenzel. *Signs* (Autumn 1981), 7(1):56–67.

—— *Le Corps-à-corps avec la mère*. Montreal: Les Editions de la pleine lune, 1981.

—— *Passions élémentaires*. Paris: Minuit, 1982.

—— *L'Oubli de l'air: Chez Martin Heidegger*. Paris: Minuit, 1983.

—— *Ethique de la différence sexuelle*. Paris: Minuit, 1984.

—— *Speculum of the Other Woman*. Trans. Gillian Gill. Ithaca: Cornell University Press, 1985.

—— *This Sex Which Is Not One.* Trans. Catherine Porter. Ithaca: Cornell University Press, 1985.

Irvine, Lyn Lloyd. *Ten Letter-Writers.* London: Hogarth Press, 1932.

Jameson, Fredric. *The Political Unconscious: Narrative as a Socially Symbolic Act.* Ithaca: Cornell University Press, 1981.

Jardine, Alice. "Theories of the Feminine: Kristeva." *Enclitic* (Fall 1980), 4(2):5–15.

—— "Introduction to Julia Kristeva's 'Women's Time.'" *Signs* (Autumn 1981), 7(1):5–12.

—— *Gynesis: Configurations of Woman and Modernity.* Ithaca: Cornell University Press, 1985.

Johnson, Barbara. *The Critical Difference: Essays in the Contemporary Rhetoric of Reading.* Baltimore: Johns Hopkins University Press, 1980.

Jost, François. "Le Roman épistolaire et la technique narrative au XVIIIᵉ siècle." *Comparative Literature Studies* (December 1966), 3(4):397–427.

Kamuf, Peggy. *Fictions of Feminine Desire: Disclosures of Heloise.* Lincoln: University of Nebraska, 1982.

Kaplan, E. Ann. *Women and Film: Both Sides of the Camera.* New York: Methuen, 1983.

Kauffman, S. Linda. *Discourses of Desire: Gender, Genre, and Epistolary Fictions.* Ithaca: Cornell University Press, 1986.

Kay, Kathryn and Gerald Perry, eds. *Women and Cinema: A Critical Anthology.* New York: E. P. Dutton, 1977.

Kelly, Joan. *Women, History, and Theory.* Chicago: University of Chicago Press, 1984.

Kristeva, Julia. "Une poétique ruinée." Intro. to Mikhail Bakhtine, *La Poétique de Dostoïevski.* Trans. Isabelle Kolitcheff. Paris: Seuil, 1970. "The Ruin of a Poetics." Trans. Vivienne Mylne. In Stephen Bann and John E. Bowlt, eds., *Russian Formalism.* New York: Barnes and Noble, 1973.

—— "Lutte des femmes." *Tel Quel* (Summer 1974), 58:93–103.

—— "Une femmes." *Cahiers du Grif* (June 1975), 7:22–27.

—— *About Chinese Women.* Trans. Anita Barrows. New York: Marion Boyars, 1977.

—— *Desire in Language: A Semiotic Approach to Literature and Art.* Ed. Leon S. Roudiez. Trans. Thomas Gora, Alice Jardine, and Leon S. Roudiez. New York: Columbia University Press, 1980.

—— "Women's Time." Trans. Alice Jardine and Harry Blake. *Signs* (Autumn 1981), 7(1):5–35.

—— *The Kristeva Reader.* Ed. Toril Moi. New York: Columbia University Press, 1986.

Krupnick, Mark, ed. *Displacement: Derrida and After.* Bloomington: Indiana University Press, 1983.

Kuhn, Annette. *Women's Pictures: Feminism and Cinema.* London: Routledge and Kegan Paul, 1982.

Lacan, Jacques. "Seminar on 'The Purloined Letter.'" Trans. Jeffrey Mehlman. *Yale French Studies* (1972), 48:38–72.

—— *Ecrits: A Selection.* Trans. Alan Sheridan. New York: Norton, 1977.

—— *The Four Fundamental Concepts of Psycho-Analysis.* Trans. Alan Sheridan. Ed. Jacques-Alain Miller. New York: Norton, 1977.

de Lauretis, Teresa. *Alice Doesn't: Feminism, Semiotics, Cinema.* Bloomington: Indiana University Press, 1984.

Lukács, Georg. *The Historical Novel.* Trans. Hannah and Stanley Mitchell. Lincoln: University of Nebraska Press, 1983.

McConnell-Ginet, Sally, Ruth Borker, and Nelly Furman, eds. *Women and Language in Literature and Society.* New York: Praeger, 1980.

de Man, Paul. *Blindness and Insight: Essays in the Rhetoric of Contemporary Criticism.* Minneapolis: University of Minnesota Press, 1983.

Meese, Elizabeth A. *Crossing the Double Cross: The Practice of Feminist Criticism.* Chapel Hill: University of North Carolina Press, 1986.

Miller, J. Hillis. "Narrative and History." *English Literary History* (Fall 1974), 41(3):455–73.

Miller, Nancy K. *The Heroine's Text: Readings in the French and English Novel, 1722–1782.* New York: Columbia University Press, 1980.

—— ed. *The Poetics of Gender.* New York: Columbia University Press, 1986.

—— "Changing the Subject: Authorship, Writing, and the Reader." In Teresa de Lauretis, ed., *Feminist Studies/Critical Studies.* Bloomington: Indiana University Press, 1986. Rpt. in Nancy K. Miller, *Subject to Change: Reading Feminist Writing.* New York: Columbia University Press, 1988.

Mitchell, Juliet and Jacqueline Rose, eds. *Feminine Sexuality: Jacques Lacan and the "Ecole freudienne."* New York: Norton, 1982.

Mitchell, W. J. T., ed. *On Narrative.* Chicago: University of Chicago Press, 1981.

Moi, Toril. *Sexual/Textual Politics: Feminist Literary Theory.* London: Methuen, 1985.

Mortimer, A., ed. *Contemporary Approaches to Narrative.* Tübingen: Gunter Narr, 1983.

Mulvey, Laura. "Visual Pleasure and Narrative Cinema." In Kathryn Kay and Gerald Perry, eds., *Women and the Cinema: A Critical Anthology.* New York: E. P. Dutton, 1977.

Perry, Ruth. *Women, Letters, and the Novel.* New York: AMS Press, 1980.

Rabine, Leslie W. *Reading the Romantic Heroine: Text, History, Ideology.* Ann Arbor: University of Michigan Press, 1985.

Rigolot, François. "Montaigne's Purloined Letters." *Yale French Studies* (1983), 64:146–66.

Rousset, Jean. *Forme et signification.* Paris: José Corti, 1962.

Scarry, Elaine. *The Body in Pain: The Making and Unmaking of the World.* New York: Oxford University Press, 1985.

Showalter, Elaine, ed. *The New Feminist Criticism: Essays on Women, Literature, and Theory.* New York: Pantheon, 1985.

Scott, Joan. "Gender: A Useful Category of Historical Analysis." *American Historical Review* (December 1986), 91(5):1053–75. Rpt. in Joan Wallach Scott, *Gender and the Politics of History*. New York: Columbia University Press, 1988.

Smith-Rosenberg, Carroll. *Disorderly Conduct: Visions of Gender in Victorian America*. New York: Oxford University Press, 1985.

Stanton, Domna, ed. *The Female Autograph*. Chicago: University of Chicago Press, 1984.

Suleiman, Susan, ed. *The Female Body in Western Culture: Contemporary Perspectives*. Cambridge, Mass.: Harvard University Press, 1986.

Suleiman, Susan and Inge Crosman, eds. *The Reader in the Text: Essays in Audience and Interpretation*. Princeton: Princeton University Press, 1980.

Todorov, Tzvetan. *Littérature et signification*. Paris: Larousse, 1967.

Wilden, Anthony. "Par divers moyens on arrive à pareille fin: A Reading of Montaigne." *Modern Language Notes* (May 1968), 83(4):577–97.

—— *System and Structure: Essays in Communication and Exchange*. London: Tavistock, 1980.

Wittig, Monique. *The Lesbian Body*. Trans. David Le Vay. Boston: Beacon, 1975.

—— "One Is Not Born a Woman." *Feminist Issues* (1981), 1:47–54.

BAKHTIN AND THE DIALOGIC

Bakhtin, Mikhail. *La Poétique de Dostoïevski*. Trans. Isabelle Kolitcheff. Paris: Seuil, 1970.

—— *The Dialogic Imagination: Four Essays*. Ed. Michael Holquist. Trans. Caryl Emerson and Michael Holquist. Austin: University of Texas Press, 1981.

—— *Problems of Dostoevsky's Poetics*. Ed. and trans. Caryl Emerson. Minneapolis: University of Minnesota Press, 1984.

—— *Rabelais and His World*. Trans. Hélène Iswolsky. Bloomington: Indiana University Press, 1984.

Bann, Stephen and John E. Bowlt. *Russian Formalism*. New York: Barnes and Noble, 1973.

Barker, Francis, Peter Hulme, Margaret Iversen, and Diana Loxley, eds. *Literature, Politics, and Theory: Papers from the Essex Conference, 1976–1984*. London: Methuen, 1986.

Bialostosky, Don. "Booth's Rhetoric, Bakhtin's Dialogics, and the Future of Novel Criticism." *Novel* (Spring 1985), 18(3):209–16.

—— "Dialogics as an Art of Discourse in Literary Criticism." *PMLA* (October 1986), 101(5):788–97.

Booth, Wayne. "Freedom of Interpretation: Bakhtin and the Challenge of Feminist Criticism." In Gary Saul Morson, ed., *Bakhtin: Essays and Dialogues on His Work*. Chicago: University of Chicago Press, 1986.

Carroll, David. "The Alterity of Discourse: Form, History, and the Question of the Political in M. M. Bakhtin." *Diacritics* (Summer 1983), 13(2):65–83.

Clark, Katarina and Michael Holquist. *Mikhail Bakhtin*. Cambridge, Mass.: Harvard University Press, 1984.

Eagleton, Terry. *Against the Grain: Selected Essays*. London: Verso, 1986.

Emerson, Caryl. "The Tolstoy Connection in Bakhtin." *PMLA* (January 1985), 100(1):68–80.

—— "The Outer Word and Inner Speech: Bakhtin, Vygotsky, and the Internalization of Language." In Gary Saul Morson, ed., *Bakhtin: Essays and Dialogues on His Work*. Chicago: University of Chicago Press, 1986.

Greenblatt, Stephen, ed. *Allegory and Representation: Papers from the English Institute, 1979–1980*. Baltimore: Johns Hopkins University Press, 1981.

Holquist, Michael. "The Politics of Representation." In Stephen Greenblatt, ed., *Allegory and Representation*. Baltimore: Johns Hopkins University Press, 1981.

—— "Answering as Authoring: Mikhail Bakhtin's Trans-linguistics." In Gary Saul Morson, ed., *Bakhtin: Essays and Dialogues on His Work*. Chicago: University of Chicago Press, 1986.

Hirschkop, Ken. "A Response to the Forum on Mikhail Bakhtin." In Gary Saul Morson, ed., *Bakhtin: Essays and Dialogues on His Work*. Chicago: University of Chicago Press, 1986.

La Capra, Dominick. *Rethinking Intellectual History: Text, Contexts, Language*. Ithaca: Cornell University Press, 1983.

Medvedev, P. N./M. M. Bakhtin. *The Formal Method in Literary Scholarship: A Critical Introduction to Sociological Poetics*. Trans. Albert J. Wehrle. Baltimore: Johns Hopkins University Press, 1978.

Morson, Gary Saul, ed. *Bakhtin: Essays and Dialogues on His Work*. Chicago: University of Chicago Press, 1986.

Perlina, Nina. "Bakhtin-Medvedev-Volosinov: An Apple of Discourse." *University of Ottawa Quarterly* (January–March 1983), 53(1):35–47.

—— "Mikhail Bakhtin and Martin Buber: Problems of Dialogic Imagination." *Studies in Twentieth Century Literature* (Fall 1984), 9(1):13–28.

Todorov, Tzvetan. *Critique de la critique*. Paris: Seuil, 1984.

—— *Mikhail Bakhtin: The Dialogical Principle*. Trans. Wlad Godzich. Minneapolis: University of Minnesota Press, 1984.

—— "A Dialogic Criticism?" Trans. Richard Howard. *Raritan* (September 1984), pp. 64–76.

—— *The Conquest of America: The Question of the Other*. Trans. Richard Howard. New York: Harper and Row, 1985.

Volosinov, V. N. *Freudianism: A Marxist Critique*. Trans. I. R. Titunik. New York: Academic Press, 1973.

—— *Marxism and the Philosophy of Language*. Trans. Ladislav Matejka and I. R. Titunik. Cambridge, Mass.: Harvard University Press, 1986.

White, Hadyn. *Tropics of Discourse*. Baltimore: Johns Hopkins University Press, 1978.

—— "The Authoritative Lie." *Partisan Review* (1983), 50(2):307–12.

Yaeger, Patricia. " 'Because Fire Was in My Head': Eudora Welty and the Dialogic Imagination." *PMLA* (October 1984), 99(5):995–73.

Young, Robert. "Back to Bakhtin." *Cultural Critique* (Winter 1985–86), 2:71–92.

VIRGINIA WOOLF

Auerbach, Nina. "Demonic Acting: A Victorian Ophelia's Prophecy." Paper presented at the University of Michigan, Ann Arbor, April 12, 1984.

Bell, Quentin. *Virginia Woolf: A Biography.* New York: Harcourt, 1972.

Carroll, Berenice. " 'To Crush Him in Our Own Country': The Political Thought of Virginia Woolf." *Feminist Studies* (February 1978), 4(1):99–131.

Chapman, R. T. " 'The Lady in the Looking-Glass': Modes of Perception in a Short Story by Virginia Woolf." *Modern Fiction Studies* (Autumn 1972), 18(3):331–37.

Clemens, Patricia and Isobel Grundy, eds. *Virginia Woolf: New Critical Essays.* London: Vision Press and Barnes and Noble, 1983.

Davies, Margaret Llewelyn, ed. *Life as We Have Known It* by Co-operative Working Women. Intro. Virginia Woolf. New York: Norton, 1975.

DiBattista, Maria. *Virginia Woolf's Major Novels: The Fables of Anon.* New Haven: Yale University Press, 1980.

Deiman, Werner J. "History, Pattern, and Continuity in Virginia Woolf." *Contemporary Literature* (Winter 1974), 15(1):49–66.

Freedman, Ralph, ed. *Virginia Woolf: Reevaluation and Continuity.* Berkeley: University of California Press, 1980.

Furman, Nellie. "*A Room of One's Own:* Reading Absence." In Douglas Butturff and Edmond Epstein, eds., *Women's Language and Style.* Akron: University of Akron, 1978.

Gilbert, Sandra. "Costumes of the Mind: Transvestism as Metaphor in Modern Literature." *Critical Inquiry* (Winter 1980), 7(2):391–417.

Gillespie, Diane Filby. "Virginia Woolf's Miss La Trobe: The Artist's Struggle Against Masculine Values." *Women and Literature* (Spring 1977), 5(1):38–46.

Gordon, Lyndall. *Virginia Woolf: A Writer's Life.* New York: Norton, 1984.

The Hogarth Letters. Intro. Hermione Lee. Athens: University of Georgia Press, 1986.

Hummell, Madelaine M. "From the Common Reader to the Uncommon Critic: *Three Guineas* and the Epistolary Form." *Bulletin of the New York Public Library* (1977), 80:151–57.

Kamuf, Peggy. "Penelope at Work: Interruptions in *A Room of One's Own.*" *Novel* (Fall 1982), 16(1):5–18.

Lilienfeld, Jane. " 'The Deceptiveness of Beauty': Mother Love and Mother Hate in *To the Lighthouse.*" *Twentieth Century Literature* (October 1977), 23(3):345–76.

Macciocchi, Maria-Antonietta. "Female Sexuality in Fascist Ideology." *Feminist Review* (1979), 1:67–82.

Marcus, Jane. "'No More Horses': Woolf on Art and Propaganda." *Women's Studies* (1977), 4(2–3):264–90.

—— "Art and Anger." *Feminist Studies* (February 1978), 4(1):69–98.

—— ed. *New Feminist Essays on Virginia Woolf.* Lincoln: University of Nebraska Press, 1981.

—— ed. *Virginia Woolf: A Feminist Slant.* Lincoln: University of Nebraska Press, 1983.

Miller, J. Hillis. *Fiction and Repetition: Seven English Novels.* Cambridge, Mass.: Harvard University Press, 1982.

Proudfit, Sharon Wood. "Lily Briscoe's Painting: A Key to Personal Relationships in *To the Lighthouse.*" *Criticism* (Winter 1971), 8(1):26–38.

Quennell, Peter. "A Letter to Mrs. Woolf." In *The Hogarth Letters.* Athens: University of Georgia Press, 1986.

Roberts, John Hawley. "Vision and Design in Virginia Woolf." *PMLA* (September 1946), 61(5):835–47.

Rose, Phyllis. *Woman of Letters: A Life of Virginia Woolf.* New York: Oxford University Press, 1978.

Rosenbaum, S. P., ed. *The Bloomsbury Group: A Collection of Memoirs, Commentary, and Criticism.* London: Croom Helm, 1975.

Schreiner, Olive. *Story of an African Farm.* Harmondsworth: Penguin, 1982.

Silver, Brenda. "Virginia Woolf and the Concept of Community: The Elizabethan Playhouse." *Women's Studies* (1977), 4(2–3):291–98.

"Some Sources for *Between the Acts.*" *Virginia Woolf Miscellany* (Winter 1977), 6:1.

Spalding, Francis. *Vanessa Bell.* New Haven: Ticknor and Fields, 1983.

Spivak, Gayatri. "Unmaking and Making in *To the Lighthouse.*" In Sally McConnell-Ginet, Ruth Borker, and Nelly Furman, eds., *Woman and Literature in Language and Society.* New York: Praeger, 1980.

Squier, Susan. "Mirroring and Mothering: Reflections on the Mirror Encounter Metaphor in Virginia Woolf's Works." *Twentieth Century Literature* (Fall 1981), 27(3):272–88.

Warner, Eric, ed. *Virginia Woolf: A Centenary Perspective.* New York: St. Martin's Press, 1984.

Wilson, J. J. "A Comparison of Parties, with Discussion of Their Function in Woolf's Fiction." *Women's Studies* (1977), 4(2–3):201–17.

Woolf, Virginia. *The Captain's Deathbed and Other Essays.* New York: Harcourt, 1950.

—— *A Writer's Diary.* New York: Harcourt, 1954.

—— *To the Lighthouse.* New York: Harcourt, 1955.

—— *Orlando: A Biography.* New York: Harcourt, 1956.

—— *A Room of One's Own.* New York: Harcourt, 1957.

—— *The Second Common Reader.* New York: Harcourt, 1960.

—— *Three Guineas.* New York: Harcourt, 1966.

—— *Between the Acts.* New York: Harcourt, 1969.

—— *The Death of the Moth and Other Essays.* New York: Harcourt, 1970.

—— *A Haunted House and Other Stories.* New York: Harcourt, 1972.

—— *Mrs. Dalloway's Party.* Ed. Stella McNichol. New York: Harcourt, 1973.

—— *The Letters of Virginia Woolf.* Ed. Nigel Nicholson and Joanne Trautmann. 6 vols. New York: Harcourt, 1975–80.

—— *Moments of Being: Unpublished Autobiographical Writings.* Ed. Jeanne Shulkind. New York: Harcourt, 1976.

—— "'Anon' and 'The Reader': Virginia Woolf's Last Essays." Ed. Brenda Silver. *Twentieth Century Literature* (Fall–Winter 1979), 25(3–4):357–435.

von Wysocki, Gisela. *Weiblichkeit und Modernität: Über Virginia Woolf.* Frankfurt am Main: Qumram, 1982.

Zwerdling, Alex. *Virginia Woolf and the Real World.* Berkeley: University of California Press, 1986.

CHRISTA WOLF

Abel, Elizabeth. "(E)merging Identities: The Dynamics of Female Friendship in Contemporary Fiction by Women." *Signs* (Spring 1981), 6(3):413–44.

Arendt, Hannah. *Rahel Varnhagen: The Life of a Jewish Woman.* Trans. Richard and Clara Winston. New York: Harcourt, 1974.

von Arnim, Bettina. *Die Günderode.* Leipzig: Insel, 1925. Rpt. 1982.

Beckermann, Thomas. "Das Abenteuer einer menschenfreundlichen Prosa: Gedanken über den Tod in der sozialistischen Literatur." *Text und Kritik: Christa Wolf* (June 1980), 46:31–38.

Bovenschen, Silvia. *Die imaginierte Weiblichkeit: Exemplarische Untersuchungen zu kulturgeschichtlichen und literarischen Präsentationsformen des Weiblichen.* Frankfurt am Main: Shurkamp, 1979.

Dischner, Gisela. *Bettina von Arnim: Eine weibliche Sozialbiographie aus dem neunzehten Jahrhundert.* Berlin: Wagenbach, 1977.

Drewitz, Ingeborg. *Berliner Salons: Gesellschaft und Literatur zwischen Aufklärung und Industriealter.* Berlin: Haude und Spener, 1965.

—— "Bettina von Arnim—Portrait." Trans. Charles V. Miller. *New German Critique* (1982), 27:115–22.

Ecker, Gisela, ed. *Feminist Aesthetics.* Boston: Beacon, 1985.

Fehervary, Helen. "Christa Wolf's Prose: A Landscape of Masks." *New German Critique* (Fall 1982), 27:57–87.

von Günderrode, Karoline. *Der Schatten eines Traumes: Gedichte, Prosa, Briefe, Zeunisse von Zeitgenossen.* Ed. and intro. Christa Wolf. Darmstadt: Luchterhand, 1979.

Hilzinger, Sonja. *Christa Wolf.* Stuttgart: J. B. Metzler, 1986.

Kähler, Hermann. "Christa Wolfs Elegie." *Sinn und Form* (1969), 21(1):251–61.

La Roche, Sophie von. *Geschichte des Fräuleins von Sternheim: Von einer Freundin derselben aus Original-Papieren und anderen zuverlässigen Quellen gezogen.* Munich: Winkler, 1976.

Lenk, Elisabeth. "Die sich verdoppelte Frau." *Aesthetik und Kommunikation* (1976),

25:84–87. Trans. "The Self-Reflecting Woman." In Gisela Ecker, ed., *Feminist Aesthetics*. Boston: Beacon, 1985.

Lennox, Sarah. "Trends in Literary Theory: The Female Aesthetic and German Women's Writing." *German Quarterly* (January 1981), 54(1):63–75.

Love, Myra. "Christa Wolf and Feminism: Breaking the Patriarchal Connection." *New German Critique* (Winter 1979), 16:31–53.

Mauser, Wolfram, ed. *Erinnerte Zukunft: Elf Studien zum Werk Christa Wolfs*. Würzburg: Königshausen und Neumann, 1985.

Mayne, Judith. "Female Narration, Women's Cinema: Helke Sander's *The All-Round Reduced Personality/Redupers*." *New German Critique* (Fall–Winter 1981–82), 24–25:155–71.

Mohr, Heinrich. "Produktive Sehnsucht: Struktur, Thematik und politische Relevanz in Christa Wolfs *Nachdenken über Christa T.*" *Basis* (1972), 2:191–233.

Sauer, Klaus, ed. *Christa Wolf: Materialienbuch*. Darmstadt: Luchterhand, 1979.

Seghers, Anna. *Über Kunstwerk und Wirklichkeit: Die Tendez in der reinen Kunst*. Berlin: Akademie, 1970.

Stephen, Alexander. *Christa Wolf: Autorenbuch*. Munich: C. H. Beck, 1979.

Tezner, Gerti. *Karen W.* Darmstadt: Luchterhand, 1979.

Was zählt, ist die Wahrheit: Briefe von Schriftstellern der DDR. Halle: Mitteldeutsch, 1975.

Weigel, Sigrid. " 'Woman Begins Relating to Herself': Contemporary German Women's Literature (Part One)." Trans. Luke Springman. *New German Critique* (Winter 1984), 31:53–94.

—— "Overcoming Absences: Contemporary German Women's Literature (Part Two)." Trans. Amy Kepple. *New German Critique* (Spring–Summer 1984), 32:3–22.

Wolf, Christa. *The Quest for Christa T.* Trans. Christopher Middleton. New York: Farrar, Straus, and Giroux, 1970. *Nachdenken über Christa T.* Halle (GDR): Mitteldeutsch, 1968. Rpt. Darmstadt: Luchterhand, 1971.

—— *The Reader and the Writer: Essays, Sketches, Memories*. Trans. Joan Becker. New York: International Publishers, 1977.

—— "Interview with Myself." In *The Reader and the Writer*. "Selbstinterview." In *Lesen und Schreiben*.

—— *Lesen und Schreiben, Neue Sammlung: Essays, Aufsätze, Reden*. Darmstadt: Luchterhand, 1980; rpt. 1982.

—— "Nun ja! Das nächste Leben geht aber heute an—Ein Brief über die Bettine." In *Lesen und Schreiben*.

—— "Der Schatten eines Traumes: Karoline von Günderrode—Ein Entwurt." In *Lesen und Schreiben*.

—— "Shall I Garnish a Metaphor with an Almond Blossom?" Trans. Henry J. Schmidt. *New German Critique* (Spring–Summer 1981), 23:3–11. "Büchner-Preis-Rede 1980." In *Lesen und Schreiben*.

—— *No Place on Earth*. Trans. Jan Van Heurck. New York: Farrar, Straus and Giroux, 1982. *Kein Ort. Nirgends*. Darmstadt: Luchterhand, 1979.

—— "Come! Into the Open, Friend." Trans. Maria Gilarden and Myra Love. *Connexions: An International Women's Quarterly* (Summer 1984), 13:12–14. " 'Komm! ins Offene, Freund!' Können wir den Frieden retten?" *Süddeutsche Zeitung,* February 20–21, 1982, p. 100.

—— *Cassandra: A Novel and Four Essays.* Trans. Jan Van Heurck. New York: Farrar, Straus and Giroux, 1984. *Kassandra: Erzählung.* Darmstadt: Luchterhand, 1983 and *Voraussetzungen einer Erzählung: Kassandra; Frankfurter Poetic-Vorlesungen.* Darmstadt: Luchterhand, 1983.

—— "A Letter, About Unequivocal and Ambiguous Meaning, Definiteness and Indefiniteness; About Ancient Conditions and New View-Scopes; About Objectivity." In *Cassandra.* "Vierte Vorlesung: Ein Brief über Eindeutigkeit und Mehrdeutigkeit, Bestimmtheit und Unbestimmtment; über sehr alte Zustände und neue Seh-Raster; über Objektivität." In *Voraussetzungen einer Erzählung: Kassandra.*

INDEX

Adorno, T. W., 60
Alcoforado, Mariana, 36
Alterity, 7, 23, 27, 53–54, 60, 121, 145,
    147, 148
Althusser, Louis, 90
Altman, Janet, 158n21
An/other woman, 3, 36, 63, 66, 77, 88,
    147, 149; as epistolary addressee, 43, 58,
    59; as female friend, 62, 67, 73, 76, 77,
    88; as mother, 62, 67, 88; see also Female
    subject; Literary precursor
Arnim, Bettina von, see von Arnim, Bet-
    tina
Austen, Jane, 108–9, 114, 115–18, 120, 129

Bachmann, Ingeborg, 52
Bakhtin, Mikhail, 7, 11, 96; as split signa-
    ture, 11–13; and the gaze, 17–18; and
    Lacan, 17–18; and the letter, 38–40; and
    the elegy, 68; and parody, 122; and
    drama, 124–25; and landscape, 129; see
    also Dialogic
Barrett, Michèle, 21
Barthes, Roland, 95
Bell, Quentin, 2

Bell, Vanessa, 2, 73, 75
Berger, John, 28–29
Booth, Wayne, 20
Brontë, Charlotte, 108

Cameron, Julia Margaret, 2
Carnival, 16, 18, 127–28; see also Bakhtin,
    Mikhail; Salon
Chodorow, Nancy, 21
Costume, 84, 86–87, 139–42, 144; see also
    Transvestism
Cross-dressing, see Transvestism

Davies, Margaret Llewelyn, 54
Davis, Natalie Zemon, 94
de Man, Paul, 96
Derrida, Jacques, 35, 43
Dialogic, 4, 14–15, 49, 90, 155n45; as
    avoiding double-bind in feminist critical
    theory, 5, 150; as struggle between com-
    peting discourses, 6, 12, 14, 148; as
    gender-blind, 7, 20; vs. dialogue and di-
    alectic, 15; as social practice, 18, 148; re-
    lation to epistolary addressee, 34, 42, 45,